Inga Clendinnen

Ambivalent Conquests

Maya and Spaniard in Yucatan, 1517~1570

CAMBRIDGE LATIN AMERICAN STUDIES

GENERAL EDITOR
SIMON COLLIER

ADVISORY COMMITTEE
MARVIN BERNSTEIN, MALCOLM DEAS
CLARK W. REYNOLDS, ARTURO VALENZUELA

61

AMBIVALENT CONQUESTS

AMBIVALENT CONQUESTS

Maya and Spaniard in Yucatan, 1517–1570

INGA CLENDINNEN

Senior Lecturer in History, La Trobe University

CAMBRIDGE
UNIVERSITY PRESS

Published by the Press Syndicate of the University of Cambridge
The Pitt Building, Trumpington Street, Cambridge CB2 1RP
40 West 20th Street, New York, NY 10011-4211, USA
10 Stamford Road, Oakleigh, Melbourne 3166, Australia

© Cambridge University Press 1987

First published 1987
First paperback eition 1988
Reprinted 1989, 1990, 1991 (twice), 1992, 1993, 1994 (twice), 1995

Printed in the United States of America

Library of Congress Cataloging-in-Publication Data is available.

A catalogue record for this book is available from the British Library.

ISBN 0-521-33397-0 hardback
ISBN 0-521-37981-4 paperback

To the memory of France Vinton Scholes

When the Spaniards discovered this land, their leader asked the Indians how it was called; as they did not understand him, they said *uic athan*, which means, what do you say or what do you speak, that we do not understand you. And then the Spaniard ordered it set down that it be called *Yucatan* . . .

Antonio de Ciudad Real, 1588

Contents

Illustrations

Maps

Preface

South and west of Cuba a great limestone peninsula thrusts into the warm waters of the Caribbean. The Maya Indians who lived there called it 'The Land of the Turkey and Deer', for they thought it a rich place. In the early years of the sixteenth century Spaniards came; some in search of a golden kingdom, some to extend the Kingdom of God. They found a harsh and stony land which they conquered and settled nonetheless. They named it 'Yucatan'.

This is a story of how the Land of the Turkey and the Deer was made into Yucatan. Proud of their exploits, the conquerors recorded them in detail, so the tale of exploration and war can be told, first, from their point of view, and in their terms – of courage, unabashed cupidity, and that extraordinary European conviction of their right to appropriate the world. Later we hear Spanish voices still, but Spanish voices raised in confused and bitter conflict, as settlers and missionary friars fought a dangerous battle for the power to determine the kind of Yucatan they would make. They fought not only over the use of land and control of labour, the conventional problems of colonial politics, but over contrary accounts of the conduct and the nature of the subject native people. In the course of that struggle about the nature of the alien and other, they were sometimes forced to unsought and profoundly disquieting discoveries about themselves – which is always a danger in the hall-of-mirrors world we make when we seek to possess the strange and make it part of ourselves.

Then, finally, I turn to the Maya: to discover, through analysis of deeply partisan Spanish accounts, what they did, and from their own few and fragmentary writings what they meant by what they did. It takes patience and perseverance to hear those faint long-ago Indian voices at all, speaking as they do from an unfamiliar world and an unfamiliar experience. The attempt also requires from both reader and author a tolerance of ambiguities, and of inherently contestable judgments. But to offer interpretations without acknowledging their uncertain ground would be less than candid, while to state only what is certainly known would be to leave unexplored what matters most.

Acknowledgments

Any study which has migrated between bottom drawer and desk top as often as this one picks up many obligations along the way. I think others will understand if I single out June Philipp, Greg Dening and Rhys Isaac for special thanks. Each read all of an earlier draft, and through the cogency of their distinctive criticisms forced the rethinking of large parts of it. They will recognise their influence in many passages, and regret its absence in others. I am deeply grateful to them. John Horacek, Margot Hyslop and the rest of the staff at the Borchardt Library have been ingenious in the pursuit of hard-to-get material, and Merelyn Dowling and Shirley Horton have chosen to accept my messy manuscripts as a happy challenge, instead of the disgrace they are, converting them into elegant typescript with sunny good humour. And somehow, through all the years, my husband John has contrived to find the doings of friars and bishops and Indians perennially interesting. These people, and many others, have made work a steady pleasure.

I owe a special debt to the magnificent team of Carnegie Institution scholars who worked on sixteenth-century Yucatecan material in the 1930s and 1940s: France Scholes and Robert Chamberlain on Spanish documentation; Ralph Roys on Maya writings; Eric Thompson ranging everywhere. Without their heroic labours we would know little of that first crucial fifty years of Spanish–Indian contact on the peninsula. Among them I met only France Scholes, in the last years of his life. I'll not forget his magisterial scholarship, nor his extraordinary kindness to a stranger. Increasing years and cares prevented the completion of his own massively researched biography of Diego de Landa. This small study is not the book he would have written, but it is, in an important sense, of his making, and in affection and admiration I dedicate it to his memory.

Melbourne, 1986   INGA CLENDINNEN

xi

Map 1 Yucatan in the conquest period.

PART I

Spaniards

1

Explorers

We seldom or never find any nation hath endured so many misadventures and miseries as the Spaniards have done in their Indian discoveries. Yet persisting in their enterprises, with invincible constancy, they have annexed to their kingdom so many goodly provinces, as bury the remembrance of all dangers past . . . Many years have passed over some of their heads in the search of not so many leagues: Yea, more than one or two have spent their labour, their wealth, and their lives, in search of a golden kingdom, without getting further notice of it than what they had at their first setting forth . . .

Sir Walter Raleigh, *The History of the World*, 1614

In 1502, on his fourth and final voyage, Christopher Columbus happened upon a great trading canoe just off the coast of Honduras. It was 'long as a galley', as Ferdinand, the Admiral's thirteen-year-old son recalled, and carved from one great tree trunk. Neither its twenty-five naked paddlers nor the richly clad men who appeared to be their masters offered any resistance as the Spaniards seized the craft, and they remained paralysed with fright as the bearded strangers rifled through the cargo. It was only when some cacao beans were allowed to spill from their containers in the course of the looting that they momentarily forgot their fear, scrambling to retrieve them 'as if they were their eyes'.[1]

Along with the precious cacao beans were copper axes and bells; razors and hatchets of a translucent yellow stone, probably Mexican obsidian; heavy wooden war clubs studded with flints; pottery; and garments of many-coloured woven cotton. The small huddle of women and children clustered under a canopy were probably also part of the cargo, to be sold, together with some of the paddlers, along the coast.

Columbus and his men picked over the cargo, keeping whatever took their fancy, and then let the canoe go on its way, detaining only the old man who seemed to be its captain to test his usefulness as a guide. Precisely what the natives made of the encounter we don't know. The canoe was certainly part of the great and enduring trading network linking Honduras and Mexico, in which merchants from the Yucatan peninsula controlled the traffic between Honduras and Xicalango, where the Aztecs, overlords of much of Mexico, maintained a station.[2] We can be sure that news of the strangers, and of their uncouth and piratical ways, ran through the whole complex system, although only a hint of that disquiet survives in the records: it was at about this time, very early in the century, that Chilam Balam, a prophet-priest of northern Yucatan, prophesied the invasion of the pensinsula by bearded strangers who were perhaps the emissaries of the self-exiled culture hero Kukul Can, the Feathered Serpent.[3]

If for the Indians the encounter was threatening, it was for the Spaniards profoundly cheering: Columbus' determined praise of the lands he had discovered had become increasingly defensive, for nowhere to that point had his men found any evidence of the rich civilisations he had promised them. The Indians of the islands they had touched on, whether ferocious Caribs or timid Arawak, were miserable creatures, living like beasts in the forest or in shelters too mean to be called huts; going shamelessly naked, or with mere wisps of loincloths scarcely covering their genitals. The Indians of the great canoe had a proper sense of shame: the Spaniards noted approvingly that the women modestly held their shawls before their faces, like the Moorish women in Granada, and that when the paddlers' loincloths were snatched from them – a glimpse of rough-and-thorough Spanish search techniques – they hastily covered their private parts with their hands. The trade canoe, with its varied cargo, the technical sophistication implied by its hierarchy of well-clad supervisors and docile labourers, represented in miniature the thriving civilisation Columbus had sought so long.

He was not to find it himself. More than a decade was to pass before Spaniards were to penetrate the tangle of islands and the restless currents and winds of the Caribbean to the extraordinary worlds which lay beyond. But the story of the great trading canoe became part of the folklore of the Indies, and lay like a promise in men's minds.

Early in 1517, a small slave-hunting and exploring expedition made ready to sail out of Cuba. Cuba had been conquered – or more correctly over-run, as its predominately Arawak Indians had offered no resistance – six years before, and had attracted the usual swarm of

Spanish adventurers hungry for a share of whatever spoils there might be. Among them was Bernal Díaz del Castillo, twenty-four years old, already four years in the Indies, and as yet unremarkable among his equally poor and hopeful companions (in old age he was to write his *True History of the Conquest of New Spain*, or 'Mexico' as we now call it, one of the greatest participant histories ever written). He had come, along with many others, from Darien, where there was a superfluity of Spanish soldiers, and for a time was sustained by the expectation that his distant kinsman Diego Velázquez, Governor of Cuba, would honour his promise to give him some Indians 'as soon as there were any available'. But Indians were in short and dwindling supply, the Cuban natives dying almost as fast as the men brought in from other islands to replace them, and the few there were had already been distributed among the powerful men of the island. So Diáz, and about another hundred men who, like him, were weary of cooling their heels, pooled their meagre resources to buy two caravels and a brigantine on credit. They provisioned them, minimally, with cassava bread, pigs – at scandalously inflated prices, Díaz believed, given the way pigs multiplied on the island – oil, and a few beads and other trifles for trading with the natives, and set off to try their luck under the leadership of Francisco Hernández de Córdoba, one of the few men of any substance to invest in the ramshackle enterprise.[4]

If the expedition suffered the defects of its *ad hoc* beginnings, it was fortunate in its pilot. Antón de Alaminos was a native of Palos, the port which had produced some of the first and continued to produce many of the best of Spain's seafarer-explorers. He knew the waters of the Caribbean as well as any other man, or, at least, any other Spaniard. He had been around them long enough to have learnt to read the messages coded in the surge and ruffle of water and the driftings and pilings of cloud. He could recognise the small signs – the slow oily swells, the restless surface play of dolphins – which were the muted warnings of the onset of the great 'norther', the terrible wind which leapt from nowhere to whip water and sky into shrieking confusion, and which had littered the reefs and beaches of the Caribbean with the shells of vessels whose pilots had run from the turmoil for the illusory safety of the shore.

Alaminos had been with Columbus as pilot on the old admiral's last voyage: he had seen the trading canoe, and all it promised. It had come, he remembered, from the west. It was Alaminos' confidence, and his reputation, which swung the Córdoba expedition away from the slender but easy pickings of slaving among the known islands towards an authentic voyage of exploration. Passing San Antonio, Cuba's westernmost point, the three ships maintained their course west.

After twelve days sailing the little fleet had left known waters, but Alaminos still held toward the setting sun, 'knowing nothing of the depth of the water, nor the currents, nor of the wind that normally prevailed in that latitude', recalled Bernal Díaz, who was no mariner and who had no trust in signs or those who claimed to read them.[5] Then came two days and nights of terror as the ships were buffeted and tossed by a storm. When the wind at last dropped, all three were still afloat, and still together. Seven days of easy sailing more, and they knew their luck held: a long, low coast slowly lifted above the horizon. This (though the Spaniards didn't know it) was the northeastern point of the great peninsula they would call 'Yucatan'. Edging cautiously towards the shore – the water shallowed a great distance out – they saw two leagues back from the beach, on slightly elevated land, and sharply defined in the clear air, a great town. It was the first town seen in the Indies, and the jubilant men instantly named it 'el Gran Cairo', the 'Great Cairo', for its size, its white pyramids, and their own vaulting hopes.

The next morning, as the two ships of the least draught probed about for a secure anchorage, ten huge canoes, bearing sail and driven by paddlers, came swooping out to meet them. These natives showed no sign of fear. As the Spaniards made banners of their capes in welcome, more than thirty Indians swung themselves aboard the flagship and swarmed over its length and breadth. They cheerfully accepted strings of green beads, and the leader among them, whom the Spaniards called by the Arawak title '*cacique*', meaning chief, appearing anxious to be hospitable in his own turn, indicated by signs that the strangers should come ashore, and that he would return the next day with canoes enough to ferry them all to the beach. Then he and his men dropped back into their craft and swept back to land.

There must have been celebrations aboard the Spanish ships that night. These Indians, decently clad in loincloths and vivid jackets, living in towns – both central requirements in Spanish notions of civility, and a promise of productivity and exploitability – these were a far cry from the sorry wretches of the settled islands, miserably crouched in their scattered huts with scarcely a rag to cover themselves. They were also well-disposed, and gratifyingly unsuspicious. Córdoba's ragged Spaniards knew that as their discoverers they could become their masters – provided Governor Velázquez

European hegemony

should not prove too greedy, and provided they could amass so substantial a claim by priority and effectiveness in action as to outweigh their own poverty and lack of status. The natives also proved men of their word. The next morning the chief came back as he had promised, still smiling and still affable, with twelve canoes manned by sturdy rowers, and again urged the newcomers ashore. The Spaniards were wary. The caravels had to be anchored a good league out to sea, and they could see that the beach where they were to land was one solid mass of Indians. But there could be no question of refusal: honour, curiosity and avarice drove them on. They packed into the brigantine and the ships' boats, with the most venturesome perched in the native canoes. Córdoba, still cautious, contrived that the whole flotilla came into the beach at the same time. Once landed, the *cacique* beckoned them towards the town, saying something which sounded like '*cones catoche, cones catoche*', which the Spaniards guessed meant 'come to our houses', and which was to lead them to name the headland Cape Catoche. Again, there was no serious alternative: clutching their weapons, and moving in the loose but conscious formation they adopted so naturally in situations of potential threat, they began the march along the path towards the town glistening white in the morning light. Then, as they drew level with some brush-covered hillocks the chief shouted, and Indian warriors, crested and painted, bodies swathed in quilted cotton armour, and armed with stones, bows and arrows, and flint-studded lances, leapt from hiding and attacked. The first flight of arrows wounded thirteen Spaniards. It says much for the discipline of men who had never fought together before that they did not break under that first rush, but were able to regroup, protect their wounded, and after sharp fighting drive the Indians off. Then they pushed quickly on to the small security of a little plaza, presumably on the fringe of the city, where there were three stone temples to the Indians' idols.

Bernal Díaz described the Indians' surprise attack as an ambush. It probably was. Ambush was a favourite tactic in Indian warfare. Deceptive displays of friendship were also not unusual. But there might have been no deception here. Certainly they intended war: their warrior regalia makes that clear. It is possible that the Spaniards' armed advance along the beach was taken as tacit acceptance of an Indian challenge: improvised sign language is not a particularly precise mode of communication. The Spaniards, reading the chief's demeanour as 'friendly', assumed their own physical security, but a courteous reception of strangers did not preclude combat in Indian etiquette. While the hostilities may have been a conventional response to uninvited intrusion, they may have been fuelled by more particular knowledge. If the excited Spaniards had had little sleep the previous night, we can be sure the Indians had no more. Stories of Spanish doings in the islands had certainly crossed to the peninsula; while there was no established trade between the two areas there were a multitude of less formalised contacts (a later Spanish expedition came across a woman from Jamaica, a member of a fishing party blown off course, who had fetched up on the peninsula's east coast). The purposeful investigation of the Spanish ships the previous day suggests the Indians had made the connection between these vessels and those others which had intercepted the trade canoe and made off with its captain fifteen years before. The Indians of Yucatan also had other sources of information regarding Spanish nature and intentions of which Córdoba and his men knew nothing: a small party of shipwrecked Spaniards had drifted to that coast six years before, and two survived still.

For Córdoba's men, some still bleeding, it was an 'ambush'. But as they rifled through the temples they cared little for Indian motivations. They were not vexed by Indian perfidy, nor deeply perturbed by the grotesque idols, nor even by the possibility, suggested by some strange sculpted figures, that these people lacked a proper abhorrence of sodomy, for in those temples they also found a few chests containing objects made of gold. The objects were small – a few 'diadems', some roughly-shaped ducks, some fishes; the gold was low grade. But it was gold. Returning exuberantly to their boats, the Spaniards hustled along with them two captured Indians as potential interpreters. In a country so full of promise, and hazard, communication by sign language could no longer be regarded as adequate.[6]

Fifteen days more of slow and cautious sailing, hugging the coast west and then south, and Spanish spirits were lower. They had learnt that while the slender Indian arrows struck with no great force the flint heads usually shattered on impact, making for a foul wound and a slow and ugly death. Two men had died since Cape Catoche, and their comrades had watched their bodies slide overboard to the patient sharks. Water was becoming the desperate problem it was to remain for the rest of an increasingly desperate voyage. The casks so hastily purchased in Cuba had begun to leak, Díaz thought because unscrupulous merchants had taken advantage of their need and poverty to sell off defective casks; but perhaps because in those early days of settlement men lacked the skill and the tested knowledge of local timbers to make them tight. But whether due to avarice or ignorance, the consequences were grave. From that time forward decisions as to where to make landfall were dictated not by calculations of security, but by the coercive need for water. And as the big ships could not come in closer than half a league, water-getting was a prolonged, exposed and risky business.

When an inlet was sighted, giving promise – falsely, as it turned out – of a stream, the Spaniards knew they had to go ashore, even though too many of their men were wounded, and even though another great town was clearly visible from the ships. They called the town 'San Lazaro', because it was on his day they first saw it, but they soon came to know it by its Indian name of Campeche.

The ships' boats and the brig carried a sizeable force of men ashore, where they found a pool of 'good water', and hastily filled their casks. As they were wrestling them back into the boats the Spaniards saw about fifty Indians come out from the town, and move steadily towards them. Unarmed and dressed in fine mantles, they had more the look of a delegation than the advance guard of an army. Through signs they asked the Spaniards what they wanted. The Spaniards, who had as yet no notion that water was a scarce resource throughout most of the peninsula, and its taking no light matter, urgently mimed the innocence of their presence: they had landed solely to fill their casks, and desired nothing more than to get them and themselves back to the ships riding at anchor out to sea. The Indians did not respond to the Spaniards' urgency. Pointing in the direction of the sunrise, they spoke with what seemed a questioning intonation a word which sounded to the desperately attentive listeners like 'Castilan, Castilan'. Then they turned, and signalled the Spaniards to follow them into the town.

It was a formidable dilemma. Another mauling like the one at Cape Catoche, too many wounded men, and they would have to call off the exploration of this intriguing coast, and their tenuous rights as its discoverers would be extinguished by more powerful men. Yet there was the compulsion of reputation. Refusal, or even too prolonged hesitation, could be read as fear. Fear could provoke attack. After a rapid consultation the Spaniards took the only course open to them. Shouldering their weapons, they let themselves be led into the town. This time there was no surprise attack. Their guides brought them to an open space before some large buildings made hideous, at least in Spanish eyes, by the great serpents and idols and strange cross-like symbols painted on their walls. To the front was a structure like an altar covered with what looked to be clotted blood. The Spaniards, huddled nervously together, took brief comfort in noting that there were women in the great crowd of Indians, strolling about with reassuring casualness. Then the press drew back and hushed to an expectant silence.

A group of Indian men, wearing ragged mantles and carrying loads of reeds, advanced, piled their reeds before the Spaniards, and withdrew. Behind them followed two squadrons of Indian warriors, painted, befeathered and fully armed, who halted at a little distance. Then ten men came swiftly out of one of the temples. Their long white mantles fell straight to their feet, but it was their hair which caught and held the Spaniards' incredulous attention, for it hung long and strangely thick, impenetrably matted and crusted with dried blood.

They came steadily forward through the silent crowd swinging their incense burners, finally wreathing the Spaniards in the sweet heavy smoke of the copal resin. In eloquent dumbshow they indicated that the strangers were to leave before the piled reeds were destroyed. They thrust fire into the heap, turned, and reentered the temple. The formal warning had been given with chilling confidence as to its intelligibility. Then the Spaniards heard for the first time a sound they were to learn to dread; the high whistling of Maya warriors on the attack. But no attack came. Despite the whistling, despite the thump of drums and the blasting moan of the conch-shell trumpets, the warriors held their ranks. The piled reeds still burned. There was neither time nor need for consultation. Pressing close together in tight defensive formation the Spaniards pulled back – not to their original landing-place, because that was too far, and too thick with Indians, but cutting directly to the shore, and then along the beach to where the brigantine and the boats, their anxious crews following events as best as they could from the water, came sidling in to scoop them up and to pull fast away to the security of the ships.

It was a bruising experience, to have run from a mere warning, and unnerving to recollect the dread that had made them run. There could, after all, be problems in the subjugating and management of these 'civilised' Indians. But the water had been got aboard, they had discovered another substantial town, and punishment for impudence and instruction in proper attitudes could always come later. Córdoba and his men pushed on.

Six fair days sailing, and then four days and nights of storm, and again water was desperately short, for now the casks gaped open and needed constant replenishing. The ships limped along, clinging as close to the coast as they dared, until again an inlet – again alarmingly close to a large town – promised a river. The boats were lowered, crowded with nervous men, and at a cluster of small stone huts they found good water. And again, as they struggled with the casks, Indians issued from the town.

This was no peaceful delegation, but squadrons of armed warriors. They came in silence along the beach. Their captains seemed to enquire whether the Spaniards had come from the direction of the rising sun. The Spaniards heard again the syllables which had so baffled them at Campeche, 'Castilan, Castilan', but despite being as Díaz recalled 'at their wits' end considering the matter' they could not make out what was meant. They had landed soon after midday, but by the time the casks had been filled and the parley with the warriors was over the sudden dusk of those latitudes had fallen. The squadrons were concealed in the darkness, but the Spaniards could hear the muffled sounds of large numbers of men moving close around. They posted sentinels, and considered their position. Some were for immediate embarkation. Most were against: in the confusion of getting aboard they would be too vulnerable to attack – and they could not easily bear to run away again. All through the night they argued and watched, until with the paling sky of dawn they saw they had waited too long. Great armies of Indians, their tall feathered crests and banners brilliant in the delicate grey morning light, had massed on the beach, joining those who had kept watch on the interlopers through the night. The drums sounded, the whistling clamour erupted.

Eighty Spaniards were wounded by the first shower of stones, arrows and darts. Then the Maya closed, wielding their double-edged war clubs, stabbing with their short lances. The closing came with terrible speed. Two men were seized alive, and dragged away; all were wounded, and most, including the captain Córdoba, the special target of Indian arrows, were bleeding from many wounds. The Spaniards held for as long as it took them to steady, and to drive through the pack to the water's edge. Then their discipline deserted them, as they clawed and scrambled and fought to get into the boats, half-swamped by the surge of desperate men. As they clung to the sterns or struggled in the water, Indian archers and lancers waded out to pick them off at leisure. When the survivors reached the haven of the ships, they found that more than fifty men, over half their number, were missing; of the rest all were wounded, some severely. Five were to die

1 Spanish explorers, conquerors, missionaries at work.

in agony over the next few days. And most of the casks – the precious,
cursed casks – were still on the beach. The whole disastrous affray had
occupied only an hour.[7]

The behaviour of Córdoba and his men after the Campeche disaster
compels respect. They had suffered a major defeat, and a major
humiliation, at the hands of men they had designated their prey and
their predestined subjects. Their condition was deplorable, and they
were far from aid. Dubbing the spot 'the Coast of the Disastrous
Battle', they turned to salvage what they could. Too many sailors had
been wounded to get all three ships back to Cuba, and even those
most jealous of their discoveries and most mistrustful of Velázquez
knew that now they had to go back. Therefore they abandoned the
smallest ship – the brigantine held on credit from the Governor – and
distributed the men between the two caravels. The handful of sailors
who had manned the ships during the battle, and who were therefore
the only men with whole skins, with three soldiers who had been

lightly wounded, went ashore on a lonely beach to dig for water. They found some, but it was such bitter stuff that those few who forced it down suffered for it. After forty-eight hours of storms, with the men suffering badly from thirst, Alaminos decided to run for Florida. There they found sweet water, but only at the cost of a sharp brush with tall Indian bowmen and the loss of two men: one a guard, wandering too far from his companions and carried off bodily, or so it seemed from the faint traces of his struggle among the trees, and the other one of the parched wounded on board ship, who drank so deeply of the water that he died within a day.

At last the little expedition found its way back to Cuba. Hernández de Córdoba was to die of his wounds soon after his ships made port, but before he died he wrote a report to Governor Velázquez celebrating the land he had discovered, with its fine cities of masonry houses, its abundant populations, its plantations, and its gold.[8] Above all, the gold. The gold which obliterated the memory of suffering, and transmuted disaster into triumph.

It is difficult for us to grasp the peculiar glamour and significance the yellow metal held for the conquistadores. We respond instantly to the cool irony of a Hernán Cortés explaining to a Mexican chief that Spaniards suffer from a disease of the heart, for which gold is the only specific; but in that coolness and irony, as in almost everything else, Cortés is atypical.[9] The Genoese Columbus tells us more, as he writes the closing lines of a letter to the Spanish monarchs: 'Gold is most excellent; of gold there is formed treasure and with it whoever has it may do what he wishes in this world and come to bring souls into Paradise.'[10]

'To do what he wishes in this world.' For Columbus gold would buy the universal triumph of Christianity. Less pious men dreamed different dreams, but to see sixteenth-century adventurers as hard-headed pragmatists and materialists is, despite their tireless measuring and counting, and their endless talk of profits, to risk missing the point. Gold was entrancingly tangible: it could be held in the hand, weighed in the palm. Some men did take what they could and return to Spain to buy a more elegant and expansive life within the confines of traditional structures; others chose to live well in the rougher but more open societies of the Spanish colonial towns. But for many gold's lustre lay not in its power to summon material goods, nor (although this was more important) in its capacity to dazzle lesser men: it derived its radiance from the dreams of a liberty and independence of action possible only in a new and transformed world. When Hernán Cortés cut from his cloak some knots of gold so that one of his men could buy a horse, he was displaying a casual munificence towards a dependant which echoed the gestures not of sixteenth-century Spain, but of its mythic *Reconquista* past.[11] The golden knots were to buy a horse for the great venture into Mexico. Cortés as the Marques del Valle, on a pinnacle of economic and social power, endlessly fretted to escape the confines of that eminence into still another grand, taxing, absorbing adventure. Francisco Pizarro, conqueror of Peru, contrived to get himself killed in the broils and squabbles which were the distorted echoes of the irreplaceable, unforgettable excitements of exploration and conquest. Pedro de Alvarado, Cortés' lieutenant in the conquest of Mexico and hero of a dozen extravagant exploits, died at fifty-six, subduing yet another clutch of rebellious natives in an obscure corner of northern New Spain. Gold spoke to such men of the chance not to live soft, but to live at full gambler's stretch. Bernal Díaz, who at the end of his long life had won little enough gold, living quietly on his Guatemalan estate, retained the habit of wistful restlessness, and was up several times every night, he tells us, to look at the stars, and to remember those other watchful nights of strung-bow tension lit with fear and hope.[12] Even in those early days of 1517 the little ducks and fishes, the three small diadems looted from the temple at Cape Catoche, far outweighed the stories of suppurating wounds and men whimpering with thirst, of lithe warriors and sinister priests. The two Indian captives, who had somehow survived the terrible voyage back to Cuba, along the way acquiring a smattering of Spanish together, we must assume, with some understanding of their masters' obsessions, swore under insistent questioning that there were great supplies of the yellow metal in the peninsula. Velázquez wrote triumphantly to the Council of the Indies in Spain announcing what he presented as his discovery, and by January of 1518 a new and better equipped expedition was ready to sail under the command of Juan de Grijalva, with the indispensable Alaminos as chief pilot.[13]

Most of the down-at-heel men who had survived the Córdoba expedition were too broken in health and credit to find a place among the 240 men recruited: as they had bitterly foreseen, the new expedition was dominated by men already powerful in Cuba. In the ruthless competition which was the mapping and claiming of the New World there were no prizes for participating, but only for winning. Governor Velázquez attempted to protect his claim to overall authority by providing all four ships, together with crossbows, muskets and some items to barter, perhaps including some of the Spanish wine for which Córdoba had reported that Indians – presumably during the initial friendly exchanges at Cape Catoche – had shown so marked a liking. The gentlemen appointed captains of the ships, and therefore potentially administrators in the new lands, strengthened their claim to later privilege by supplying the required salt pork and cassava bread, much of it produced on their own estates. Lesser men supplied themselves as best they could, attaching themselves to one or other of the captains. Bernal Díaz, penniless and therefore dependent on favours, won a place in the expedition when his kinsman Velázquez secured him a minor post.

At least one of the two men seized at Cape Catoche was also taken along. Grijalva seems to have been genuinely anxious to fulfil Velázquez' instructions to explore rather than to settle, and avoided conflict where he could. At the island of Cozumel, their first landfall, he kept his Spaniards in tight check, though he was unable to coax the island's timid inhabitants to respond to his friendly gestures. The fleet made a sortie down the east coast to the great bay they named the Bay of Ascensión, and sighted several substantial towns along the way, but the captain refused to let the restless men land. Turning back, he coasted the peninsula to Campeche, where he attempted initially to negotiate for water, in face of his men's impatience to use their small cannon, but Indian intransigence gave them the opportunity they wanted, and this time it was the Indians who broke and fled. The Spaniards took possession of the well-remembered town, but it was almost empty of people. Despite Grijalva's message of peace and hopeful gifts of green beads sent out into the forest with Indians too old or too slow to escape, the forest remained silent and the town deserted, so the Spaniards took ship and sailed on.

As the Spanish ships prodded their way along the coast, the great canoes of the Maya raced away to carry word of their coming, and warning of the new, noisy weapons which belched fire and could kill at a distance. At Champoton, the town which had been the scene of the disastrous battle on the beach, the Indians showed little of their old aggression: a few big war canoes made tentative approaches, but a couple of cannon shots put them to flight. Grijalva forced his grumbling men on, refusing to let them pause to teach the Indians manners, and choosing to make camp to rest worn men and refurbish worn ships at a beautiful but unpopulated bay. Sailing on to the river we call the Tabasco, he found numbers of armed warriors and fleets of canoes assembled, but as the Indians still seemed disinclined for battle, keeping a wary distance from the ships, Grijalva seized the chance to communicate through his interpreters his peaceful intentions, and his readiness to exchange beads and Spanish wine for food and other necessities.

The Indians acquiesced. It seemed they had decided on a policy of meeting manageable demands, and so moving their unpopular visitors out of their territory. They certainly knew what bait to use. Along with the food they offered a few trifling gold ornaments – not worth above 200 *pesos*, Díaz estimated – but they kept earnestly indicating that in the direction of the sunset there was an abundance of gold, and, as Díaz recalled it, 'they said, "Colua, Colua, México, México", but we did not know what this Colua or México could be'.[14] They were soon to find out. Sailing on, they passed a sandy beach where warriors pranced and cavorted – warriors whose great tortoiseshell shields glinting in the sun were taken for gold by the more hopeful and naive soldiers – into the golden domains dominated by the people called the Azteca or the Mexica, and ruled by the great lord Moctezuma: the land the Spaniards formally named 'New Spain', but which came to be known as 'Mexico'. Grijalva, faithful to Velázquez' instructions, collected enough evidence that Mexico was indeed a golden prize, and turned for home. There were brushes with the natives at Champoton and Campeche, but again Grijalva refused his men the gratification of vengeance.

Grijalva had sent one ship ahead to carry word to Velázquez of the marvellous new land and its gold. When the rest of the fleet came into port they found the next expedition already in preparation. It was to be led by Hernán Cortés, at that time distinguished by little more than a smooth tongue and extravagant tastes in entertaining, but to prove himself the most brilliant strategist and leader the New World was to produce. The Cortés expedition effectively ignored Yucatan, making landfall only at Cozumel Island. That pattern was to persist for the decade the Spaniards took to dismember and to distribute the spoils of the Aztec empire. With the prospect of Mexican riches the inhospitable coasts of Yucatan had lost all attraction. Cozumel became the favoured, first and often the only landfall for the watering and refurbishing of ships *en route* to Mexico.

The Indians of Cozumel had never offered resistance, except by flight, and Cortés contrived to gain the cooperation of the chief Naum Pat, and persuaded his men to treat the Indians of the island with unaccustomed gentleness.[15] Prudential considerations probably led later visitors to respect the convention he established. The people of Cozumel had long experience of accommodating outsiders who came in peace, as the island was sacred to the Maya goddess Ix Chel, and her shrine was a place of pilgrimage for the mainland Maya. A peculiarly treacherous current running in the narrow sea between mainland and island was a further barrier to violent invasion. Certainly Naum Pat and his people enjoyed immunity from the endemic Indian warfare which constituted normal relations between the mainland provinces, and saw themselves as outside the Maya political arena. Their tranquil cosmopolitanism seems to have extended to incorporate the Spanish ships which were to come and go with increasing frequency over the next years.

It was on his first landfall at Cozumel that Cortés solved the mystery of those strange syllables 'Castilan' which had so puzzled Córdoba's men. He discovered through an interpreter that traders visiting the island had spoken of two Spaniards being held as slaves somewhere on the mainland. Cortés sent out local emissaries·with letters and promises, and through luck and patience was able to retrieve one of the men, whose lord consented to release him. Gerónimo de Aguilar's Spanish had grown rusty, but he was able to tell Cortés how he and a handful of other Spaniards, survivors of a shipwreck, had stumbled ashore on a northern beach some time in 1511; how all but he and one other had been sacrificed, or had died of hunger or disease; and that the other survivor was called Gonzalo Guerrero, and was still alive somewhere in the south-east.

On Aguilar's rescue, it is reported, he 'wept for joy, and kneeling down, he thanked God, and asked the Spaniards if the day was Wednesday . . .' having contrived to count off his days of servitude among the pagans by the Christian calendar. He had also been left his breviary, 'with which he kept run of the feast days', and, if some later special pleading is to be believed, had won the awed respect of his *cacique* by his dour defence of his chastity in face of the most calculated and delicious temptations.[16] But his rescuers probably eyed him uneasily: he had lived among the devil worshippers, after all, for a full eight years, and spoke their strange tongue and knew their strange ways. Further, he brought news almost incredible to Spaniards proud of race and faith. Gonzalo Guerrero had refused to be 'rescued' because he had gone over to the natives. He had married an Indian woman, and had children by her. He had been tattooed, and wore the ear-plugs of a warrior. Aguilar also understood he had become a war-captain, and had urged and organised the attack on certain Spanish ships, probably those of the Córdoba expedition, at Cape Catoche the

year before. Small wonder that bringing such news Aguilar trod
warily.

Aguilar, with his acquired Maya and his remembered Spanish, was
to go on to be a crucial link in the chain of interpreters who permitted
Cortés to talk rather than fight his way into Moctezuma's great
imperial city of Tenochtitlan. Guerrero was to remain a peculiarly
threatening figure to his fellow Spaniards. However gratified by
indications of Indian 'civility', however impressed by demonstrations
of Indian courage, these Spaniards knew Indians to be irrevocably
inferior. Indian 'religion' was a filthy mixture of superstition and
devil worship. For one of their own to acquiesce in such filthiness,
and to choose it over his own faith and his own people, was to strike
at the heart of their sense of self. In the defeats and baffling reversals
they were to suffer through the whole of the wearisome conquest of
the peninsula, they were to identify, wherever they were to occur and
however implausibly, the mark of his baffling dark intelligence.

What it was that held Aguilar to his Spanish and Christian sense of
self, yet allowed Guerrero to identify with native ways, is mysterious.
We know nothing of how Guerrero's remaking as a Maya came
about; whether isolation and despair led to collapse, and then a slow
rebuilding, or whether knowledge of many ports (he was thought to
be a sailor), an ear quick for foreign sounds, a mind curious for
foreign ways, allowed an easier transition. What startles is the tenacity
and passion of his war against his erstwhile countrymen. It was not
until 1534 or 1535, when the tattooed body of a white man was found
among the Indian dead after a skirmish in the territory of Honduras-
Higueras to the south of Yucatan, that Spaniards could be sure that
Guerrero was dead, and his malice at an end. His hatred of his
countrymen had been so compelling that he had led a canoe-borne
attack far beyond his own territory, and had died for it.[17]

Over the next several years the mainland Maya were to be little
troubled by Spaniards. One of the Spanish barques skirting their
coasts might turn and come in for water, taking it with or without a
fight, but usually the ships sailed out where the water was deep,
remote as passing gulls. The Maya probably believed the ships held
well out through respect for their own fighting abilities. They knew
of the fate of Mexico, and suffered some repercussions: the market for
their finest cotton garments and their brown cakes of salt had closed,
and merchants from Aztec lands no longer brought the brilliant
skeins of dyed rabbit fur, the fine worked gold ornaments, the
obsidian knives, to the entrepôt at Xicalango.[18] Instead there came

stories of sieges, mass enslavements, and unfamiliar cruelties; of floggings, of cutting off of hands, of men and women burned alive.

The Maya also received another sign of the Spanish presence, though they probably did not recognise it as such. At about the time of the Córdoba expedition a new and terrible disease devastated the peninsula. It was almost certainly smallpox, perhaps introduced by the expedition, though there is nothing to suggest that in the records, or by some forgotten victims of shipwreck, or brought by a long chain of Indian carriers from Panama. The Franciscan Diego de Landa was later told by some of those who had seen it at work that it was characterised by 'great pustules, which rotted [the] bodies with a great stench, so that the limbs fell to pieces in four or five days'.[19] Oddly, no Spanish observer commented on the tell-tale pock marks, possibly because they were accustomed to such disfigurement of both Indian and Spanish skins. The lower level of aggression displayed by the Indians to Grijalva and his men was perhaps due to disruptions wrought by the disease, but unhappily we know almost nothing of how the Maya responded to the epidemic, to the shrinkage of their trade world, or to the steady movement of the foreign ships across their horizons. And then, a decade after Córdoba's ships had made their first landfall on the peninsula, there came another Spanish fleet.

2

Conquerors

With the spoils of Mexico divided, Spanish interest had turned again to Yucatan. Late in 1526 Francisco de Montejo, who had served as a captain in both the Grijalva and the Cortés expeditions, obtained a charter from the Crown for the pacification of the peninsula. He proclaimed his proposed conquest throughout a Spain enchanted afresh by a New World which had already yielded one Mexico.[1] Within a few months he had secured four good ships, cannon, excellent small arms, horses, and what he believed to be abundant supplies of meat, oil, wine, vinegar and biscuits. He had recruited a surgeon, two pharmacists, three churchmen – two seculars and a Carmelite – and several Catalan merchants, complete with merchandise to trade with the Indians and, when they should get established, with the conquistadores-turned-settler. Among the usual adventurers attracted to Montejo's standard were a few men of significant rank. When the smart little fleet dropped down past San Lúcar de Barrameda late in the June of 1527, it looked, as Montejo believed it to be, 'the best that has come out from Castile'.[2] Arrived in Hispaniola, the expedition was stiffened by the intake of some seasoned men, and horses enough to bring the cavalry up to fifty – an indication of the tough reputation the Maya warriors of the coastal towns had won for themselves. But there was one surprising lack. Montejo had known and spoken with Aguilar, and with Cortés' more famous interpreter Doña Marina. He knew the 'pacified' Indians of Tabasco spoke a tongue intelligible to the Yucatan Maya. But he provided himself neither with an interpreter, nor even with a basic Mayan vocabulary. It was an extraordinary omission, and suggests that Spanish confidence in their destiny to master Indians was so complete as to obviate the requirement to hold human converse with them along the way.

Leaving Santo Domingo, the fleet sailed to Cozumel, where they were given the usual friendly reception by the amiable Naum Pat. They crossed the dangerous strait to the mainland without incident, making landfall near a small village called Xelha. There Montejo decided – apparently with minimal reflection – to establish the first Spanish settlement in Yucatan. The stores were dragged ashore, the cluster of rough shelters went up, and Montejo dubbed the whole collection 'Salamanca de Xelha', in nostalgic tribute to his own birthplace.

Within two months fifty of his men were dead.[3] They died, most of them, close by the little collection of huts on the beach, from disease, hunger or exhaustion. The 'abundant supplies' brought from Spain had melted away with terrifying rapidity. Montejo commandeered the foodstuffs so hopefully imported by the Catalan merchants; those too were consumed. For a time the small population of local Indians had been bullied and coaxed into bringing the hungry Spaniards offerings from their own meagre diet of beans and squashes, peppers and maize, but what would sustain them for a month was consumed by Spaniards in a day, and they hid from the desperate men. The Spaniards found that swords and muskets were useless when Indians would not stand to fight nor stay to be intimidated, but simply withdrew into the wilderness of the forest. The raiding parties made up of the fitter Spaniards sometimes stumbled on a mean village, but the few handfuls of dried maize-cobs they netted did little for the shivering, fever-ridden men back at the main camp.

When murmurings about the dreadful futility of their miserable 'settlement' got too loud Montejo, in a gesture which at this distance looks like a parody of the great Cortés, destroyed his ships to cut off the chance of escape. That action, irresponsible though it was, paid off: as the months passed, the men slowly became seasoned, and learnt to survive in that hostile terrain, until there were men fit enough for Montejo to lead a party out of the settlement to explore to the north. Saved from starvation by a chance meeting with Naum Pat, who had come to the mainland to attend a wedding – a tantalising glimpse of the continuing pulse of ordinary Maya life – Montejo and his men moved on to Ecab, the 'Gran Cairo' of the Córdoba expedition, and then through other major towns of the north-east, before swinging back to Salamanca de Xelha. There they found their numbers, counting their own losses, had been reduced to a third; but the arrival of a ship carrying supplies and reinforcements gave them strength for a sortie southward, to the thriving port of Chetumal. At Chetumal Montejo discovered that the renegade Gonzalo Guerrero was somewhere near, and decided to make one more attempt to recall him to his senses and his duty. A version of the letter he sent by a native messenger, and of Guerrero's putative response, was recorded by the man appointed official chronicler of the Indies, Oviedo, and is worth quoting for the themes Montejo – or Oviedo – thought to play upon. It runs:

Gonzalo, my brother and special friend. I count it my good fortune that I arrived and have learned of you through the bearer of this letter, [through which] I can remind you that you are Christian, bought by the blood of Jesus Christ, our Redeemer, to whom I give, and you should give, infinite thanks. You have a great opportunity to serve God and the Emperor, Our Lord, in the pacification and baptism of these people, and more than this, [opportunity] to leave your sins behind you, with the Grace of God, and to honor and benefit yourself. I shall be your very good friend in this, and you will be treated very well.

And thus I beseech you not to let the devil influence you not to do what I say, so that he will not possess himself of you forever.

On behalf of His Majesty I promise you to do very well for you and fully to comply with that which I have said. On my part, as a noble gentlemen, I give you my word and pledge my faith to make my promise to you good without any reservations whatsoever, favouring and honouring you and making you one of my principal men and one of my most select and loved groups in these parts.

Consequently [I beseech] you to come to this ship, or to the coast, without delay, to do what I have said and to help me carry out, through giving me your counsel and opinions, that which seems most expedient.

The chronicler also recorded Guerrero's reply, scrawled in charcoal on the obverse, and if anywhere near authentic demonstrating Guerrero's literacy, perhaps surprising in a mariner of 'low origins', as well as his fine sense of irony. He is said to have written:

Senor, I kiss your Grace's hands. As I am a slave I have no freedom [to join you], even though I . . . remember God. You, my lord, and the Spaniards will find in me a very good friend.[4]

If Guerrero 'remembered God', his actions gave no hint of it, while their freedom and range indicate that he was no slave. His 'friendship' he was to demonstrate vigorously over the next several years, advising the native chiefs, organising their strategy, and then carrying his personal vendetta against the Spaniards beyond Yucatan to Honduras-Higueras and his death.

Rebuffed by Guerrero, and with the eastern and north-eastern fringes of the peninsula now roughly explored, Montejo turned his attention to the west coast, establishing his main camp at Campeche. Most of the men still with him had been recruited in New Spain or the islands, and were very much tougher than the eager young men from Spain who had sickened and died in the swampy coastal fringes of the eastern forests. Between 1529 and 1534 his forces penetrated through most of the north and centre, and one party had cut across the peninsula from Campeche to Chetumal. Only the eastern and southern interior remained largely unexplored. In those five years they had learnt some lessons, none of them welcome, about Yucatan, and about the Maya.

They learnt that there was no golden city lying hidden in the forest awaiting its conqueror. The towns of the deep interior failed to match those on the coast either in size or in prosperity. Even on the coast, where fishing and canoe-borne trade allowed the maintenance of much larger populations than in the agriculture-dependent interior, actual populations were probably smaller than first impressions had suggested. The chronicler Oviedo had been told by men who had taken part in the first Yucatan expedition that Champoton, for example, contained 8,000 houses, and Campeche 2,000.[5] Maya towns were certainly large in area. One soldier recollected that he and his companions had passed the outskirts of the great town of Chauaca in the copal-growing region of the north-east at midday, and had reached the lords' houses and temples marking the town centre only at 'vespers'. Even now, after European reorganisation, Maya towns strike strangers as very spread out. Then, as now, each house was surrounded by a substantial house-yard, big enough to allow for the raising of animals, vegetables, and fruit trees, and often enough a handy supply of maize. The yards also had to provide space for a multitude of domestic activities, with the small, dark house interiors being used for little more than sleeping. Not all houses were occupied: the Maya frequently abandoned a dwelling after the death and burial (usually under the floor) of the head of the household. And from tense, excited soldiers guessing at the size of their prize in the lottery of the New World we must expect both conscious and unconscious exaggeration.

The towns of the interior, where the exigencies of slash-and-burn agriculture combined with a Maya preference for the security and excitements of collective life to put an upper limit on population, rarely held more than four thousand people, and usually fewer.[6] They were modest places altogether, with often enough the only stone building being the pyramid-platform of the temple. The houses of the lords were rarely built of stone, and were distinguished only by size and preferred position from the wattle-and-daub dwellings of the commoners.

The Spaniards were aware of the imbalance between the towns of the coasts and of the interior, but they gave little attention to the reasons for it. They noticed the great salt-pans of the northern coast, they were disturbed by the strange scent which hung in the air as they rode through the groves of copal, the native incense, in the region around Chauaca, and from time to time they caught the tell-tale flash of scarlet blossom which betrayed cacao trees clustered in some especially favoured hollow. It is unlikely that they recognised or cared to consider the importance of any of these products in native trade, inside and outside of the peninsula. To moderns trained to respectful curiosity regarding the exotic ways of other cultures – a curiosity developed by dozens of popularised ethnographies and scores of lushly photographed documentaries – the vision of the Spaniards seems curiously blinkered. They noted, or at least recorded, only those aspects of native life immediately relevant to themselves. They were attentive to the substantial native traffic in slaves, because of their own interest in labour which cost only its keep. They commented on the magnificent loincloths, skirts and mantles woven by the women of Yucatan – garments so splendid they could find eager buyers even among the fastidious Aztec lords of Tenochtitlan – but only as general evidence of the 'civility' of the natives; they were, as yet, little interested in what they signified for commercial exploitation. They noted the maize cakes, the honey, the fruits, the little dogs, the 'chickens', as they generically labelled the turkeys and ducks raised by the Maya, brought to them as offerings of peace as they approached certain towns, but they were concerned with them as food first, tokens of submission second, and as evidence of native agricultural techniques and modes of production not at all. They had not come to Yucatan to farm, or to trifle with native products: after all, some men had staked already-established and substantial ranches and other holdings in this venture. They had come to subjugate the Indians and to find riches; and riches meant, quite specifically, precious stones, silver, and gold.

That first task of conquest proved difficult. Although they spoke a common tongue the Maya were not politically united: indeed, the Spaniards were long puzzled to discover any stable political group-ings in the country. Initially, the physical appearance of things, their reading of Indian behaviour, and their own cultural predilections had inclined them to identify the town as the key social and political unit. The deference shown the town chief, the *'batab'* as they discovered he was called; his and his lords' authority to settle disputes; the social gradations mapped in size and location of dwellings – all these powerfully suggested that each town constituted an autonomous system, especially as each treated with the Spaniards with an independence so developed as to appear capricious. They learnt that a town which had once welcomed them with gifts might on their next entry greet them with arrows. Even more bewildering, if less dangerous, that order was sometimes reversed.[7] More frustrating, especially for Spaniards, who at least officially placed a high value on the binding power of oaths, the Maya seemed to suffer from selective amnesia. Treaties and agreements were forgotten when the actual physical presence of the Spaniards was withdrawn, leaving battles to be fought and submissions to be exacted all over again. It seemed that, for the Maya, oaths were written in water.

Unsurprisingly, these first invaders never grasped the importance of less visible authorities and relationships: the exigencies of survival focussed their curiosity on the most obvious elements in the Maya political order: towns, and chiefs. With time and continuing failure, their understanding became more sophisticated, and they began to see, behind the apparently atomistic structures, the outlines of larger and more compelling loyalties. While the Maya spoke the same tongue, and in some sense thought of themselves as one people, their most clear allegiance appeared to be towards a particular territory, and the particular lineage which ruled it. The Spaniards came to recognise that at least in some 'provinces', as they tentatively called them, the town chiefs who had seemed to act so independently in fact owed their allegiance, and their position, to a head chief who ruled the whole province – the *halach uinic*, or 'real man', as he was titled. Even where no such developed structure existed the chiefs of a particular province, while they might occasionally fight one with the other, always united against outsiders, and thought of themselves as a distinct people. Thus the Indians of Campeche region called themselves the Pech, and many of their town chiefs were of that lineage. Around Champoton the Couoh ruled; in Mani the Xiu; in Sotuta the Cocom; in Ah Kin Chel the Chel, and thus for perhaps sixteen or more distinct provinces.[8] Despite endemic war and slave-raiding, there were, it seemed, connections between the ruling lineages, and mutual respect and recognition of the legitimacy of their authority. When Montejo's son led an expedition of two hundred men to establish a Spanish settlement at Chichen Itza, the Cupul lord in whose territory Chichen lay demurred when the Spanish leader demanded his submission to the Crown of Spain, saying: 'We already have kings, o noble lords, King Cocom of Sotuta, Naum Pech, King Pech, Namax Chel . . . of Dzinzantun. Foreign warriors, we here are the Itza!'[9] The 'Itza', invaders themselves from Toltec Mexico three centuries before, had established the rule of their several lineages through much of the peninsula. Later events had created divisions, and in the struggle for Chichen Itza the Cocomes, the Cupules, the Cochuah and the Tases cooperated against the Spaniards, while the Xiu, the Ah Kin Chel and the Ceh Pech lent the outsiders rather tentative support. But while the Spaniards could at last begin to see some pattern in what had seemed irrational or wilfully fickle responses of particular Maya towns, and to recognise the reality of frontiers which bore no visible markings, in none of the early campaigns were they able to locate a clear and permanent line of cleavage between the provinces. That they needed, desperate as they were to emulate Cortés' dazzling exploitation of tribal divisions in the Mexican conquest which had already become a model of strategy and audacity for all who sought to conquer in the New World.

If crucial political boundaries lay unmarked, the landscape itself resisted mental mapping, and offered its own harassments. While there were some pockets of relief – the rolling parklike land of the far north-east, the occasional grove of softer vegetation – most of the land, the Spaniards found, was blanketed by a thick, tough growth; scrubby to the north and west, taller as the rains increased to the south and east, but always baffling to the eye and confusing to the mind. Scattered through the forest were the villages and towns, each sustained by the cleared patches or *milpas* where the Indians grew their maize and the other basic crops, but without local knowledge of the vague tracery of paths webbing the forest it was easy to pass them by. There were no vantage points in that flat land from which distances gained could be measured, future objectives identified – what small elevations there were revealed only the grey scrub stretching to the rim of the horizon. And there were physical hardships. The air, dankly chill at the end of the wet season, was thick and hot for most of the year. Land flat and featureless to the eye was bruisingly uneven underfoot, the loose stones sliding away, the crests and ridges of rock jarring. The forest growth crowded close along the paths, high enough to blinker vision and distort sound, and to seal away any grateful breath of wind, but too low to offer the sweating, cursing men any respite from the sun. Paths comfortably wide for the smooth-trotting Maya, body bowed, possessions slung neatly in a carrying net along the back, were miserably narrow for the European footsoldier, lugging his clumsy weapons and, where natives could not be pressed into service, whatever food he had been able to gather or loot. For the horseman, hacking away at overhanging branches, his mount plunging and slithering, it was frustrating, constant, unproductive exertion.

Even the vegetation proved malicious, nearly all of it hooked or prickled or barbed. The tender acacia fronds fringing the paths concealed savage thorns eager to tear flesh. Insects made their contribution to misery. Mosquitoes swarmed along the coasts, and to brush carelessly through any foliage was to risk attack by the big black ants which stung as badly as any hornet, or the less immediate but more prolonged anguish of a cascade of *garrapatas*, the tiny burrowing ticks which first set up an intolerable itch, and then turned flesh into a swollen suppurating mass if left untreated too long.[10]

The Spaniards had been quick to realise that Maya projectile weapons were not sufficiently powerful to justify the weight of European armour, so they replaced it with a Spanish variation of the quilted cotton armour of the Indian warriors. Footsoldiers habitually wore knee-length tunics and Spanish-style caps, with chin pieces and visors all reproduced in quilted cotton. The horsemen added long leg-protectors in the same stuff, and the precious horses were shrouded in protective skirts. The improvised armour was light and flexible, but still uncomfortably hot. The nights brought little relief, as ears strained to identify the cries and mutterings of unfamiliar nocturnal creatures, and mosquitoes kept up their tireless attack. For most of the time they were thirsty. As the little bands struggled in from the coasts the men came to discover that the whole northern section of the peninsula had no rivers, no streams, and no drinkable surface water at all, save that little caught in hard rock depressions, man-made or natural, during the rains. The whole peninsula was a great limestone shelf, and permanent water could be found only where the surface crust had broken away to form sinkholes, or '*cenotes*' as the Spaniards – prepared in this vital matter to follow Maya usage – learnt to call them, giving access to the water table beneath (in the south, where soil was deeper and rain heavier, there was too much water, and expeditions struggled and floundered through endless morasses and swamps). There were *cenotes* enough, if you knew where to find them. Any human settlement meant there was a *cenote* somewhere in the vicinity, and there were many others hidden in the forest. Local Indians could sometimes be forced to tell where they were, though some chose to remain mute, and died silent, and some of those who spoke then led the Spaniards into ambush. Sometimes – increasingly often, as the years of war dragged on – the intruders found that before the villagers, warned by their noisy approach, had fled to take refuge in the forest, they had found time to fill or foul the wells, and to burn the village foodstocks; a procedure inconvenient to the Spaniards, and possibly fatal to themselves, but giving sinister warning of Maya capacity for war *à outrance*.[11]

Direct attack, when it came, was chillingly effective. Spaniards learnt that Indian hands could insinuate thick rope-like vines so skilfully through and between the growth along the track to give no sign of their presence, until the sudden stirring in the leaves, the hiss of arrows, sent men and horses trapped in single file plunging and lurching in a desperate struggle to escape the swarming dark figures, who killed, and killed, and then, as the Spaniards fought down their own and their horses' panic, and steadied themselves for revenge, melted back into the forest.[12] Land and people denied the Spaniards opportunity to display their distinctive forms of courage and audacity. The subjugation of Yucatan demanded not heroism, but a kind of dour tenacity little valued and therefore little practised in Spanish performance. But all could have been borne had it not been for one lack. What made the hardships intolerable and the place and the people detestable was that there was neither gold nor silver nor precious stones in the peninsula.

Hope had died slowly: in April 1529 Montejo, while allowing that the country had its difficulties, with much of it bush-covered and rough, was still confident, informing the Crown:

The land is heavily peopled and has very large and beautiful cities and towns. All the towns are a [veritable] fruit garden . . . I have found many signs of gold . . . I went over a great part of the land and I heard many reports of the gold and [precious] stones that are in it . . .[13]

By August of 1534 he could no longer deceive himself. Nor had he any interest in deceiving the King: he and his men had heard news of golden Peru, and Yucatan could hold them no longer. Montejo summed up what he had learnt of the place in the seven years since he had raised the banner of the conquest in Seville:

In these provinces there is not a single river, although there are lakes, and the hills are of live rock, dry and waterless. The entire land is covered by thick bush and is so stony that there is not a single square foot of soil. No gold has been discovered, nor is there anything [else] from which advantage can be gained. The inhabitants are the most abandoned and treacherous in all the lands discovered to this time, being a people who never yet killed a Christian except by foul means and who have never made war except by artifice. Not once have I questioned them on any matter that they have not answered, 'Yes', with the purpose of causing me to leave them and go somewhere else. In them I have failed to find truth touching anything.[14]

By 1535 there were no Spaniards in the peninsula. While later a tiny group under orders from Montejo clung on at Campeche, it was not until 1540 that the Maya were once again under foreign attack. Those Spaniards who regrouped under his son in 1540 to renew the assault on the peninsula were determined but disillusioned men. They knew the country held no promise of treasure; they knew its resistant people and its resistant terrain. They returned because they no longer hoped for riches. They knew they had missed the big prizes. Many of them middle-aged, many of them with family responsibilities, they sought some modest but secure recompense for their years of marching and fighting and going on short rations in the New World. And Yucatan, poor as it was, had some potential. The intricately embroidered cotton garments now spoke to more chastened men of a raw material, local technical skill, and the chance of a commercial product tuned to European needs. Honey, wax, indigo, cacao, all suggested the possibility of a modest but useful trade. Above all, there were the Maya themselves, sturdy, vigorous, accustomed to regular labour, and conveniently close to the chronically labour-hungry mines of the islands, which had only sick and dying Indians to work them. The enslavement and export of the native population was the most promising road to profit.

The Maya had not used their five years' grace well. They probably believed the foreigners had quit their territory for good; after all, they had driven them away before: at Campeche, at Champoton, they had beaten the invaders back to their boats, so they had not dared to venture inshore again for many years. Then they had come back, blundering from province to province, but they had finally given up, and gone away. Guerrero's advice, and their own observations, must also have informed the Maya of the centrality of gold as a fuel of Spanish energy. Yet their behaviour over that half decade seems to go beyond misplaced insouciance. It suggests that Spanish intrusions, both direct and indirect, into the rhythm of Maya life had been more socially disruptive and psychologically disturbing than the flawed mirror of Spanish accounts implies. A missionary friar was later to record what he was told had happened in those years. First, after the Spaniards had left, there came a great drought. Few communities had been left with reserves. The bearded foreigners had neither planted nor harvested, and fought and looted when they chose, even through the time for planting, when no Maya thought of war. So famine followed on the heels of drought, and the people had to abandon their villages to live as best they could. It was in these desperate circumstances, with the ritual life of the villages tattered, that the Xiu of Mani decided to make pilgrimage to the Sacred Cenote at Chichen Itza, to make offerings to the gods of rain. To reach the Sacred Cenote they had to cross the territory of their traditional enemies the Cocom of Sotuta. They therefore explained their mission – which was clearly of crucial importance to every province in the peninsula – and requested, and were granted, safe conduct. Then, at the Cocom town of Otzmal, where the Xiu lords had been lodged together in one large house, the Cocom set the structure on fire, and killed all those who managed to escape the flames.[15]

That, at least, is the story as the friar recorded it. One of his major informants was a Xiu, and it is possible the deliberation of the Cocom in the matter was exaggerated. Other accounts emphasise the Xiu's earlier flirtation with the Spaniards, and see the killings as fitting punishment for quislings.[16] But treacherous attack was a Maya technique: the settled hostility between the Cocom and the Xiu derived from an earlier betrayal and massacre, when the Xiu lords had led a successful insurrection against the Cocom, at that time rulers of most of the peninsula, and had slaughtered all the male Cocom they could lay their hands on. Still, the violation of a safe-conduct on a religious occasion is a rather different matter. The Cocom had no respect for the Xiu, but they had a great deal for the gods of rain. Whatever the precise events, the outcome was disastrous. 'Great wars' erupted, and, while the Maya fought, locusts ravaged the few *milpas* planted, so that 'nothing green was left. And they experienced such a famine that people fell dead on the roads, so that when the Spaniards returned, they no longer recognised the country . . .'[17]

There was some consolation for the Spaniards, despite the ruined landscape: the Xiu, ambiguous allies in the earlier campaigns, were at last ready to pursue the destruction of the hated Cocom by unequivocal alliance with the outsiders. Within twelve months the provinces of the north and west had been pacified, and were lending the Spaniards vital support in supplies, carriers and fighting men. To the south and east were the irreconcilables, led by Nachi Cocom, head chief of Sotuta. The Spanish founding of the town of Mérida on the Indian site of Tiho in 1542 – achieved only after bitter, obstinate resistance by the local people – brought an onslaught of 60,000 Maya warriors if we are to believe a Spanish account of the struggle.[18] Even if the figure is inflated, so large a mass of fighting men points to a supra-provincial coalition. The establishment of the next Spanish town, Valladolid, at its first site of Chauaca, again provoked a frantic attempt at organised resistance by the warriors of the eastern tribes, as if they understood the symbolic significance of these statements of the permanence of the Spanish presence; but this time they were demoralised by the swiftness of the Spanish response, and nascent organisation fractured into dispersed local actions. The Maya attempted no more pitched battles after Tiho, perhaps because they recognised that style of fighting favoured the Spaniards, or more probably because they no longer had the men to put together a significant army. Over its last years the struggle settled into the terrible unaccommodating impersonal intimacy of guerrilla war.

Whatever their mutterings about the miserable poverty of the country and the suicidal obstinacy of its intractable inhabitants, the Spaniards would never again withdraw. Nor would they repeat the errors of the first phase. There were no more ambitious wanderings by small, isolated bands: now each group operated from a secure base, and ventured out only in effective force. Methods changed. As the Maya fouled their precious wells, destroyed their food supplies, and even performed the sacrilege of smashing down the growing corn to deny the invaders any prize beyond the blackened shell of what had once been a village, so the Spaniards destroyed those villages they could take by surprise, and massacred or enslaved their inhabitants. In the southernmost province of Uaymil-Chetumal, where the renegade Spaniard Gonzalo Guerrero had once exhorted and explained and organised, the Spaniards pursued deliberate policies of terror which must have vindicated his worst warnings. It was in the south that Montejo at last got his permanent 'Salamanca', with the founding of Salamanca de Bacalar on the south-western shore of Lake Bacalar late in 1544. It was an ironic monument to his earlier dreams. Eight Spanish citizens formed its corporation. They ruled what had once been one of the most populous and prosperous of the provinces, now effectively depopulated, haunted only by a few ghostly survivors of the years of war.[19]

The Maya had defended their villages for as long as they could, and then destroyed them. Scattered through the forest, they had watched, and killed when they were able. After five years of fighting it seemed their resistance was at last an end. An unknown number withdrew, as the Maya had done and would do again in other times of foreign intrusion, first to provinces not yet subjugated, and then, as Spanish pressure increased, to the swamps and lagoons of the southern rainforests, the independent Itza kingdom at Lake Peten, or the remote zones of refuge which were to offer sanctuary to those other irreconcilables, the Maya rebels of the Caste War of the mid nineteenth century, when once again the Maya demonstrated their hatred of foreign masters. But most drifted back to their villages, and so became vulnerable to Spanish control and exploitation.

A question remains. Why was a people so resolute and so resourceful defeated by a band of adventurers? On that issue the few Maya writings are laconic to the point of muteness, but Spanish accounts, angled though they were to maximise Spanish gallantry and Spanish tenacity, yield enough to puzzle. The Maya had enjoyed the substantial advantage of local knowledge of a terrain hostile to outsiders. Despite progressive and accelerating depletion, they had at all times overwhelming numerical superiority: Montejo rarely had more than 400 men under his command, and those men were distributed between three or four separate camps. Historians' acknowledgment of that great imbalance in numbers (true for Mexico and for Peru, as well as for Yucatan), is usually accompanied by an obeisance (slightly baffled) to 'European technical and cultural superiority' or a reference (slightly embarrassed) to the unfortunate rigidity of 'traditional native thought' when confronted by novel challenges. It is worth bringing these abstractions down to the ground of actual episodes and encounters, to see what sense there is in them.

'European cultural superiority' is usually seen as manifesting itself in a greater capacity for flexible and rational thought, and a pragmatic allocation of energy and material resources. It is difficult to see much of either in the Spanish campaigns, especially those led by the senior Montejo, where bad decisions were taken, and obstinately adhered to. The early stages of the campaign resemble nothing so much as a disorderly game of Blind Man's Buff, with the Spaniards, blundering about with very little sense of direction or purpose, in the role of victims; being spun and shoved from town to town, province to province, and finally out of the peninsula altogether. The conduct of the campaigns improved under Montejo the Younger, but it remains difficult to regard it as distinguished by rationality.

Possibly more important, at least for Spanish survival if not for final victory, was the Spaniards' superb discipline under pressure (and only under pressure; solidarity evaporated like morning dew as soon as necessity was removed). The last stages of the conquest were fought by seasoned men, who learnt to move almost instinctively into the tight formation fighting which had made the steadiness of Spanish swordsmen and pikemen a legend in Europe. Awareness of the military value of every Spanish life, intensified by the deeper loyalty to one's own kind in a world both alien and hostile, meant that no man in jeopardy would be abandoned if his comrades could prevent it. In warfare at least, Spanish lives were neither lightly wasted nor easily yielded. Above all, while the Indians were fighting on their home ground, with all that implies of inhibition, vulnerability, and anxiety for the morrow, the Spaniards could move through the land with no scruple as to the destructiveness and the human cost of their actions: those considerations could wait on victory. The 'technical superiority' argument usually pays particular attention to Spanish military equipment. Yucatan did not provide a favourable venue for the Spanish cavalryman, the tank of the New World. The man on horseback enjoys enormous advantages in height and reach and – less measurable, but perhaps even more potent – in psychological superiority over the man on foot, as anyone unlucky enough to have confronted a mounted policeman knows. Those advantages evaporate where the horse is not sure of its footing, as on the nightmare causeways of Tenochtitlan, where the incomparable Cortés suffered a smashing defeat – or along the narrow stony paths of Yucatan. In those few places in the peninsula where the terrain happened to suit them, Montejo's horsemen enjoyed their usual success. But it was the crossbows and muskets, together with Spanish mastiffs, the great dogs trained for war, which the Spaniards most valued and the Indians most feared.

Modern commentators have had some harsh things to say about the sixteenth-century musket and crossbow. They point out that they were painfully, even perilously slow to load, and that they could be put out of action by mechanical breakdown, loss of parts, or even prolonged wet weather. This is all true enough. But it is also true that Bernal Díaz, who as a swordsman was jealous of what three feet of

Toledo steel in skilful hands could do, nonetheless was always careful
to note just how many musketeers and crossbowmen were present in
any especially tense situation. It was effective projectile weapons that
the Maya (along with most of the other Indians of the New World)
lacked, as Spanish readiness to adopt native cotton armour shows. A
particularly lucky shot, or a multitude of minor wounds, might bring
a Spaniard down, but Indian weapons could not kill at any distance.
Spanish crossbows, muskets and cannon could.

But the puzzle remains. Most of the encounters were fought at
close quarters, and in hand-to-hand combat the Maya were skilled
and tough. Each community sustained a body of at least semi-
professional fighting men, and prowess was valued and measured in
the endemic slave-raids and more formal battles between towns and
provinces. The Spaniards had no doubt as to the Mayas' toughness:
the Mérida *cabildo* judged them 'bellicose, valiant and experienced in
war', and Spaniards did not distribute such reputations lightly,
especially to Indians.[20] Is the crucial factor then some real difference
in 'how natives think', some stultifying rigidity which rendered them
helpless before European invention?

We have examples of Maya 'creative innovation' in response to
European threats. Pits with stakes devised to cripple the horses were
effective, and on the organisational level we can trace throughout the
course of the conquest a development in the range and reliability of
Maya alliances. The coalitions of forces resulting from those alliances
could win major victories, as when Montejo the Younger, desperately holding out at Chichen Itza against a great Maya army
drawn from four or five provinces lost 150 men, with all of the
surviving one hundred men badly wounded, in the course of a single
day. Yet there are oddities in Maya behaviour, at least as we can
reconstruct it from the sketchy and partial Spanish accounts. The
aftermath of that spectacular Maya victory at Chichen Itza provides
an instructive example. The little Spanish encampment was meant to
be held under close seige, but the bloodied, fatigued Spaniards
managed to escape by a stratagem. Their trail was quickly picked up
by the Indians. The Spaniards laid an ambush; there was a brief, sharp
encounter, and the Indians pulled back. Then they followed the
fleeing Spaniards at a wary distance, escorting rather than molesting
them, until Montejo the Younger was able to join forces with his
father at Tiho, with consequences ultimately disastrous for the Maya.[21]
There was, on that occasion as on others, a curious lethargy in Maya
response, a tentativeness in following through the victory – at least

according to our expectations. Are we then looking at an example of 'native thought', capable only of reaction and not effective prosecution? Was each group of Maya still obstinately parochial, despite their coalitions, and concerned only to see the intruders leave their own territory? Or were they persuaded, on sufficiently 'rational' grounds, given past experience, that the Spaniards were essentially birds of passage who would, if sufficiently discouraged, remove themselves from the peninsula once more and for good?

Probably — as far as the relatively opaque sources permit us to see — something of each of the last two elements shaped Maya response. Throughout the conquest, whenever the Spaniards made unequivocal their intention to settle, by establishing permanent towns and demanding regular tribute, even 'pacified' and previously docile Indians rose in revolt. At other times, when they appeared as transients, the Spaniards were permitted to wander blindly through the forests, meeting opposition only when they attempted to retrace their steps. We also have hints of discord between different provinces, and of some unreadiness to pursue the Spaniards across local boundaries: intent on the familiar game of peninsular politics, the Maya were too little aware of the threat the new players posed to the game itself.

It is also true that some Maya 'strategies' appear at first sight to be self-defeating. In the early as well as in the later stages of the campaign it was a standard Maya response to withdraw from a threatened town. After the Spaniards had entered unopposed and taken possession of the town, attack sometimes followed, with the attackers being, of course, at a significant disadvantage. These Maya actions, superficially irrational, make more sense when we recall that in traditional Maya warfare the taking of loot and captives, not the possession of places, was the prime aim. The Maya were capable of drawing radical lessons from their experience, as when they signalled their recognition of the Spaniards as a new kind of enemy by their own unprecedented destruction of their precious wells, and the sacred maize.

The meaning of other strategies, or at least frequently reported actions, is harder to penetrate. As the campaigns dragged on, the Spaniards often encountered defensive earthworks and barricades on the approaches to a town or village — earthworks which must have taken many man-hours to construct. Yet they were frequently left unmanned, or so lightly defended as to be easily brushed aside. We could perhaps be looking here at some magical exercise, or only partially realised innovation, but my own guess is that we are glimpsing desperate attempts, defective and inadequate in their own terms, by communities exhausted and depleted but still determined to resist.

There is, unhappily, no direct way of demonstrating the truth of that guess. I have already commented on the acute selectivity, the characteristically blinkered vision, of the Spanish reports, and in these early encounters the Spaniards were not, nor could we expect them to be, sensitive to indications of flux and disorder. Yet the Maya must have been constantly responding to novel experiences: to the intrusion of new diseases, and of enemies who thought and who fought in new ways. We cannot know how those experiences were accommodated in social relations, but major adjustments must have been necessary, if only because of a massive reduction in population. Chauaca, the town so large that it took the best part of an afternoon to march from its outskirts to the town centre, could muster only 200 tribute payers in 1549, and Champoton, with its estimated 8,000 houses in 1517, had a population of not more than 2,000 thirty years later.[22] From a native population of perhaps 800,000 at the time of the first smallpox epidemic, before the beginning of the military campaign, Yucatan was reduced to about 250,000 people when the fighting stopped.[23]

It is difficult to begin to grasp the human experience distilled in those figures. We do not even know what age groups were most vulnerable, or in what form death most often came. Introduced diseases probably killed indiscriminately, and perhaps the men killed in battle did not outnumber the women and children and the old people who died of exposure, hunger or at the hands of the Spaniards during the prolonged anguish of the conquest. Certainly the depleted populations and the forced migrations must have fractured social life, and frighteningly disrupted the reassuring pulse of collective ritual activity. The survivors were reduced to being refugees in their own land, striving to pull together some of the old strands of life as they regrouped in the desolate villages, among the empty houses and the silent places. If we remember the psychological tension which must attend the attempt to deal with strangers who appeared ignorant of the most taken-for-granted rules of conduct – who fought even when with the coming of the rains the planting had to begin, or during the inauspicious and deeply dangerous days which fell between the old and the new year; who had no understanding of the warrior codes – Maya behaviour ceases to puzzle. Roles must have been elided, transformed, even excised, as men strove to sustain the activities and routines they identified as most essential, while organising to meet as best they could, with what time and energy they could muster, the unpredictable threat from outside. When that threat was removed, or rather institutionalised, by the fact of defeat, and the villages were left by their Spanish masters to reconstitute themselves, those little societies had already been profoundly transformed.

3

Settlers

The institutions evolved in the long struggle against the Moors in homeland Spain had the attraction of obvious appropriateness to the conquerors on Spain's frontiers in the Americas. In Yucatan Montejo deployed notions of government derived from Spain's medieval and unequivocally military past. His own title of *adelantado*, and the extensive judicial, military and executive powers which went with it identified him with the Marcher Lords of the *Reconquista*, who had also directly represented the Crown in their frontier zones. When Montejo exercised that authority to establish government of the new territories he drew on another institution of the *Reconquista*, the *encomienda*, used throughout Spain's American empire in its first phase. The essential form of the *encomienda* was simple enough. The Crown, or in this case, the Crown's delegate, granted to an individual worthy of reward the right to exact tribute and labour from a specified number of royal tributaries. In return the grantee, or *encomendero*, undertook to care for the material and spiritual well-being of his charges, and to maintain himself in readiness for military service. The neat economy of such a system, providing as it did instant rewards to the conquerors with instant control and exploitation of the conquered, was as irresistible in Yucatan as it had been elsewhere in the Indies: by the close of 1545 Montejo had parcelled out the native towns and villages of the peninsula in *encomienda* grants among his followers.[1]

The *encomienda* system did not disturb the internal organisation of the native political structures. Spaniards had no interest in vengeance, once the fighting was over, and readily used the traditional Indian lords as agents for the collection and delivery of what the new masters saw as their due. Even the notorious Nachi Cocom was permitted to continue as chief of the head town of Sotuta and as *de facto* head man of the whole province, the Spaniards being ready to respect rank and toughness, especially when they could be made to serve Spanish interests. Montejo could draw on another institution to aid his administration of the peninsula, and although prominent in the *Reconquista* this one had even longer historical roots: the independent Spanish town corporation, or *cabildo*. Yucatan's conquerors knew they could never amass enough wealth to return to Spain. They would have to make their homeland in the peninsula. To live alongside the Indians of their *encomiendas* would be to live in exile: as Spaniards they had a developed preference and talent for the pleasures of urban life, with *civitas* identified with 'civilization'. The focus of their loyalty, the locus of their most significant activity, and the most enduring symbol and statement of their Spanish identity in that inhospitable and alien landscape would be the Spanish town. Hernán Cortés, at a very low point in Spanish fortunes in Mexico, had in a superb gesture of dominance and confidence paced out the phantom shapes of La Villa Rica de la Vera Cruz – the Rich City of the True Cross – on the sandy wastes of the Gulf Coast. In Yucatan, the sites for the four towns which were to dominate the peninsula, at least in Spanish minds, had also been selected and their essential shapes laid out with careful and loving formality long before the fighting was over. With an end to the fighting those phantom structures of the mind were being replaced by others more solid, if less imposing: Campeche on the west coast, Valladolid to the east, the little fortified settlement of Salamanca de Bacalar far to the south, and Mérida, at the bitterly contested site of Tiho. Among the towns Mérida, as seat of the royal government, was to be the most important. The Mérida of Spain was, in the manner of European cities, a clutter of overlapping social groups and competing activities, the plan of the old Roman city having been long obscured by centuries of casual growth. The new Mérida was a very conscious creation, neatly mapping its citizens' shared understanding of the right order of men and things, and carefully demarcating and framing those areas where what to the Spaniards were the crucial exchanges of social life were to take place.[2]

The centre of life and the city was the great plaza, the main stage for the sauntering display and the elaborate verbal exchanges which were the delights of town living, and the lack of which made rural life a savourless exile. The first site allocated, on the eastern flank of the plaza, was set aside for the cathedral, when they could afford to build one; until that time, a small temporary church met their needs, and gave the few Spanish women in Mérida a familiar legitimate excuse for escaping the almost Moorish seclusion of their domestic lives – a seclusion presumably doubly trying for those few who had experienced the perils and freedoms of the military phase of the conquest.[3] To the north, the government buildings, royal and municipal, were soon under construction, as was the grandiose mansion built for Montejo, head of the royal government, and therefore source of whatever favours and honours and whatever poor imitation of court life the land could provide.

What strikes oddly about the scheme of the town is its failure to make provision for any kind of work, save the work of government. During the long process of the *Reconquista* where the military frontier offered the simplest route to high status, those values we identify as 'aristocratic' came to permeate the whole people. A gentleman was one who was free from the taint of all forms of manual labour, which were identified with servility. Therefore, men who had in the destructive labour of conquest spent sweat and energy to make a navvy blanch lost their legitimate occupation with victory; any form of work save that of supervision would jeopardise their tenuous claims to gentility. Not the least lure in the bloody gamble of conquest had been the promise of secure emancipation from demeaning toil through the power to command servile labour, and to participate in the honourable business of government. Montejo's soldiers, now become *vecinos*, citizens, bickered over his appointments to each town's governing council, and shared out the executive offices of the municipal authority. The councils exercised substantial authority over their hinterlands – hinterlands sufficiently extensive in the Yucatan case, the four towns dividing the whole peninsula between them, at least, on paper – being charged with collecting taxes, supervising commerce, enforcing the laws, and keeping the peace against internal or external threat.

The first threat came from within, and from a familiar quarter. Maya resistance was still not quite at an end. In the exhausted peace which settled over the eastern and southern provinces old contacts had been slowly renewed, old alliances reforged. In the November of 1546 many of the Spanish citizens of Valladolid, some with their families, had left the friendly security of the little town to stay in their *encomienda* villages, to keep a close eye on their Indians during tribute collection. It was, officially, contrary to royal law and to royal policy for Spaniards to stay in Indian communities, but the colonists, like colonists elsewhere, never doubted their right and duty to bend the policy of the central government to suit local conditions and to meet local interests. Then, on the night of 8 November –5 *Cimi* 19*Xul*,

Death and the End, in the Maya calendar – with superb coordination, the Maya of seven provinces rose. Spanish families, isolated in the villages, were seized and killed. The Maya took time over the deaths, remembering their old rituals. There were stories of Spanish children held by Maya priests over fires smoking with copal incense, and roasted; of Spanish men tied to stakes, and shot to death by Indian archers. The heads, hands and feet of the Europeans were sent out through the still-docile provinces as eloquent silent testimony that Spaniards were not invincible. The Indians destroyed all things Spanish; all things tainted by association with Spaniards. Spanish trees, Spanish plants, were ripped out of the ground; Indians who had served the Spaniards save under duress were slaughtered; even the cats and dogs were hunted down and killed. The little town of Valladolid was laid under siege; Salamanca de Bacalar was completely cut off.[4]

The Spaniards of Mérida and Campeche, after a brief period of confusion as they pieced together what had happened out to the east, organised their men and named their captains for the new campaign. They recruited the native warriors of Campeche and Champoton by the neat, economical, and (for the Maya) familiar device of authorising them to enslave any of the rebels they managed to catch, and the armed bands, each with its contingent of horsemen, went out. By March 1547, though there were still a few pockets of resistance, the revolt had been effectively quelled. Hundreds of Maya were enslaved, and six or seven native priests, assumed to be ringleaders, were burned at the stake, in ugly counterpoint to the Maya ritual killings by fire. An uneasy peace settled over the land.

The Maya were never again to challenge their Spanish masters, at least by military means, though the Spaniards were to sniff rebellion on every wind for months and years after the 'Great Maya Revolt', as they dubbed that last convulsive effort to expel them: the Spaniards never underestimated their Maya adversaries. The revolt also seemed to give a chance for profit. The Maya were rebels for their casting-off of Spanish rule. They could therefore be enslaved – and as slaves sold to the labour-hungry mines of the islands and the mainland, or so the settlers hoped.[5] The hope was short-lived. By the late 1540s the Crown no longer tolerated so profligate a use of its new vassals, and firmly closed that way to profit. The Yucatan Spaniards, their slaves already branded for export, tasted not for the last time the bitterness of having eager plans frustrated and urgent necessities denied by outside authorities moved by other and larger interests, and indifferent, ignorant or careless of their own. So peace brought no prosperity. Some settlers tried to introduce sugar cane, or indigo, or some other crop commanding a secure market among Europeans, but the enterprises remained small-scale.[6] The terrain continued to protect its children in subjugation as it had in war: lack of water, and the thinness of the soil layer above the rock crust, effectively frustrated Spanish commercial opportunism. Even cattle did poorly in the humid, tick-infested forests, and watering them was a chronic problem. The settlers had to content themselves with their *encomienda* tribute in the traditional products of Yucatan; with cotton mantles, now unadorned, and woven to a set measure, and with salt, honey and wax, to provide the basis for a small trade with Mexico.[7] They could afford to import only essentials from the motherland, and in the colony itself currency was so short as to make barter the normal mode of exchange.

Yucatan's poverty protected it from sustained attention from the Crown. In other provinces the royal government's determination to recover its dispersed authority and increasing competition for native labour led to the extinction of the *encomienda* system: in Yucatan it was to survive sturdily enough until the Bourbon interventions of the late eighteenth century. But the Crown continued to exert authority, however intermittently, through its control of the law, and through its refusal to delegate the power of ultimate judgment. First, administrative laws were obsessively detailed, in fine disregard of local realities. If the gulf between law and reality is always substantial, in the Spanish colonies it gaped hugely. Occasions for friction were deliberately maximised, with the intermixing of administrative and judicial functions in any one institution, and the overlapping of jurisdiction between them, and the development (with time) of the parallel and quasi-independent ecclesiastical hierarchy. Judgments of the local authorities could always be appealed, in the first instance to the most accessible *audiencia*, the panel of royal judges sitting in the head-town of the most important provinces, but finally – were the appellant sufficiently tenacious and confident of his longevity – to the Council of the Indies in Spain, and so to the king himself.

Longevity was a requirement because Spanish judicial mills ground only fractionally faster than the mills of God. The litigious-ness of the Yucatan settlers usually stopped within the borders of their own province, although within those limits the contests in law seem to have replaced the excitements of the campaign, to judge by the mounds of documents so generated. But if such disputes added zest to provincial life, the colonists were adequately united in their essential interests. They were, by colonial standards, a small and stable group. By 1550 Mérida had seventy or more citizens, Valladolid forty-five, Campeche perhaps forty, and Salamanca de Bacalar fifteen or twenty.[8] (For that year the whole non-Indian population has been estimated at a conjectural and to my mind high 1,550 persons.)[9] As late as the 1580s there were still only about 400 heads of Spanish households in all of the peninsula.

The Spanish townsfolk might have turned inwards and away from the people and the terrain which sustained them – their most constant association with 'Indians' was probably with the Mexican auxiliaries, now established in their own quarter on the fringe of the Spanish towns – but that education in the ways of the natives, so urgent in the time of war, continued in the gentler and less coercive rhythms of peace. The desperate mystifications and anxieties of those long-ago first encounters were now almost forgotten: conventions had developed to regularise and formalise what communications were necessary between the two peoples. Indians came regularly into the Spaniards' towns and the Spaniards' houses, bringing in their tribute and serving out their labour obligations. With that constant flow there was advantage in learning something of the language, and soon most Spaniards had at least a few words of Mayan. There were other less obvious but pervasive influences. Indians built the Spaniards' houses, in hopeful approximation to sketches of Spanish design, but with an ineradicable Indian flavour in the decorative detail. Inside those houses Spaniards slept in hammocks for coolness, like Indians, and like Indians woke to the gentle regular rasp of grinding stone on stone slab, as their Indian women ground the maize to smoothness. Wheat would not grow in that stony ground, and Spaniards of necessity developed a taste for the maize cakes of the Maya, and the flavours and textures of Indian foods, which they ate from plates and pots of Indian making.

There were other associations, rarely commented upon, but common for all that, which may have widened Spanish understanding of Indian ways. During the military phase of the conquest there had been the usual sexual abuse of native women. Old habits dying hard, some colonists continued to regard all native women as sexually available, until at last discouraged by the vigorous intervention of the missionary friars. But most were content with less promiscuous and more stable liaisons. There were few Maya women of sufficient rank to tempt Spaniards into marriage; while one or two conquerors did marry Indian women, commonly only men of low status were prepared to take native wives. Less formal but still moderately enduring relationships were the norm: there were few Spaniards who did not have one or more Indian girls tucked away in the recesses of their houses, or, more discreetly, separately housed in the Indian section attached to every Spanish town, and it is perhaps legitimate to assume, or at least to hope, that there was some increase in understanding as a result. And this was the conqueror's generation. Their children would have Mayan as their first tongue, and be tended through their first years by Indian hands.[10]

But these fragile bridges brought Indians into the Spanish milieu. Few settlers were interested in making the reverse journey. Here and there a Spaniard and the Indian chief of one of the villages in his charge could develop an acceptable if unequal working relationship, but inter-racial interactions were largely routinised into conventionalised and therefore not too abrasive forms. Travelling through the country, Spaniards demanded service of any Indian, but they travelled rarely. Ensconced in their towns, caught up in the engrossing daily round of local politics, local conflicts and local society, the settlers were content to treat the world of the native villages – provided the native chiefs had the tribute delivered on time, provided the agreed number of Indians arrived punctually for the agreed period of service – as a world apart.

If Spanish settlers had no interest in tampering with the institutions of native life at the village level, another group of Spaniards, who had had to restrain their impatience until the military phase was over, were determined to reshape those institutions root and branch. I mean, of course, the Spanish missionary friars.

4

Missionaries

The Indians have friers in great reverence: the occasion is, that by them
and by their meanes they are free and out of bondage; which was so ordeined
by Charles the emperor: which is the occasion that now there is not so much
gold and silver coming into Europe as there was while the Indians were
slaves . . .

Henry Hawkes, 1572

Franciscans were to dominate the missionary enterprise in Yucatan,
as they had in Mexico. If to a twentieth-century mind the motives of a
Bernal Díaz, for all their distinctive accenting, are sufficiently familiar
to be intelligible, missionaries, and Franciscans, are less accessible.
What would move a Spanish youth in the early decades of the
sixteenth century to join the Franciscan order, and then to opt for
service in a remote corner of a remote New World? What vision
would lead him to those actions, and how might that vision be
sustained or modified by experience in the field?

First, he would be choosing not the complete withdrawal from the
world of the closed orders of monks, not the integration into the
world of the secular priest working within the parish system, but
membership of an institution designed to mediate between the
elevated-spiritual, and the earthy-mundane. While friars of the
mendicant orders maintained the prayerful discipline of monks, they
also undertook preaching rounds to reanimate the faith of the people,
and cultivated a popular touch. But they were (at least ideally) to be
firmly separated from the world they served, most dramatically by
those rituals of admission in which a youth cast off the garments, the
name and the nature he had once owned to be reborn into his new
family of male celibates, collectively committed to living in accordance with the detailed prescriptions for behaviour and sentiment
laid down in a 'Rule'.

To choose the Order of St Francis over other mendicant orders was to choose the largest order in Spain, and arguably the most vigorous. The Franciscan Rule had been purged to a determined rigour and simplicity in the first years of the century. Some houses had carried that reform to a high emphasis on austerities, and to an evangelical mission to the spiritually neglected 'Old Christians' of remote areas, and the 'New Christians' of the Moslem south.

There were other, more subtle attractions. The Rules of every order bound 'nature' to an unnatural rhythm: 'natural' sleep broken by obligatory prayer, 'natural' hunger rebuked by penitential fasting, 'natural' wilfulness chastened by unreflecting obedience to a superior. To that regimen the Franciscans added a commitment to the peculiar beauty of poverty, humility and simplicity of soul, together with an elevation of ecstatic experience, a trusting spontaneity in faith, over merely human intellect and learning. These were, of course, the emphases of St Francis, but in rank-mad, gold-dazzled expansionist Spain they took on the special poignancy and authority of a deliberate denial and inversion of the values dominant in secular society. The singular power of that systematic denial is indicated by the many men who after gathering the successes of this world discovered in themselves a deepening reverence for St Francis and his followers, and begged permission to be buried in the Franciscan habit.

Once a Franciscan, why choose the mission to the New World? The strength of that attraction must have varied significantly through the century. In the mean and brutal early years when Spaniards enslaved and killed their way through the islands of the Caribbean, those few friars in the field, Dominicans mostly, could do little but bear horrified witness to the carnage: the natives died too quickly for there to be any harvest of souls. But Mexico was a different matter. Its great populations lived in ordered communities, and were already disciplined to regular observances of a public religion. And Mexico's conqueror had learnt the object lesson of the islands: he was determined to bridle Spanish greed. Hernán Cortés was also one of those worldly men with a special tenderness for St Francis and his followers. Shortly after he had achieved his conquest he petitioned Pope and Crown that the establishment of the new Church in the Indies be entrusted to the Franciscans, whose simplicity, self-forgetfulness and devotion to poverty fitted them for the massive task.

Pope and Crown concurred. The establishment of the secular hierarchy of parish priest to bishop could wait on the completion of the spiritual conquest. The Pope accordingly extended to the prelates of the orders all the powers normally exercised by bishops – save where a bishop was within two days' travel – through the bull *Exponi Nobis Fecisti*, which was to become the charter for Franciscan action in the New World. The Crown was probably also responsive to Cortés' reminder that the friars would ask for minimal material support, for the Crown would bear the cost of the mission. But the most significant factor influencing the decision was the appropriateness of the reformed Franciscans' poverty and simplicity, and their proven missionary zeal. As Christ had led his twelve simple and poor men to transform the world with his teaching, so there would be Twelve Apostles to carry the word of God to the newly discovered peoples of the Indies. Martín de Valencia, Provincial of the remote and strenuously reformed province of San Gabriel, was named with twelve of his brothers to found the Apostolic Church in Mexico.[1]

Twelve could seem a ludicrously small number of men to entrust with the conversion of an Indian population estimated in millions, even allowing that Spain's population was small, and the numbers it could spare for New World ventures smaller still. While the initial core of Mexican Franciscans grew rapidly, their total number always remained low: in 1536 perhaps sixty, in the late 1550s, thirty years after the conquest, no more than 380, with that number including administrators and those too old or frail for the rigours of the field.[2] The missionaries themselves were always acutely aware of the desperate shortage of manpower, but they did not on that account despair. First, they worked within a context of coercion. Among Indian commoners, adults were obliged to attend weekly, and children daily instruction in the catechism. More important, those natives in authority were compelled to accept baptism, while the sons of native lords were gathered up and sequestered in the schools attached to every monastery, to be drilled in the catechism, in Christian–Hispanic patterns of living, and in contempt for their fathers' ways.[3] Later the lads staffed the village schools, teaching children and adults what they understood of Christian doctrine and obedience, and representing religious authority in the long periods between the occasional visits of the friars.

In those early days – as, indeed, later – 'teaching' focussed more on training in correct external behaviour than on the transference of knowledge; on bowing the head, on kneeling, on maintaining a hushed silence and stillness in the manner of Spanish piety. The four main prayers were taught by rote, the unfamiliar syllables being counted off by stones, or by more ingenious devices, as a Franciscan chronicler recorded:

The word [in the Aztec language] which comes closest to the pronunciation of 'Pater' is 'pantli', which means a little flag, which is their sign for the number of twenty. So, in order to remember the word 'Pater' they draw the flag 'pantli' and so say 'Pater'. For 'noster' the closest word they have is 'nochtli', which is the fruit called by the Spanish here 'tuna', and in Spain 'the fig of the Indies' [prickly pear] . . . therefore to call to mind the word 'noster' they draw a tuna fruit alongside the little flag they call 'pantli', and so they are able to continue along until they finish the prayer, and in the same way they find other similar characters and ways by which they are able to teach themselves those things they must commit to memory.[4]

Given our notions of the centrality of intellectual conviction and the comprehension of beliefs in matters religious, we doubt that a mere sequence of sounds can have any efficacy. But the friars knew those sounds could open the way to God's grace, and that sacramental grace could descend even on the ignorant. Indians were baptised after minimal instruction: one Franciscan recorded the feat of a brother in baptising 'four or five or six thousand' in a day, switching the jar of holy water from arm to aching arm, while callouses thickened on his hands and the Mexican sun burned his tonsured head raw.[5] There was a special urgency about the mass baptisms, because these Indians too were dying; like those in the islands because of Spanish greed, but also, the friars thought, because of some fatal weakness or frailty, a 'childishness' in their physical as in their mental constitutions. (They could have no understanding of the way new European diseases scythed through a population with no developed immunity.) The millenarian strand was strong in Franciscan thinking; for many the unassuageable deaths of these last people of the world to hear the Word pointed to the end of things.

That intuition led not to resignation, but to a furious activism. They had been charged with the care of Indian souls: they undertook the care of their bodies too. Spaniards who thought conquest and Christianity together gave them uncontested rights over their Indian subjects found those rights passionately contested by men whose institutional network stretched back to Spain and to the ear of the king; who were long practised in opposition; and who enjoyed the incomparable advantage of acknowledging no material interests in the matter of the exploitation of Indian labour. The friars mounted a magnificent campaign to reduce all exactions on the Indians to law, and then they policed the law: tireless vigilantes for the Royal conscience.

Those political struggles, like the hardships of the mission field itself, could only have been sustained by men of unusual physical and spiritual toughness. Here, selection must have played a part: only men of a certain temperament are attracted to far lands. Spirits which had chafed in the cloister and energies which under the restrictions of the Old World could too easily sour into fretfulness found joyful fulfilment in hardships artificially contrived in the Old World, but part of the texture of days in the New: the weary distances travelled, always on foot; the strange food and stranger diseases; the exhaustion of the struggle to identify, in a flow of sound, the contours and intentions of human speech.[6] Those burdens became their glory. The official chronicler of the Mexican mission, memorialising the heroic dimensions of individual Franciscan achievements was to write:

In Spain we know it for a common thing that when priests have to preach a sermon they are so tired and in such a sweat that they have to change their clothes . . . And if after he had preached, a priest were told to sing a Mass or comfort a sick man or bury a dead one, he would think it the same as digging his own grave. But in this land it happened every day that one lone friar would count the people in the morning, then preach to them and sing Mass, and after that baptise both children and adults, confess the sick no matter how many, and then bury any dead there might be. And so it was for thirty or forty years, and in some places so it is still. There were some (and I knew them) who preached three sermons in different languages, one after the other, and then sang Mass, and did everything else that had to be done, all before having anything to eat.[7]

While their political and social situation clearly mattered, the core of the friars' self-understanding, and the sinew which bound them to the task, must have been spiritual. It is not easy to penetrate the nature of that spirituality. Protestant missionaries to lonely places have left records of their spiritual travails in their letters to their home congregations, or in the diaries in which they wrestled with doubts or an obstinately elusive God. Franciscans left no such records: they spoke to their confessor and to their God directly. Nor had they much of the paraphernalia which sustained and regulated religious life in the Old World, and so gave it meaning: the exigencies of the missionary situation and the parsimony of the Crown took care of that.[8]

Here the superb flexibility of the organisation of the order, and its determined independence of externals, must have come into play.

Community life could not be maintained: the little collections of thatched huts which were the first 'monasteries' usually housed only two friars, and one of the two was normally out on circuit through the surrounding villages. Yet the friars could continue to take comfort and guidance, as so often, from the example of St Francis, 'who when travelling made a superior of his companion, so as to be always under obedience'.[9] That dyad of one who orders and one who obeys was the essential unit of the Franciscan structure: where it was, so was the order. And if the community was physically dispersed, it was present still in the steady and unchanging rhythm of the daily observances, marking the hours with the familiar prayers, the sacrifice of the mass, and in the larger patterning of the liturgical year. The very meagreness of Franciscan possessions, even to the familiar patches of the habit which served as blanket by night and garment by day, must have woven a web of security around the immediate environment unknown to those who travel amid a clutter of refractory possessions.

The habit, the crucifix, the routines of prayer, the protocols of fraternal speech and conduct marked and made those who possessed them 'Franciscan'. How to be a Franciscan missionary they discovered and invented in the doing of it. Written texts had little part here: they would carve out of their own days the texts by which they would live. Perceiving the necessity for providing public exemplars to Spaniards and to Indians, they were also providing exemplars for themselves. They mapped the slow making of a Christian landscape out of the events of their daily work: here where a child was saved by the prayers of its desperate parents; here where prayer and procession brought rain; here where the cord from a Franciscan habit averted pestilence. Those episodes and a thousand lesser ones were woven into the constantly elaborated, constantly enriched mythic history of the order, in which every brother was to be systematically eulogised, the small events of his individual life knitted into the great mantle of the order's being in the New World.[10]

The most richly coloured events from that glowing fabric must have been carried back to Spain by friars entrusted with the delicate task of recruitment for the mission – delicate because of the Crown's parsimony; because of the disinclination of Provincials to see their best young men drained away; and because the desperate need for men, so clear in Mexico, was increasingly obscured in Spain by other desperate needs. As the years passed and the Lutheran heresy spread through Catholic lands the 'best young men' could find challenge enough in Europe. And the millenial lustre of the Mexican mission dimmed with those passing years. The thousands of Indians who had begged and moaned for baptism, even the young men specially groomed for admission to the order, had grown sullen and careless, and drink was eroding the social fabric of the Indian towns. Other issues too were less clear cut, as the friars, who had their own requirements for buildings and supplies and carriers, came in time to find their reading of local needs closer to agreement with the colonists' than with the detached and overly Utopian fiats of a distant Council of the Indies. The early Franciscan monopoly in Mexico had lasted only a few years: then came unedifying squabbles between the orders, and between the orders and the growing number of secular priests. Even within the Franciscan order itself there was dispute, as yet muffled, especially about the effectiveness of that exuberant early soul-saving campaign, and some of those who found the missionary life unendurable had managed to return to Spain, carrying their disaffection with them.

Despite the decline in early idealism, and despite the difficulties of replenishment the Mexican mission accepted its responsibility to 'seed' new missions; in 1544 eight veterans, four from Guatemala and four from Mexico, were named to initiate the conversion of the Maya Indians of Yucatan.[11] How they felt about their nomination we do not know: burdens came from God, and Franciscans were vowed to obedience. But the task could have been attractive. It was true that the Yucatan *encomenderos* were already well-entrenched, and, most of them having come as conquerors, possessed of a high sense of their own prerogatives which went well beyond those actually granted by the Crown. But they were a small group, and a stable one, and the lack of commercial opportunity in the peninsula could be expected to keep demands on the Indians at an endurable level. The Indians themselves spoke only one language – welcome news after the multiplicity of tongues spoken in Mexico – and were a town-dwelling people, accustomed to public forms of worship. And Yucatan, they were assured, would be a Franciscan monopoly.

The first days of the Yucatan mission must have recalled the heady first days in Mexico when the Twelve Apostles had brought their message to a newly conquered people. Three of the four friars from Guatemala came overland to Campeche by way of Acalan and Champoton, but the fourth, Fray Lorenzo de Bienvenida, travelled by canoe to the Golfe Dulce and from there continued on foot to

Salamanca de Bacalar, and then north, to traverse the peninsula, preaching, as well as he was able, as he went. Most of the territory he covered – alone, shunning identification with Spanish soldiery – had been only recently and imperfectly pacified.

Meeting in Campeche, the four were well received by the Montejos, as were the four veterans of the Mexican field who joined them later in the same year. The first essential steps were taken: a monastery with its infirmary and school was established in each of the two Spanish towns of Mérida and Campeche, and Fray Luis de Villalpando settled to unravelling the complexities of the native language, striving to develop a dictionary and a grammar so that the essential translations could be made. Although the Maya lords yielded up their sons no more readily than had the lords of Mexico, there were soon more than two thousand boys in the school in Mérida, being taught to read and to write Mayan in European script, to sing in choir for the services which marked out their days and, most important of all, to learn the elements of the Christian faith. Perhaps to reduce the burden of cost, perhaps because of difficulties in keeping the peace between lads from hostile lineages, the boys were less securely sealed away from old influences than their Mexican counterparts, living in separate dwellings with others from their home province and being served and provisioned by their own retainers.[12] Like their brothers in Mexico, and despite frequent royal directives, the Yucatan friars showed little enthusiasm for teaching their charges Spanish, for knowledge of Spanish would open the way to corrupting influences by challenging their own role as mediators between Spaniard and Indian.

The colonists initially had been ready to welcome the friars, as a mark of the increasing stability of their settlement; and as the next stage in the process of conversion, which they as soldiers had begun by bringing the Indians into submission. But the fragility of the alliance was exposed when news of the Maya uprising of November 1546 was received in Mérida. The friars learnt how little heed Spanish soldiers gave to the requirements of a mission programme, or indeed of simple humanity, when they were out to break the spirit of the natives. It seems that Fray Lorenzo de Bienvenida contrived to accompany the punitive expeditions – his account reads like an eyewitness report – but he could do nothing to save the Indian women casually mutilated, the Indian children casually murdered, the men rounded up, branded and chained. In a long furious letter to the Crown he made clear how complete was his identification with his new flock, how total his repudiation of his compatriots, and how powerfully in this new milieu the friars' sense of themselves as the Indians' protectors against rapacious and brutal *encomenderos* had been reinforced.[13]

Yet for a little time longer the Franciscan–Montejo alliance held: Montejo after all exercised secular authority in the peninsula, and he had not been personally implicated in the excesses of his lieutenants. Meanwhile the friars considered their mission strategy. The Mexican Franciscans had concentrated on the great centres of population, and had seized the chance to knit the agricultural cycles of Mexico's valleys and hillsides into the web of Christian ritual, organising masses and processions in direct competition with the native agricultural gods. In Yucatan the *milpas*, or cornplots, were scattered through the dry, dense, grey forests which hemmed the villages; and the dim paths which led to them blurred easily into bush, at least to European eyes. The exigencies of slash-and-burn agriculture had dispersed villages and hamlets over the whole rocky face of the peninsula. And that was dangerous. Native chiefs were confirmed in their offices only when they submitted to baptism, but the friars did not deceive themselves as to the conviction of those 'conversions'; the chiefs could certainly not be relied on. Clearly, the role of the native schoolmasters would be crucial. It was as if the landscape itself conspired to prevent easy access and supervision by outsiders: Bienvenida, doughty traveller though he was, lamented to the Crown that some of the villages were so remote that 'only birds could visit them freely'.[14] Might not the grey wilderness simply swallow up the missionaries' passion and devotion? The friars apparently thought so, for they committed their initial strength and their personal presence to areas most firmly under Spanish control: the more remote southern and eastern provinces were to be, at least for the time, ignored.

The first Franciscan house in 'native' territory was set up at Oxkutzcab in Mani, the province of the Xiu, allies of the Spaniards in the last stages of the conquest. Villalpando and Bienvenida set up the house with its dependent school in 1547, and began the round of teaching, tending and supervision which was to become so familiar. But even in so tamed a province resistance still flickered. One of the boys of the school came secretly to the two friars to reveal that some of the lesser chiefs, disgruntled by the friars' refusal of baptism until they had freed all their slaves, were plotting to burn monastery and friars together. Through the night the two watched and prayed, their steadfast courage, they thought, holding their would-be assassins at bay, until with the morning came the providential arrival of a body of armed Spaniards.

As so often with tales of threatened revolts or dangerous sullenness, it is impossible to judge at this distance how real was the threat, and how reliable the boy's story. For the friars, it was certainly real. But even this distressing sequence they turned to advantage, with a pragmatism as characteristic as their courage. When twenty-six Maya nobles thought to be implicated were on the point of being burned alive in the public square of Mérida, with all the pomp and ceremony the dusty little town could muster, Father Villalpando dramatically interceded for them, and won from Montejo their unconditional pardon. Understandably, the chiefs were thereafter docile, and baptisms followed apace. The lord of Mani, Ah Kukum, who the Spaniards believed not to have been involved in the conspiracy, was baptised as Don Francisco de Montejo Xiu, Montejo graciously acting as his godfather. As the new Don Francisco was head-chief of the province the friars took swift advantage of his submission, transferring their monastery to the head-town of Mani.[15] The Xiu 'conspiracy' was the last overt Maya attempt – if attempt it was – to resist the conversion programme by offering violence to its agents, and its successful resolution strengthened the Franciscan preference for psychological manipulation over physical punishment.

The incident nonetheless probably reinforced the friars' unwillingness to penetrate too far into the interior, away from the slender protection of Spanish arms. Their infant mission, now with its own core of veterans, could expect no more help from Mexico; so one of their little band, Nicolas de Albalate, was sent back to the mother country in 1548 to recruit volunteers from the Franciscan houses there. In expectation of his return two more monasteries were established, one at Conkal, a few leagues north-east of Mérida, and one at Izamal in the province of the Ah Kin Chel, who had offered little resistance to the Spaniards. In 1549 Albalate was back, bringing with him perhaps nine friars.[16] Among the nine was one young man, Diego de Landa, who was to play a leading part in the Yucatan of both Indians and Spaniards.

Despite their necessary dependence on the local government and colonists both for protection and the maintenance of discipline over the Indians, tension between the friars and their fellow Spaniards steadily increased, as episode after episode dramatised their division. The Adelantado Montejo was removed from office in 1549, in part because of the friars' increasing impatience with his regime, but his removal only worsened conflict. The colonists, despite the vehemence of their internal bickerings, were united by shared interests as by shared experience, and by a conviction of the legitimacy of the interests derived from the experience. Essentially, they believed their Indians to be indeed theirs. That conviction the friars met with their own, equally firmly based: the settlers had only closely restricted rights to labour and tribute; physical and spiritual control of the Indians belonged to the friars. Of course they had no force at their disposal: they depended on the secular government for the execution of their policies. But their strength was formidable for all that, residing in their privileged access to the Crown and in their celebrated immunity to the pleasures of domination and material possessions. So they watched, recorded, and had no hesitation in urging the Crown to remove the *encomiendas* from – that is, to ruin – those Spaniards whose behaviour exceeded proper bounds.

In October of 1550 Fray Luis de Villalpando, head of the mission, wrote a long letter to the Crown in which he named and listed the delinquencies of ten *encomenderos*, with equally careful listing of the villages and the numbers of tributaries they held in *encomienda*. Villalpando knew the power of detail. Somewhat disingenuously, he included in his account some hangings and killings of 'three and a half years ago', without making clear that those events took place during the aftermath of the revolt. However most of his stories related to 'normal' times, and 'normal' relationships, and demonstrated the ease with which Spaniards could give way to unrestrained violence when angered. He told how an *encomendero* took an Indian woman, stripped her, tied her naked to a post, and flogged her with willow switches in a petulant fury at some imagined failure in compliance, until she died; of how the same man gave the chief of one of his villages a great blow with his cudgel when Villalpando was present; how the Indian, streaming with blood from his wound, defecating helplessly with terror, fled to the friar for protection, who took him in his arms; 'and the Indian thus clinging to me and I to him, running with blood, filthy and stinking, [the *encomendero*] tore him away from me, dragging him by his hair from my arms, who could not help him, in front of all the people and of a Spaniard who was standing there . . .'[17]

For Villalpando, as for his fellow missionaries, that moment caught in an eternal *tableau-vivant* their role as they understood it: transcending considerations of race, of conventional fastidiousness, of personal danger, to embrace and protect the suffering victim of brutish violence. That violence came not only from individual *encomenderos*, but was endemic to the corruption and brutality of the whole system of government in the peninsula, with local administr- ators winking at such offences, or imposing trivial penalties 'because they are neighbours and because one is a judge one year and the other one the next year one sentences the other to pay two *maravedis* for some offences and for others they are set at liberty . . .' His last case implicated even royal officials in the conspiracy of brutality. Eight months before, a tax collector who had killed an Indian lord was set at liberty on the purchase of 'two pounds of blue beads . . . to give to the wife and children of the dead man, with no other penalty . . . large or small'. The man had been killed in front of the assembled village because the Spaniard 'asked the said lord for some carriers and he did not bring them as quickly as he wanted'. Villalpando concluded, 'it costs more to kill a cow or a horse in Yucatan than to kill an Indian'.[18]

Denunciations and counter-denunciations were the stock-in-trade of colonial disputes as men competed to catch the attention of the distant Council of the Indies, and tales of *encomendero* brutality were unhappily commonplace. But those of the Yucatan friars must have had some impact, because in 1552 the Crown resorted to its usual strategy to damp down provincial wrangles by sending a judge to Yucatan, vested with royal authority, to take over the administration, to bring the wranglers to a respect for decorum and for the law, and to devise regulations sufficiently specific to inhibit further squabbles over local rights and powers.

5

Conflict

Tomás López Medel was a member of the Guatemala *audiencia*, one of those panels of judge-administrators to whom the Crown entrusted the execution and, to a carefully limited extent, the interpretation of its law in the Indies. López Medel gave the colonists their most sustained view of the new breed of royal official. Austere, energetic, inflexible, his presence reminded them (as intended) of the formal, complex world of Spain, which distance and the disorder of faction had allowed them to forget. The new broom swept vigorously, reducing to law the previously haphazard and too often opportunistic relations between the old and the new vassals of the Crown of Castile: forcing agreement between the Spanish town councils and the friars on the amount of tribute and service to be extracted from the Indians, and fixing wage scales for the human carriers who transported most of the goods of the colony.

López Medel also turned his attention to the bringing of a more visible order and regularity to the life of the Indian villages, and here he spoke in the accents of the friars, and with their superb confidence in the power of detailed prescriptions to regulate life. There were, he noted, too many lords being offered service and deference by the commoners. Henceforth only 'the oldest and the most virtuous' were to continue to enjoy noble status; the surplus was thenceforth to consider themselves and be considered as commoners. Chiefs and lords 'greatly venerated because of the antiquity of their lineage' persisted in calling their people together 'in out of the way and hidden places . . . to preach to them their rites and ancient ceremonies'. Such activities were forbidden, and anyone knowing of them was obliged to denounce them. All village gatherings were to be curtailed: the informal meetings of the lords in the evening, when they indulged in 'idle and illicit chat, not conducive to their spiritual or temporal good'; the great feasts of the lineages with their 'drunkenness and disorder'; the dancing in the evenings where 'dirty things of their pagan days' might be sung; all these were forbidden, and a general curfew imposed 'after the bell had sounded for the souls in purgatory'. López Medel also dealt with another matter. Despite their attachment to their 'traditional rites and ancient ceremonies', some chiefs showed a puzzling eagerness to set up secret churches and schools of their own, in which they pretended to teach Christian doctrine, and to marry, baptise and divorce their followers with fine disregard to the friars' monopoly over those functions. Nor was this alarmingly selective enthusiasm for the new faith restricted to the chiefs. Some Indians sought out baptism, 'having once been baptised returning to be baptised again, deceiving the ministers of the evangelist', saying they had submitted to the ritual 'to aid them in augury under the urgings of the devil'. These same Indians then persuaded other Indians that 'baptism kills little children and that baptised children die soon and that those that are not baptised grow up', so that anxious parents hid their little ones from the friars. López Medel did not concern himself with what was wilful and what was naive in the garblings, contenting himself with imposing a blanket prohibition on all these bewildering and contradictory actions. He then proceeded to a string of regulations aimed at enforcing Spanish notions of propriety in sexual and familial relationships. The sprawling multiple-family households of the Maya were to give way to single-family conjugal units. The friars were to ascertain which of a man's several women was his 'legitimate' wife, and compel him – by flogging, if necessary – into accepting her. Certain procedures were to be followed at meals: the sitting around the table, the cleanliness of the table cloth, the folding of the hands, the saying of Grace, all being laid out in obsessive and wistful detail. (The Maya lacked tables, chairs, and tablecloths.)[1]

Given the protective screen of the forest, and the paucity of the friars' manpower, the López Medel ordinances could have become yet another example of the chronic utopianism of Spanish colonial legislation. But López Medel had added another clause which was to make the rest very much more consequential. He had noticed, he said, that too many Indians still lived scattered in the bush. He therefore ordered those Indians to be gathered together 'in good and convenient places . . . in properly organised villages'. Then, his job done, he returned to Guatemala.

This last clause brought the simmering tension between friars and settlers to violence. López Medel had been a reminder of the power and majesty of the imperial government, but with his withdrawal to

Guatemala the image of that authority also receded. The *audiencia* of Guatemala, under whose jurisdiction Yucatan officially lay, was in any case too remote, and its provincialism perhaps too unimpressive, to exert any continuing influence over the affairs of Yucatan. For the next eight years secular authority in the peninsula was to pass through the hands of a sequence of colonists distinguished neither by wealth, rank, training nor interest from the men they sought to govern. And then there were the Franciscans, outside of the secular authority's jurisdiction, pursuing their own, antipathetic, ends, yet – officially – dependent on those secular authorities for executive action: above all for the apprehension and the custodial care of delinquents, and then the exaction of fines and the administration of physical punishments. The Crown's careful devising of overlapped and cross-cutting authorities in the new kingdoms, designed to discourage the growth of any overmighty faction, worked well enough in more developed colonies, but in the radically simplified frontier situation of Yucatan it could only raise in poignant and painful form the question it was designed to suppress: who, finally, was to rule?

There were two possible solutions. Either the colonists would shape their lives as they chose, with their town councils emerging as the effective organs of provincial government, or the friars would succeed in identifying the issue of conversion as the primary concern of government, and make effective the putative powers implied in the López Medel ordinances.

The friars seized the initiative. Under the shaky warrant of López Medel's recommendations that Indians be 'gathered together', they proceeded (in the areas within their reach) to concentrate scattered Indian settlements. Depleted villages had new populations grafted on to them: others were forcibly cleared and burnt. Often with no more warning than the unheralded arrival of a solitary friar, Indians were ordered out of their houses, which were then put to the torch, along with their carefully nurtured fruit trees and their few meagre possessions. Then the dazed and weeping Indians were herded off to the new sites the friars judged 'convenient'. The friars did not force villagers to shift beyond the boundaries of their original provinces. Probably they glimpsed the political complications that that would introduce, and they intended those compelled to move to go on cultivating their old *milpas*. But there were too few friars, and too much political urgency, for the transition to be made easily. Many Indians died from hunger and exposure, and others, we are told, 'from the great sadness in their hearts'.[2]

Local *encomenderos* cursed the interfering friars who dared to move their Indians around the countryside without a by-your-leave. Worse, the friars' actions struck at their already meagre incomes. If *encomenderos* exaggerated the population losses caused by the resettlements – up to seven out of eight Indians died, some said – official counts indicate that a loss of fifty to seventy per cent of tributaries (whether through death or flight) was not uncommon. The tough *encomenderos* of the Valladolid region, where the friars behaved with singular ruthlessness, were especially outraged, and apparently twice burnt down the local Franciscan monastery to express their feelings.[3] It was from among those intransigent Valladolid settlers that the champion of the *encomenderos* appeared.

Francisco Hernández was one of the original conquerors of the province. He held two villages, Chikindzonot and Tepich, in *encomienda*, and was a member of the town council of Valladolid. He was also a touchy man. When, with the establishment of the Valladolid mission, Fray Hernando de Guevera collected and took away Indian youths from his village for Christian instruction (an action few *encomenderos* would have thought to contest) Hernández was sufficiently outraged to travel to Guatemala to complain to the *audiencia*. He charged the friar with having flogged some Indians so savagely that they had died – a double offence, against humanity, and against the secular authorities who alone were empowered to inflict legal punishments – and with interfering with political arrangements in the villages, which again fell within the jurisdiction of the secular government.[4]

Returning through Honduras some time in 1556 Hernández took the opportunity to buy some loads of cacao for sale in Yucatan. Arrived in the peninsula, he had difficulty in recruiting Indian carriers in one village, at least at the rates he was prepared to pay, and smelt the influence of the friars. So he turned his tongue on them, haranguing the Indians on the subject of Franciscans. His diatribe came straight out of the folk-lore of pre-reform Spain. The friars were professional drones who entered the order only to get out of working. They came around the villages only to get their hands on the women. They were liars who only pretended to be real priests, but their baptisms were no more than sprinkles of water. And all their teachings were false.

How much the Indians understood of this diatribe is uncertain, but Hernández' general demeanour was clear enough. Later in the same day, when some boys he had hailed to get fodder for his horse instead went into the village church, he chased after them and abused and cuffed them out of the building. Then, his anger at least temporarily assuaged, he went on to Valladolid. By September of 1556 he was in the public jail of that city, awaiting trial before the ecclesiastical authorities – which, under the terms of the papal bull *Exponi Nobis Feciste* meant the local Franciscans – for his scandalous behaviour.

What was to happen to Hernández over the next five years is a tale too complex for complete telling. He was totally persuaded – Papal Bulls, the realities of the Yucatan situation, and the actual conduct of its austere friars notwithstanding – that friars were not true priests, but meddlesome, hypocritical parasites. That conviction was to steel his resistance during what became a merciless legal battle. Judged before Francisco de Navarro, the newly elected Custodian of the Franciscan order, he was found guilty and sentenced to public humiliation, a five-year exile, and a heavy fine. To ensure his submission his property and all the income from his estates were to be sequestered. Hernández somehow managed to escape – perhaps because the men charged with keeping the public jail were no more fond of friars than he was – and fled to Guatemala, where he laid his case before the panel of royal judges.

The *audiencia* initially attempted to mediate, releasing Hernández' property, and urging the secular authorities in Yucatan to try to adjudicate. Then they revoked Navarro's decision, and required the rehearing of the whole case – before ecclesiastical authorities in Yucatan. However, the *audiencia* did stress that Hernández would have the right to appeal from any judgment those authorities should hand down.

To offer Hernández even this discreet encouragement was probably no kindness, for when the retrial began in October of 1558, Hernández no longer faced Navarro, but the newly elected Custodian Diego de Landa. The friars had also found their champion. Landa was to display over the next years great flexibility of tactics but a terrible tenacity of purpose, together with a superb intransigence in face of attempted interventions of 'authorities' he judged to have no standing in the matter at hand.

Landa's first move was to recommit Hernández to jail. He then forestalled Hernández' attempts to appeal the case back to the Guatemalan *audiencia* on the grounds that an appeal was premature – until he himself chose to enter a judgment. With Hernández still desperately refusing to acknowledge ecclesiastical jurisdiction, the Custodian excommunicated him – only to lift the excommunication when Hernández sought an appeal to the Holy See. Then, after a satisfactorily long delay, and with Hernández still refusing to accept his jurisdiction, Landa remitted the whole tangled matter to two lawyers resident in Mexico City. The strategy must have been depressingly clear to its victim. The crucial aim was to keep Hernández incarcerated, and to break his spirit. In prison he was subjected to constant harassment: he was charged with having failed to make his confession during Easter, despite his sworn statement, supported by another from a secular cleric, that he had tried to do so. It is possible that this systematic persecution won the sympathy of his jailers, for once again Hernández contrived to escape, and to make his way once again to Guatemala, and the *audiencia*. Unluckily for him, Landa was still in pursuit, and argued convincingly to have the jurisdiction of the prelate of the Franciscans ratified. By the time Hernández could make his way back to the peninsula Francisco de la Torre had replaced Landa as Custodian – but Landa's zeal was such that de la Torre agreed to leave the Hernández affair in his hands.

Hernández still had one card to play. He had been in contact with the Archbishop of Mexico who by virtue of his office did not favour any very broad interpretation of the *Exponi Nobis Feciste*. Hernández travelled to Mexico, and placed himself under the archbishop's protection.

The archbishop ordered Landa to desist from the case, and designated the priest Monterroso, curate of Mérida, as commissioned judge. Landa briskly repudiated the archbishop's authority, claiming that, acting as he was for the prelate of the order in Yucatan, he was therefore subject only to the Pope or to the Holy Office of Spain. Monterroso he intimidated into silence, threatening to harry him out of the land should he attempt to implement the archbishop's instructions. The archbishop sought to stiffen Monterroso's spine by naming another secular priest, Hernando de Andrade of Valladolid, to aid him, but when Andrade tried to publish the archbishop's censure of the Franciscan, Landa made good his threat and had him removed from his benefice and from the peninsula.[5]

In May of 1561 Hernández unwisely returned to Yucatan, where soon a new charge, of having urged the Indians of his *encomienda* not to attend mass, was brought against him. Landa, now Provincial, and so head of the order in Yucatan, had already established some influence over the newly appointed *alcalde mayor*, Don Diego Quijada, and set him to collecting evidence on the case – meanwhile returning Hernández to the familiar public jail. Hernández was at first obdurate, continuing to reject the authority of the friars, incurring excommunication once more. But the constant travelling, the constant tension, and the rigours of imprisonment, were taking their toll. He fell seriously ill. Despite the pleas of his friends, Landa refused to soften the harsh conditions of his confinement. On 29 October 1561, Francisco de Hernández at last conceded defeat. He intimated his readiness to make a full confession.

The next day Landa's Provisor came to his cell, taking the sick man through the whole sorry tale, exacting submission on every issue. The 'confession' was very much more to do with legal than with spiritual matters. The submission made, Landa's interest in the case ceased. He had no personal malice towards Hernández, and the essential matter, the matter of authority, was now resolved. Hernández was released on the same day into the care of his friends. He made his will on 9 November, and died a few days later. He was about forty-two years old.[6]

The Hernández case is wearisome in the telling, even in this pared-down form. It must have been a slow nightmare in the living. Hernández had been an original conqueror, with all that implied in local prestige and local camaraderie. He had shouted aloud what many of his fellows had muttered. He had fought with all the weapons elaborate Spanish law had seemed to offer him. He was ready to use all his resources to win the contest he had so readily invoked. And he had been destroyed, in his property, his person, and his honour.

The colonists did not forget Hernández. They would brandish his sad ghost when changed circumstances at last made Landa vulnerable. But for the moment it had been demonstrated that Yucatan was indeed a frontier society where institutionalised authority was too weak or too remote for its interventions to be decisive, and where power would lie with those most relentless in its pursuit, most ruthless in its exercise, and most jealous in its possession. Landa had displayed to a sufficiently attentive audience his total belief in the righteousness of his own authority. No-one in the peninsula would lightly challenge his definition of his powers.

With the winning of that very public battle the Franciscans had forced acquiescence in their own definition of the proper and legitimate scope of ecclesiastical authority in Yucatan. But Yucatan would continue vulnerable to the uninformed and destructive interference of outsiders – like the Archbishop of Mexico – for as long as it lacked a bishop. The Crown had earlier named Juan de la Puerta, one of the founding fathers of the mission, to the post, but he had died before he could take office, so in 1559 Landa and two other friars had renewed their petition, sending it off to the Crown in the hands of Lorenzo de Bienvenida, another of their most senior and experienced friars. The three also requested that the only friars permitted to enter the province be Franciscans, so that harmony would be maintained; that some upright and conscientious magistrate with clearly defined powers be appointed to bring the province to order; and that supervisory jurisdiction be transferred from the *audiencia* of Guatemala to that of Mexico, a mere five or six days' journey away.[7]

Some time during 1560 Garci Jufre de Loaisa had travelled to the province as *juez visitador*, to assess how far local administrators had failed to implement his predecessor López Medel's ordinances, but he had proved too accommodating to *encomendero* interests, and so a disappointment to the friars. The Crown at last acted. In January of 1560 Yucatan was transferred by royal order to the jurisdiction of the *audiencia* of Mexico, and in February Don Diego Quijada, a professional bureaucrat, was named *alcalde mayor*, and so head of the secular government. On the issue of the bishopric the Crown failed to take the hint, if hint it was, regarding Bienvenida, but at least appointed a Franciscan to the post. In July of the same year Francisco de Toral, at that time Provincial of the order in Mexico, was named Bishop of Yucatan and Tabasco. It would be months before he could actually take up the appointment, as he would journey back to Spain to be consecrated as bishop before entering his diocese, but he had the essential attributes: he was a Franciscan, and a Franciscan versed in the ways of Indians, Spaniards, and friars. Lorenzo de Bienvenida, still recruiting friars in Spain, must have carried the welcome news back to the peninsula on his return in 1561.

The new *alcalde mayor* took up his duties in Mérida in the late June or early July of the same year. He had reason to be pleased with his appointment. After serving in a number of minor capacities in the royal administrations of Guatemala, Nicaragua and San Salvador he had travelled to Spain to solicit some more important and secure post. Yucatan was something of a backwater, and his decisions would be liable to review by the Viceroy and the *audiencia* of Mexico, but for a man of his unremarkable record and undistinguished rank the new post was desirable indeed. The Crown had secured itself a zealous and grateful servant.

Quijada's first task was to conduct the *residencia* of his predecessor. The *residencia*, the judicial review of conduct in office, probably did something to inhibit excessive corruption or indolence among agents of the Crown, but at the cost of plunging the incoming official into

the accumulated grievances and factionalism of the new ter:
into swift decisions on complex and emotionally charged lc
Quijada handled the test well, remitting the most serious
the Crown for judgment, and sensibly dismissing as trivia̱ ᴛʜᴇ usual
charges of favouritism or malice towards individuals.[8] The *residencia*
completed, he received news of an attack on Campeche by French
corsairs, and had to hurry to the port town to assess the damage and
reorder its defences. After some weeks of agitated work he was able to
assure the king that he had reconciled feuding citizens, put the
administration into working order, and shaped the Campeche
colonists into an effective little army capable of repelling any more
attacks.

It seems the *encomenderos* were ready to forgive his small part in the
Hernández affair: by October of 1561 the Mérida town council was
urging the Crown to increase Quijada's salary, to match the high cost
of living in 'these harsh, stony and dry lands', and that his term of
office be extended to ten years, for 'in the time he has been in this
province what he has begun and done shows his great zeal for the
service of God and Your Majesty, and . . . for the benefit and common
good of all'. The councillors were also anxious, on more selfish
grounds, that Quijada's powers be extended to permit the granting of
encomiendas.[9] In the following April, in a long, discursive, touchingly
informal letter to the Crown, Quijada made the same pleas for
himself. The province had suffered too long from temporary
governors: it needed long-term projects, like the construction of
roads and the breeding of horses to free the Indians from the task of
porterage. As for himself, he felt too old and ill and tired of travelling
to want to move again – unless, of course, His Majesty's service
should require it. If he could distribute Indians in *encomienda*, and if he
had the authority to award pensions, he could, he said, care for the
needy, and properly reward the deserving.

There were probably more immediate reasons for Quijada to want
to develop a local group of supporters with solid reason for gratitude.
Some colonists were beginning to reconsider their initial enthusiasm.
And there was disaffection in another and more dangerous quarter.
Quijada had noted that the Franciscans had granted dispensations to
some of the leading men of the province to marry within degrees of
relationship usually prohibited. The *alcalde* had no intention of
intervening, as he had no desire to disturb the people involved or to
antagonise the friars: he wanted only to ask the king to discuss the
matter with the Franciscan Commissary General, so that he would

know his duty. But his discreet enquiries had been noticed locally, and Quijada was uneasy. For the first and last time in his rambling letter he named the person who was causing him disquiet. He wrote:

There is in this province a friar called Fray Diego de Landa who, because I have taken this matter up, bears me ill will: he enjoys broils and having a finger in every pie, and he expects to rule in both spiritual and temporal matters. He is a choleric man, and I am afraid he will write to Your Majesty's Council to my injury: I wish Your Majesty to understand that he has always been inflamed against those who have governed here, as he is against me . . . may Your Majesty never believe that I harbour ill will against him or any other man of religion, for they I support to the limit of my strength, for in their hands lies the Christian welfare of the Indians, and without them, all is in vain.[10]

Paradoxically, it was Quijada's determination to support the friars 'to the limit of his strength' in the events which followed which was to destroy his reputation and his career, and in those events the 'choleric man' Diego de Landa was to have a most powerful influence.

It is commonplace that men both shape and are shaped by their environments – a commonplace which dulls our recognition of those interesting occasions when there is a peculiar and fortuitous matching between previously dormant talents and the demands of a novel situation. The New World example *par excellence* is Hernán Cortés: a smiling public man in Cuba, and then a leader of consummate political genius for the two dazzling years of the Mexican campaign. Diego de Landa worked on a very much smaller scale in Yucatan, but there is the same sense of a sudden expansion of energies to meet expanding challenges, of the deployment of an unusual configuration of capacities precisely appropriate to the unforseeable requirements of the new life. Landa had been born in Cifuentes, a town settled by 'Old Christians' after Alfonso VIII had forced out the Moors. A large Jewish colony survived there until the expulsion of 1492, and Cifuentes still sustained a colony of 'converted' Moslems into the sixteenth century. Perhaps Landa's zeal for the preservation and propagation of the Faith had been honed by the abrasion of growing up among men of doubtful orthodoxy. Entering the monastery of San Juan de los Reyes in Toledo at sixteen, he was about twenty-five when he accepted the missionary challenge and journeyed to Yucatan.

It was an unusual man who would, in the late 1540s, choose Yucatan at all: a backwater in an Indies remote from the absorbing

2 Fr Diego de Landa, Bishop of Yucatan 1571-79.

turmoil of Europe. And the commitment would have been understood as being for life. Only those friars radically unfitted for missionary life were permitted to return to Spain. Perhaps it was the very emptiness of the prospect, and therefore its openness, which constituted its appeal: missionaries have found escape from the restrictions of the home place as liberating as do their lay counterparts, and Landa was not a man who took direction easily. But it could equally have been the scope of the challenge. Landa suffered from asthma, that scourge of active anxious spirits, and Yucatan's climate is not kind to asthmatics; yet there is no hint in his long career of any falterings or periods of withdrawal, but rather of the outflow of an endless volcanic energy, both physical and mental. He began by setting himself the task of learning Mayan, which he did with such perfection that he was entrusted with the task of the revision of Villalpando's grammar, and with the translation into Mayan of the approved catechism and of a few basic sermons to aid his less gifted brothers in their teaching.[11] Posted to the monastery at Izamal, with Lorenzo de Bienvenida as Guardian, he was caught up in the arduous but routine round of the mission station, visiting and instructing through the surrounding villages; teaching the boys in the mission school; tending the sick in the infirmary; baptising, marrying, burying the Indians of Izamal. It was a demanding and, for some, a rewarding life; but the young friar chafed under it. The cautious decision to limit missionary activity to the better-controlled regions did not suit his restless spirit. He might also have chafed under the benevolent but constant supervision of Bienvenida: Landa was to show himself impatient of effective superiors. With Bienvenida's permission he set off alone into the forest, to carry the faith to the Indians of the interior.

His chief Franciscan biographer, López de Cogolludo, writing a century later, believed Landa to have travelled all over the peninsula, save to remote Bacalar, in that extraordinary wandering mission. He penetrated the regions around Valladolid which, especially since the revolt of 1546, had a sinister reputation, and where the 'pacification' had given those Indians who survived good reason to hate the Spaniards. Landa was almost certainly the first to preach to these embittered people. Cogolludo records that in 1551, while passing through the territory of the Cupules, Landa came upon 300 Indians about to sacrifice a youth. The boy, garlanded with flowers, was tied to a post, and around him were arrayed vessels of *balche*, the honey-based mead favoured by the old gods. Landa, bursting from the thickets, released the boy, smashed the vessels, and preached to the Indians so persuasively, we are told, that they begged him to stay among them and teach them further; 'and to show their good faith they themselves smashed the idols in his presence'. Even in Mani, the province favoured by the first mission station, Landa happened upon a large assembly of Indians ready to make sacrifice to their idols, and again effected an immediate mass conversion. He was also credited with having persuaded many scattered Indians to form new settlements conveniently close to existing monasteries, so bringing them into contact with less venturesome friars.[12]

Through the obscuring mist of pieties we glimpse a man of extraordinary endurance and extraordinary courage, extending the heroic dimension of the text of 'being Franciscan' by his own strenuous living of it. He was also, it would seem, a man of sensibility to both persons and places. Landa's home village had been in a region of rugged cliffs and gentle valleys, where the vegetation grew lush and green, and the air was alive with the sound of fountains and streams. The harsh silent plain of Yucatan should have been alien indeed. But it was in those early days that Landa made Yucatan peculiarly his own. Many years later, an exile in his own land, he was to write a great *Relación* or 'Account of the Things of Yucatan' which is steeped in pride and nostalgia. The land's harshness faded in his recollection: he was to celebrate the fertility of the scanty soil, the wonders of the *cenotes*, the salt, which he proclaimed the best he'd ever eaten, the excellence and variety of the fish and fowl, the fragrance and diversity of the flowers. And, seaming through the whole, the beauty and sense of the Maya people: the babies, 'marvellously pretty and plump', the gentle and modest women, the alert, upright, disciplined men.[13]

The intimacy of his descriptions – recipes favoured by the women, the antics of pet animals, the handling of babies and toddlers – imply an acceptance of the young friar into the huts and house-yards of the Maya with an easiness which goes well beyond mere nervous tolerance. He was to penetrate an even more closed zone with his admission into the society and at least some of the secrets of the elders. They trusted him enough to lament the decline in the chastity of their women from the days 'before they became acquainted with [the Spanish] nation'. One ancient patiently unravelled the complexities of the Maya systems for measuring time. With another, 'a man of very good intelligence and of wide reputation among them', Landa pondered the meaning of a cross-like symbol he had found represented in native sacred places, finally deciding its resemblance to the Christian cross was fortuitous.[14]

Even more remarkably, he was shown some of the sacred writings preserved in the folding deerskin 'books' which were the jealously guarded, secret and exclusive possessions of the ruling lineages of each province. With Nachi Cocom, head chief of Sotuta and for so long a wily and implacable enemy of the Spaniards, he had an especially warm relationship. Landa described him as 'a man of great reputation, learned in their affairs, and of remarkable discernment and well acquainted with native matters' who was 'very intimate with the author'. He recorded that Cocom 'showed him a book which had belonged to his grandfather, a son of the Cocom who had been killed at Mayapan'.[15] There can be no doubt that this was indeed one of the sacred and secret books of the Cocom lineage, recording its history and its prophecies. The revelation of that treasure – especially to a Spanish outsider – can only be explained as the expression of a confidence and attraction so powerful as to override traditional prescriptions and even conventional caution.

Some years after being shown these sacred books, Landa, in his official capacity and in company with his fellow Franciscans, was to burn as many of them as he could discover, together with any other sacred objects which came into his hands, precisely because they were so cherished. As he recalled in his *Relación*:

These people also make use of certain characters or letters, with which they wrote in their books their ancient matters and their sciences, and by these and by drawings and by certain signs in these drawings they understood their affairs and made others understand and taught them. We found a large number of these books in these characters and, as they contained nothing in which there was not to be seen superstition and lies of the devil, we burned them all, which they regretted to an amazing degree and which caused them great affliction.[16]

For the early period of his solitary wanderings, eager as he was to reveal the mysteries of his own faith, and clearly distinguishable in dress and behaviour from the Spanish soldiery the Maya had previously encountered, he had probably been identified by the custodians of Maya religion and learning as a fellow expert in those high matters. Committed to the patient accumulation of knowledge from whatever source, they can have had no notion of the exclusivist zeal which both fuelled Landa's curiosity, and empowered him to abrogate it so decisively.

Despite his intense engagement with the Indians, Landa took more than his share of administrative and political duties within the order. In 1553 he was charged with replacing the huts of the monastery at Izamal with a permanent stone structure. Details of the construction were left to the architect, the friar Juan de Mérida. It was the design and overall layout which interested Landa. The whole was to be set out on a vast Maya platform – Izamal had been one of the most important Maya religious centres. The structures were not to be especially massive, and were in fact economical in their use of materials and labour. The design derived its undoubted grandeur from the scale and distribution of its great spaces for processions and collective ceremonial. The structure was flung across the land like the grandiose gesture it was: a most material testament of Landa's vision of the Church he and his brothers were building in Yucatan.

As relations between friars and settlers deteriorated, it was probably Landa's political skills – which in that raw colonial politics meant tenacity and clarity of purpose – which his fellows most valued, among his formidable array of talents. He had been entrusted with the disciplining of the loose-tongued Hernández, and despite the *encomendero's* twists and turns, he pursued him through the labyrinth of the colonial judicial process and had finally brought him down. In 1561 the General Chapter of the order, meeting in Spain, united the missions of Guatemala and Yucatan to form an independent missionary province. The friars of the two territories met in Mérida to elect their first Provincial towards the end of the Hernández affair. Passing over men who had been pioneers in the mission field, and veterans of many years' standing in the order, their choice fell on Landa. He was thirty-seven.

6

Crisis

1562 must have been something of a watershed year for the Yucatan Franciscans, a time for reviewing what were, on any score, formidable achievements. The worst excesses of the colonists had been curbed, and through the reduction of Hernández they had been taught a useful lesson as to the respect due to the Order. With the appointment of Quijada, the first resident 'outsider' – the judge-inspectors had been birds of passage – local control over the apparatus of the royal administration had been broken. Quijada himself was or could be made properly respectful of ecclesiastical authority. The first bishop was to be a Franciscan, and a Franciscan of impeccable credentials, seasoned in the field. And the mission – given the difficult terrain, given limited manpower, given the mere seventeen years of its existence – was thriving.

There was still only a handful of secular clergy in the province, but the population of friars had grown. Bienvenida had been twice to Spain, bringing back recruits each time. Just how many Franciscans there were in the peninsula at any time after the earliest days is uncertain, as the records have been lost, but the original eight had been joined by perhaps nine in 1549, fifteen in 1533, and ten or eleven in 1561. Death and disability must have claimed some: the sapping work and sapping heat of Yucatan took its toll. Some left: there was more movement of men between Mexico, Yucatan and Guatemala than the rigours of travel would lead us to expect.[1] But by 1562 twelve monasteries had been established, six being housed in their permanent stone structures, and if the more remote areas remained untended more than 200 villages already had their church, their school, their mission-trained schoolmasters. The chiefs and lords had accepted baptism, as had those *ah-kines*, the priests of the old religion, who had survived the time of war (the Spanish soldiery had killed them when they could). Few of the friars spoke Mayan, or at least spoke it well enough to preach fluently or to hear Indian confessions, but the native schoolmasters spoke in their native tongue on Christian texts, and if few Indians made their confessions most Spaniards did so only once a year. In essentials the web of control had been established and the people tamed to the Christian order. In the villages the days were patterned by the church bells which summoned the children to instruction, and then the adults to prayer, as the weeks and months were patterned by the obligatory Christian feasts. The friars knew some vestigial idolatry continued, out in the scattered cornfields, or in remote or recently converted regions. In Sotuta during his service there as curate between 1556 and 1560 the secular priest Lorenzo de Monterroso had to punish his Indians several times for making offerings of food and drink to some images they kept hidden at their *milpas*, as had the priest in charge of the southern province of Cochuah. These 'offences' were treated with compassion, and punished with no more than a whipping. When Landa himself uncovered what he later described as 'very great knaveries and idolatries' in the troubled region of Valladolid he had been content to have all the chiefs and lords called together, and to give them a solemn lecture before extending his pardon.[2]

Then a chance discovery placed all those understandings and all those achievements in jeopardy. Early in May 1562, two Indian youths from Mani hunting about a league from the village, stumbled upon a cave in which they found a number of idols together with human skulls. They ran back to the village and reported their find to the guardian of the monastery, Fray Pedro de Ciudad Rodrigo. Fray Pedro had the bones and idols collected and piled in a great heap in the patio of the monastery, where they were examined by six friars who happened to be in Mani improving their command of Mayan, and by a few of the local encomenderos. After consultation with his brothers, Fray Pedro had his native constables bring to the monastery about forty Indians who lived in the vicinity of the cave. The suspects were herded into the monastery jail and then taken out one by one to be questioned.

The Indians freely confessed to ownership of the idols, which they worshipped, as they were reported to have said, 'so that it would rain and that they would give them much corn and so that they would kill many deer'. Further, they said that Indians from all the neighbouring villages also retained their idols and continued to worship them. Again the constables were sent out, this time to round up most of the local commoners, so that they overflowed the little jail into the hospital and several houses and shops. Again, almost all readily admitted to idolatry.[3]

Those discoveries, and worse, those easy confessions, must have profoundly shaken Ciudad Rodrigo. Mani was the heartland of the mission enterprise, of special pride and significance to the Franciscans: their first venture among the Indians, glorified by the near-martyrdom of Villalpando and Bienvenida, the secure centre for their cautious expansion. And Ciudad Rodrigo had special grounds for believing his Indians placed exemplary trust in him. In the previous August he had been able to quell a flare of superstitious terror which swept the village of Hunacti when a curiously deformed baby had been stillborn. It seemed to the frightened villagers who attended the birth that it bore the marks of the stigmata on its feet, hands, and side, and the indentations of thorns upon its head, and that from these wounds, though the child was dead, some blood had flowed. The village chief immediately had his schoolmaster write an account to the Franciscan guardian, who ordered the little body to be brought to him. When it arrived with its escort of anxious and excited Indians he was able to assure them that the lesions were 'a natural thing', and to send them back to their village comforted. (He had also quashed some talk among local *encomenderos* that the Indians must have been up to 'some wickedness').[4]

Now he was persuaded that his Indians' apparent trusting dependence had been fraudulent. His next, unprecedented step betrays his chagrin, his pain, and the sense of outraged betrayal he and his colleagues felt. With no legal preliminaries, but with the support of the Mani friars, he had the Indians taken in job lots of twenty or thirty, and subjected them to the torture known as the *garrucha*, or the 'hoist'. A Spanish eyewitness remembered:

when the Indians confessed to having so few idols (one, two or three) the friars proceeded to string up many of the Indians, having tied their wrists together with cord, and thus hoisted them from the ground, telling them that they must confess all the idols they had, and where they were. The Indians continued saying they had no more . . . and so the friars ordered great stones attached to their feet, and so they were left to hang for a space, and if they still did not admit to a greater quantity of idols they were flogged as they hung there, and had burning wax splashed on their bodies . . .[5]

When they were finally let down, the villagers were sent off in the charge of a native constable to collect as many idols as they had confessed to owning, and were then returned to jail to await formal judgment and punishment, while the idols were added to the slowly mounting pile in the patio before the church.[6]

The friars' actions were on any score illegal. The torture was applied promiscuously, to those who had confessed culpability as well as to those who had not, and with none of the careful safeguards which regulated its use in Spanish ecclesiastical and civil courts.[7] 'Due process' in Spanish law moved through the slow accumulation of sworn and properly attested statements. Here no records of any kind were kept. And the Franciscans had no authority to inflict physical punishments: that was, officially, the preserve of the secular government.

Casual about such secular restrictions, the Mani friars were punctilious regarding the sacred and ceremonial aspects of the law. On a Sunday soon after the initial discoveries they celebrated an *auto de fe*, the judicial sentencing of offenders against the faith. The Indian penitents, idols in their hands, ropes around their necks, and some wearing the high conical cap of the *coroza*, the headdress of shame, were forced to stand through a mass and a sermon, and then suffered their prescribed number of lashes. Many were also required to pay cash fines. Those who could not pay were returned to jail.

The Provincial Landa had been informed of the discovery of the cave and of his friars' response, which he probably authorised and certainly approved, but he delayed taking charge of the investigation for almost a month. His tardiness was perhaps due to protracted negotiations with the wary *alcalde mayor*, for when Landa arrived at about the end of the first week of June he brought with him Quijada's formal authorisation, signed only on the third of that month, to command the aid of lay Spaniards in the prosecution of the enquiry. Landa needed Spanish officials because he was determined to extend the enquiry into the ranks of the chiefs and lords. The native constables appointed in each village would follow orders (however unwillingly) against the commoners, but no pressure could make them act against the lords. Spanish constables were pressed into service, and more than twenty native leaders were apprehended and brought back to Mani over the next few days.

As Provincial, Landa was empowered to conduct an episcopal inquisition under the terms of the concessionary Papal Bull. *Encomenderos* already disturbed by the Mani friars' highhanded proceedings must have welcomed his coming, with its promise of a more formal approach to the enquiry. His initial actions were reassuring. He brought with him his official notary, Francisco de Orozco;

commissioned one Spaniard as prosecutor, with the task of present-
ing charges, and another 'defender' of the Indians. Fray Pedro de
Ciudad Rodrigo, Fray Miguel de la Puebla and Fray Juan Pizarro he
named fellow inquisitorial judges. Landa established his own court in
an arbour of the monastery, where the Indian leaders were brought
separately to face him, as he sat flanked by his notary and the official
interpreter. The setting at least was of a formal episcopal inquisition.

But again formality was sustained only in the *mise en scène* and not
the procedural dimension of the judicial process. For Landa too the
discovery of the canker of idolatry at the very heart of the missionary
enterprise was deeply galling. As ruling prelate, he would soon have
to render an account of his stewardship to the incoming bishop who
must arrive within the next few months. Time was short. There is no
hint that he flinched from what had been done by his brothers, or
urged a gentler course, and he had as little concern for legal niceties as
they. Then and for the next three months he maintained the
procedures of mass arrest and savage unselective torture, extending
the enquiry into two adjacent provinces, where the violence of the
tortures and the invention of the torturers appears to have been even
more extravagant. When, after sentence, Indian penitents were tied to
the whipping-post to suffer their prescribed number of lashes, it was
reported that their bodies were already so torn from the preliminary
interrogations that 'there was no sound part on which they could be
flogged'.[8]

More than 4,500 Indians were put to the torture during the three
months of the inquisition, and an official enquiry later established that
158 had died during or as a direct result of the interrogations. At least
thirteen people were known to have committed suicide to escape the
torture, while eighteen others, who had disappeared, were thought to
have killed themselves. Many more had been left crippled, their
shoulder muscles irreparably torn, their hands paralysed 'like hooks'.[9]

Although Landa labelled it an episcopal inquisition, the enquiry
bore little resemblance to established inquisitorial forms. In Bishop
Zumárraga's inquisition into Indian idolatries in Mexico between
1536 and 1543 procedures had been carefully prescribed and as
carefully adhered to, and where torture was employed it was narrowly
regulated.[10] Spanish law recognised the danger of that weapon in the
hands of a baffled or frustrated interrogator. In Yucatan records of
interrogations were rarely kept, only sentences being routinely
recorded. The penalties imposed – floggings, heavy fines, and periods
of forced labour of up to ten years' duration, and these only on lesser

offenders – were well in excess of the limits laid down by the Mexican ecclesiastical council of 1555.[11] The unashamed violence of the Franciscan inquisition is at once the best evidence for the political domination they had achieved in the peninsula, their anger at Indian betrayal, and their sense of the desperate urgency of the situation. Landa was later to justify his disregard of legal formalities on the grounds that:

all [the Indians] being idolaters and guilty, it was not possible to proceed strictly juridically against them . . . because if we had proceeded with all according to the order of the law, it would be impossible to finish with the province of Mani alone in twenty years, and meanwhile they would all become idolaters and go to hell . . .[12]

However urgent the extension of the enquiry, the unchallengeable power of the church had also to be ceremonially displayed, given the covert defiance of the Indians and increasing criticism from lay Spaniards. In July Landa summoned Quijada to Mani, 'to guarantee order,' he said. But he had a further purpose. Landa was planning a great *auto de fe* which would go far beyond the petty affairs celebrated before his arrival. A sufficiently splendid performance, modelled on those of the homeland, would so display the terrible majesty of the combined power of Church and Crown – and the supremacy of the Church in matters spiritual – as to persuade the disaffected of the triviality of merely procedural irregularities, and the wicked of the necessity to repent.

Elaborate preparations were put under way. Indian women had begun dyeing and painting cotton lengths to make the banners which would flaunt above the procession. Some cloth remained unpainted and was dyed black, for the crosses carried were to be shrouded in the colour of mourning. One Indian undertook the unfamiliar task of painting the great red crosses on the yellow garments of shame, the *sanbenitos*, which some of the penitents would wear. Others laboured to erect a wooden platform in the little square of the village, where the Spanish dignitaries would sit to watch the punishment of the sinners below.

Soon after Quijada and an escort of six or seven armed Spaniards rode into Mani. On 12 July, the great *auto* was celebrated. The friars, in solemn procession, bearing their shrouded crosses and chanting litanies, led the shuffling mass of Indian penitents to the square and the elevated stage. Among the friars marched Quijada, bearing his staff of office, and so symbolising the unity of Crown and faith, while

Map 2 The afflicted provinces, 1562.

mounted Spaniards (signifying less formally but equally vividly the force those two abstractions could invoke) rode at the rear, scanning the great press of watching Indians. The two Indian youths who had discovered the cave, wearing the new outfits which were part of their reward, carried the banners commemorating their role. And heaped before the platform were the masks, the curiously worked wood, the pottery vessels in human or animal forms, the jewelled human skulls, that the Spaniards called 'idols'. The four inquisitorial judges and the *alcalde mayor* mounted the platform, the penitents ranged below. The Provincial rose to address a solemn sermon to the crowd, in his clear, precisely accented Mayan. Then it was the *alcalde mayor*'s turn. Sinking to his knees, he swore his unqualified support for all the friars' actions, past and to come, in their efforts to extirpate idolatry.

After the saying of the mass the interpreter Gaspar Antonio Chi proclaimed the sentences, which were immediately executed. Men were tied to the whipping post, and once again the blood ran as up to 200 lashes were laid on the flesh already lacerated from the preliminary questioning. Punishment was not restricted to those who had actually performed acts of idolatry: one youth who had failed to betray his father's ownership of two idols was given two hundred lashes. The lesser lords already tried received similar sentences, in addition to permanent loss of status, and periods of up to ten years' service to the friars or to designated lay Spaniards. Then the great mound of idols and the jewelled skulls of the ancestors were set to burn.[13]

The *auto de fe* presumably had the desired effect of impressing Spaniard and Indian alike at least with the authority of the episcopal inquisitorial office, and the power of those who filled it. Quijada's public involvement had been unequivocal. It had not been achieved without pressure. Landa had soundly abused him for allowing himself to be guided 'by the carelessness and fawning' of certain Spaniards who had displayed shamefully little zeal for the faith. Despite the clear evidence of the loads on loads of idols brought in to the monastery, despite the Indians' eager confessions and despite having seen 'the damnation of this province' these perverse men claimed the whole affair to have arisen 'from the anger and the ill will of the friars towards the Indians'. Angered by such signs of increasingly public disaffection, Landa threatened to go personally to Mexico to denounce Quijada before the viceroy and the *audiencia* unless he served the ecclesiastical arm with proper zeal.[14]

The threat had been sufficient to bring the nervous Quijada to heel, and his highly public submission followed. That declaration of unconditional support for all the friars' actions was certainly impolitic, closing as it did the only local avenue of appeal for colonists anxious to question the handling of the inquisition. As head of the secular government Quijada was obliged to assist the missionary programme, and to execute the judgments arrived at by the ecclesiastical authority. But Landa then manoeuvred Quijada into actions which carried him beyond legality by insisting that the *alcalde mayor* himself should conduct the preliminary interrogations of forty Indians, subjecting them to torture, and reporting his findings back to the Provincial.[15]

Quijada acquiesced, perhaps because his earlier attempts to resist had been so ineffectual. Good bureaucrat that he was, he kept records of his interrogations, seven of which survive. They are pathetic documents. Of the seven, only two Indians could remember the four essential prayers, though whether this is a comment on the inadequacy of the friars' teaching or the terror of the Indians' situation we cannot know. It is clear that dread of the torture was intense, with the mere threat of the hoisting being enough to make the numbers of idols soar. One terrified man who had already confessed to having inherited ten idols from his father admitted to ten more when he felt the cords being bound around his wrists, while another, having admitted to three and then to twenty more was put to the torture, and while he dangled confessed to three, then to one, and then to two more idols, before he was, at last, let down. Then, of course, he had to find and hand over the twenty-nine idols, or face more agony. There was no long-term advantage in inflating the numbers.[16]

Landa extended the enquiry to the adjacent provinces by sending Fray Juan Pizarro, assisted by Fray de Aparicio and Fray Antonio de Veruga, to Sotuta, and Fray Miguel de la Puebla, with Andrés de la Bruselas and Francisco de Gadea, to Hocaba-Homun. Landa himself remained in charge in Mani, where he drew up a formal indictment summarising the iniquities he had uncovered. After they had 'become Christians', he charged, the Indians of Mani:

returned to their ancient and evil customs, worshipping idols and sacrificing to them publicly and in secret, and so publicly that many of them have been performed at the churches, altars and crosses along the roads, and at other holy places dedicated to God, and some have gone on to blaspheme against the faith and to make pacts with devils, and to destroy the Christianity of the simple people so that, as some of them have said, in the time of their paganism they were not so given to idolatry, and others, dogmatising and teaching false doctrines . . . saying that our true Lord is not God but the devil, the enemy of their souls, and that their preachers and ministers are not really so, and therefore they should not believe what they preach and teach.[17]

Not long after the *auto de fe* Landa was urgently called to Sotuta. The hasty summons probably had to do with the suicide in prison before interrogation of Lorenzo Cocom, chief of the head village, lord of the province, and brother and successor to Juan Nachi Cocom, Landa's old informant, who had died the previous year. Cocom's suicide was interpreted as proof of his guilty involvement in idolatries.

Certainly fear ran before the friars. When Pizarro and his brothers arrived in the head village they found the villagers had fled, to return only when some of their *encomenderos* – now identified as their protectors against the assaults of the friars – arrived. In Kanchunup, a village only half a league from Sotuta village, two Indians had hanged themselves at word of the friars' coming. Such proofs of 'wickedness' strengthened the friars' resolve and the vehemence of their interrogations. One Spaniard forced to serve as constable to the Inquisition in Sotuta recalled that some chiefs and lords were hoisted as many as five times, and another swore that they were flogged while they hung suspended until the blood ran. But it was of Hocaba-Homun, with Fray Miguel de la Puebla in charge, that the darkest tales were told. While the Spaniards pressed to serve the inquisition in the other provinces carried out their duties with aversion, the enlisted constable in Hocaba-Homun seems to have taken some pride in his work. Dissatisfied with the hoist, he constructed a version of the *burro*, extensively used by the Inquisition in Spain for the administration of the torture of the water and the cords. The victim was secured face up on a wooden frame, and cords were twisted around thighs and upper arms. The cords could be tightened by the turning of a rod inserted between flesh and frame. The victim's mouth was forced open, and quantities of water were poured in, usually through a cloth to increase the sensation of drowning. In the careful protocol observed by the interrogators of the Spanish Inquisition the accused was given ample time between each 'turn' and vessel of water to confess his guilt, but the Hocaba constable observed no such niceties. His individual contribution was to trample on the distended belly of the victim, so that the swallowed water was violently discharged. At least one Indian died lashed to the *burro*.[18]

Of all these activities no records were kept, either of interrogations or of confessions. When the Hocaba-Homun inquisitors returned to

Mérida they apparently submitted only oral reports, presumably of the usual acts of idolatry. Most of what we know of their proceedings comes from Spanish colonists who later told their stories before an official enquiry. At the time, they could do little but watch. But they watched, and remembered, well. The *encomendero* of Homun village recalled that he had seen Indian suspects herded out of the jails and forced to kneel, to be questioned by native assistants to the friars. The assistants would refer from time to time to papers they held, presumably furnished by their masters, and should a suspect deny a charge he was immediately put to the torture. The *encomendero* recalled that as they writhed 'the friars would ask them how many idols they possessed, and some would say twenty, and others fifty, and others two hundred . . .' A confession once made, even under these conditions, could not be easily withdrawn. One Homun Indian under torture confessed his own idolatry, and implicated several others, who were tortured in their turn. When the time came to ratify his testimony he repudiated it, saying that he had lied, that he was a true Christian, and that his companions had been unjustly condemned. The friars' response was to have him strung up again much higher than the others, to weight his feet with stones, and to leave him to hang for two long hours. Throughout, he continued to insist he had lied.[19]

Settler anxiety, already intense, increased as the inquisition plunged on. The enquiry had begun in May, which was usually the time of the planting, but there was little planting in the central provinces that year, and *encomenderos* feared for their tribute. Labour supplies were disrupted: some Indians fled into the forest; most vanished into the friars' jails; and those released were not quickly fit for work. *Encomendero* claims to authority over their Indians were in tatters. Now it was the settlers who had to face deputations of frantic Indians weeping, displaying their wounds, begging for protection; and had to admit themselves powerless to intervene. The Church had uncontested jurisdiction over sinners and apostates.

They were fearful, too, of what would happen when the great lords still awaiting interrogation in Mérida would be stripped and flogged. Spaniards understood the importance of the inviolability of the person, especially the person of high rank. They recognised in Indian society a deference system even more pronounced than their own. Franciscans had always denied the validity of that account of things, and had insisted – through their mortifications of their own flesh, and their deliberate infliction of rituals of physical humiliation on the socially great – that men of whatever rank were equally sinners before the Lord, and prisoners in a double sense of their own carnality. If both groups of Spaniards looked towards the interrogation of the chiefs, they did so in very different spirits. And settler-conquistadores knew the fury of the aroused Maya, as the friars did not.

All these issues troubled them. But what the settlers most bitterly contested, and the theme they rehearsed in a multitude of anecdotes, was the cruelty. There was politics in that, and retaliation for Franciscan denunciations, but despite their own brutalities the protests were not disingenuous. To cudgel a man in a rage is one thing. To subject him to hours of calculated agony, outside of the context of careful legalisms which could render such considered violence legitimate, was very much another. Time and again settler observers noted the friars' failure to keep records and to take sworn statements. Spaniards were passionate litigants, and the huge edifice of Spanish legalism was built on the properly sworn statement. They were genuinely shocked by Franciscan casualness about particular cases, and about particular 'facts'. One Spaniard spent many hours and some hard riding on behalf of Diego Uz, chief of Tekax in Mani, because he was persuaded of his innocence. He had twice visited the chief in prison. On the second occasion the old man was in a desperate state. Being, as he said, 'a heavy man', he had found the agony of the hoistings unendurable, and had finally 'confessed' to the ownership of forty idols. The Spaniard (not, interestingly, his *encomendero*, which suggests a more personal bond) first appealed to Landa to set aside the confession he believed to be patently false, and then, when the Provincial rebuffed him, turned to help the chief's son to hunt up anything which could pass as an 'idol'. Other Spaniards reported that Indians were combing the ruins of Coba, more than twenty-five leagues distant, searching for idols. They pointed to some of those handed in which were suspiciously old and mossy, and others suspiciously new.[20] They thought that because they had demonstrated that not all the retrieved idols were authentic, that not all the confessions were precisely true, they had demonstrated the idolatry trials to be a cruel farce, on which no ceremonial performance, however carefully choreographed, could confer legitimacy.

For the friars such considerations were trivial. They were concerned not with legal process, nor even the particular case, but the general intention, and there they knew the Indians to be guilty, and the violence they visited on Indian bodies justified by their obligation to preserve Indian souls. Settler protest simply exposed their malice, and their reprehensible lack of zeal. Landa effectively throttled overt criticism by posting an edict in Mérida cathedral placing the whole investigation under the seal of the episcopal inquisition, which he as surrogate bishop claimed the right to conduct, and so banned any discussion of the matter under threat of excommunication.

The colonists were not without some clerical support. The secular priest Lorenzo de Monterroso, one-time curate of Sotuta village, had been summoned to Sotuta to aid the enquiry, and had been persuaded by the Indians' protestations of their innocence, and the cruel futility of the friars' 'interrogations'. In Mérida the town council, official organ of settler opinion, was sufficiently disquieted by the disruption of native life, the possibility of general insurrection, and the outrage of the settlers to send two of its senior officials, Francisco de Bracamonte and Joaquín de Leguízamo, to beg the Provincial to change the mode of the inquisition. They urged that Landa and Fray Francisco de la Torre, both senior friars and proficient linguists, should undertake a slow and careful enquiry themselves into the matter of idolatry, and that the mass terror should cease.

Even filtered through the medium of Monterroso's hostile account, the report of Landa's response has the ring of authenticity. Monterroso wrote:

This witness heard what they said to him and begged him on behalf of the council . . . and the said Fray Diego de Landa replied that whoever should rise up or rebel or hang themselves or give themselves to the devil, the matter would continue to be dealt with rigorously, as it had been from the beginning, as was fitting because they had performed many sacrifices and idolatries . . .[21]

The council had reached an *impasse*. With Landa intransigent, and Quijada committed to his support, the official 'authorities' were united. There could be no redress within the peninsula; no check on the Franciscans' continuing violence. The two delegates, together with Monterroso, decided on a desperate measure. Leguízamo owned a frigate which lay at anchor in Campeche harbour. He would attempt to embark secretly, and carry the appeal for some tempering of the friars' notion of justice to the outside authority of the *audiencia* of Mexico.

Leguízamo was saved the danger of the enterprise. Soon after the delegation returned to Mérida, they received word that the new bishop had at last arrived and, disembarked at Campeche, was ready to take charge of his diocese.

Bishop Toral came warmly recommended by the great Viceroy of New Spain, Don Luis de Velasco, as a man of holy life, zeal, and wisdom, who had served both Indians and Spaniards well in his years in New Spain. He had shown a decent humility when offered the bishopric, and had accepted it only on the orders of his Franciscan superior. He had been as energetic and determined in his endeavour to understand his Indian charges in Mexico as had Landa in Yucatan, mastering not only Nahuatl but also the difficult Popoloca language of the Puebla region, for which he produced a grammar and a vocabulary. In 1552 he had journeyed to Spain to attend the General Chapter of the order meeting at Salamanca as Custodian of the Mexican zone, and then went on to search through Spain for zealous friars ready to labour in the Lord's Mexican vineyard. He brought back thirty-six friars when he returned to Mexico in the following year, which points both to his negotiating skill, and his capacity to inspire.[22]

The one portrait we have of him shows a slight, fine-featured man, whose glance initially seems to indicate a wariness tinged with anxiety. Longer examination suggests the watchful mistrust to be at least in part inner-directed, and that this is someone capable of reflection and considered self-scrutiny. Certainly the impression of delicacy, even fragility, remains strong.

That impression is almost certainly false. All effective missionaries, and Toral was effective, had to be tough. He had the requisite political courage. As Mexican Provincial he had taken the hard decision to aid Fray Bernardino de Sahagún in the compilation of his great work on the religion and society of the Aztecs of Mexico. Many in the order were fearful of too close an examination of what was after all the devil's kingdom. And there were other problems. Sahagún, a superb linguist, with a fine observing eye, wanted to collate his material to alert his colleagues to what he identified as pagan continuities in overtly 'Christian' observances. He was coming to suspect what was later to become a bitter certainty: that the so-called conversion of the heroic days of the Mexican mission had been no 'conversion' at all. Men outside the order – including members of competing orders – had long complained that the Mexican Franciscans had been dangerously casual in their pre-baptismal instruction, and all too complacent in their later supervision of their charges. Any acknowledgment of that criticism from within the order could be read as the meanest betrayal; and this in an institution which prized and asserted total loyalty to a totally shared ideal and a shared understand-

3 Fr. Francisco de Toral, Bishop of Yucatan 1560–71.

ing of the world. Toral's decision to relieve Sahagún from routine duties and to instruct him to continue his work was therefore morally intrepid.[23] (As a consequence of that decision, we now have, after many vicissitudes, Sahagún's magnificent *General History of the Things of New Spain*, the indispensable and incomparable source for the native world of Mexico.)

As a Franciscan Toral had always been ready to fight the pretensions of the secular clergy, and to protect the Indians from what he saw as their impositions. At the Provincial Council of Ecclesiastics held in Mexico in 1555 he failed in a determined attempt to have the Indians exempted from the tithe, but the council did accept his argument that, as newcomers to the faith, they should be lightly punished for errors in religion, and that, given their existing burdens, they should not have pecuniary fines imposed on them. As Provincial he denounced to the Crown the inadequacies of the Archbishop of Mexico and the Bishop of Tlascala, and soon after he himself had become a bishop he wrote again to the Crown explicitly asserting the right and the necessity for friars to 'command and to castigate the Indians as a master and father', so demonstrating that elevation would not dim his loyalty to the order.[24] He had proved himself ready to consider the possibility that conversion programmes, however passionately prosecuted, could be defective, and Indians, however apparently responsive, could be delinquent. The question remained: how would he respond to the extraordinary situation in Yucatan?

When the Franciscan Juan de Zumárraga had entered his new diocese of Mexico as its first bishop early in December 1528, his journey from Vera Cruz to Mexico City became a triumphant procession of settlers and Indians, led by his joyful fellow Franciscans. If Toral hoped for a similar reception he was to be disappointed. Disembarked with a handful of attendants at Campeche in the steamy heat of August he was met not by the Provincial and attendant friars, but by Leguízamo's dolorous account of the events of the last few months.[25]

Toral had time to reflect on the story and to garner more information from the colonists who formed his escort, for it was not until he had approached within three leagues of Mérida that he was formally greeted by two friars from the mother house. The Provincial had been informed of the bishop's disembarkation by a hasty letter from the Mérida friars, who urged him to hurry to welcome the bishop and to place the whole idolatry enquiry in his hands. But Landa had decided that affairs in Sotuta had a higher claim upon his duty. Despite renewed pleas and a warning that his deliberate absence could jeopardise his relations with the new bishop, Landa refused to alter his decision, and insisted that the friars carry out the instructions he had already given for the Bishop's reception.

The precise nature of the instructions is unclear, but they included the conditions on which Toral would be permitted to lodge in the Franciscan monastery outside Mérida: only if the bishop had not yet been consecrated should he be received into the Franciscan house. Landa's point seems to have been that if Toral were unconsecrated, he remained a Franciscan, and so could lodge in the monastery, and, presumably, owe obedience to the Provincial.

Whatever the niceties of the political point, and however revealing of the Provincial's temper, the attempt at exclusion was ineffective. After hearing Leguízamo's tales, and seeing the disarray of the friars on his arrival, Toral was in no mood to tolerate the manoeuvrings of an obstinately absent Provincial. If any of the Mérida friars protested, their protests were brushed aside. Toral and his small entourage took symbolic and actual possession of the monastery.[26]

Toral stayed for only two days in the Franciscan house, and then sought quarters within Mérida. The town could provide little that was suitable for an episcopal palace, and he was forced to take up residence in the Casa Montejo, the mansion built for the first conqueror. Its ample rooms and airy patio were handsome, but the motif of the two great medallions flanking the entrance door, of armoured Spaniards standing at ease on the heads of wailing Indians, must have reminded Toral that his new diocese was much closer to the harsh attitudes of the conquest period than the relatively mature society he had left. One of the bishop's first actions after his arrival in the city was to alleviate the rigorous confinement of the chiefs awaiting trial, and to move them to more comfortable quarters.

Toral had entered Mérida on 14 August. It was only after he had been five or six days in Mérida that the Provincial finally appeared. The story he brought with him from Sotuta rendered insignificant the irritations of the last few days, and provided ample justification for his absence. By 11 August Landa had become convinced, in the course of what had become a routine investigation of idolatry among the Maya, that some Indians of Sotuta province had offered human victims to the old gods, as they had in the days before the Spaniards came. Among those identified as present at those ceremonies had been so-called 'Christian' schoolmasters.

Precisely when Landa was persuaded that the Maya had returned to human sacrifice cannot be established with certainty, for the Provincial was careful to keep the matter as secret as possible for those last few days in Sotuta. His caution might well have sprung in part from the fear that the information he was collecting would be distorted by irresponsible rumours. Certainly Leguízamo's delegation left for Mérida knowing nothing of this new and sinister turn of events, and Monterroso, who had watched while three or four boys from the school at Sotuta were being tortured, heard only 'later' that 'they had declared that all the Indians of the said village had sacrificed some children in the church of the village at night' during the period of his own curacy. It is perhaps more difficult to understand why Landa would allow his fellow inquisitors, working in Mani and Hocaba-Homun, to remain in ignorance; for he was in constant communication with them. Nor is there any mention of his discovery in his letters to his friars in Mérida in response to the news of the Bishop's arrival. But on the 11 August he had had his notary draw up an indictment which ran:

the principal lords and *ah-kines* and schoolmasters have made human sacrifices to god [*sic*] within the church of this village and in other places in homage to the devils, killing infants and boys and girls, Indian men and women, offering the hearts ripped living from them to the devils. And . . . they have burnt crosses, taken from the altar to burn them, mocking them . . . and they themselves have become priests, and have preached falsely that which the priests, friars and clerics were teaching them was not true or good . . .[27]

Even within Sotuta itself Landa strove to maintain discretion. The ordinary business of sentencing and penancing Indian idolators continued through the last few days of the enquiry, though it is likely that this now routine task was carried through by Fray Juan de Pizzaro, Landa being fully absorbed by the pursuit of more sinister things. On 11 August he had taken sworn testimonies from ten Indians from the villages of Sahcaba, Sotuta and Yaxcaba. At the end of that day he could glimpse the dimensions of the task ahead, but only obscurely. Too often witnesses had only hearsay evidence to offer: they had been told about some human sacrifices at some time in the past; the men they named as involved were dead, or vanished, or still waiting trial in Mérida, on charges which now seemed trivial. Even eyewitnesses were often confused on details: on times, places, where victims had come from, their names, their sex. And even after torture, even when they had been thoroughly incriminated by other Indians' testimony, some men remained obdurate, and flatly denied all accusations. But Landa had learnt that there had been a deliberate conspiracy involving *ah-kines*, the traditional chiefs, and – most woundingly of all – the 'Christian' schoolmasters, the young men who had lived with the friars and shared their lives, to destroy the friars' influence and to frustrate their efforts to lead men out of the old faith. It became clear to him that the central expression of this conspiracy had been the ritual killing of victims, usually children, usually inside the village church. The conspiracy had been organised by the head chief Lorenzo Cocom, whose suicide was now all too easy to understand. Indians had been exhorted to cling to their old gods, and even after the Mani enquiry had begun the ceremonies continued.

The leaders told the people to yield up only old and broken idols to the friars – as their brothers in Mani had done. There was no longer any mystery regarding the dilapidated state of some of the 'idols' handed in to Mani investigators.

According to confessions taken over the next few days there could be no hope that the killings had been restricted to those three villages. Witnesses from Kanchunup admitted that human sacrifice had been practised there too, and for an even longer period, the first being performed two years before. The sacrifices had continued even after the village chief and his son had been sent prisoner to Mérida. Nor were the sacrifices confined to Sotuta and the followers of the Cocom. Another witness revealed that he had been present at human sacrifices in his home village of Oxkutzcab, in Mani. Present at the sacrifices, along with other Mani chiefs, had been Diego Uz, chief of Tekax, whose protestations of innocence and whose 'unjustified' sufferings at the hands of the inquisitors had so moved his Spanish protector during the earlier phase of the enquiry, which was now revealed as not severe enough. In the one village of Mopila testimony revealed that at least fifteen children had died, in eight separate sacrifices over three years. The child victims were usually stolen from other villages, and in three cases their mutilated bodies had been smuggled back to their home villages and thrown into the *cenote*.

Landa recorded no testimonies between 14 and 16 August and the sources do not reveal his whereabouts. He had probably heard of the Bishop's arrival in the peninsula just as he uncovered the first evidence of human sacrifice. By 15 August he must have been warned of Toral's increasing impatience with his Provincial and his in-quisition. Clearly Landa could not too long delay his return to Mérida. When he returned to the formal taking of testimonies on 17 August he had brought before him more Indians from Kanchunup and Yaxcaba, and one of those witnesses revealed a new and yet darker dimension to Maya perfidy. He gave an account of a sacrifice at the foot of the cross in the cemetery of the church at Kanchunup which had taken place rather more than two years before. The two victims were young boys, Ah Chuc and Ah Chable. ('Ah' is the Maya prefix denoting the male sex, and was generically applied to males under the age of about seven.) He continued:

The one called Ah Chable they crucified and they nailed him to a great cross made for the purpose, and they put him on the cross alive and nailed his hands with two nails and tied his feet . . . with a thin rope. And those who nailed and crucified the said boy were the *ah-kines* who are now dead, which was done with consent of all those who were there. And after [he was] crucified they raised the cross on high and the said boy was crying out, and so they held it on high, and then they lowered it, [and] put on the cross, they took out his heart. And in the same way they killed the other boy who was there . . . and the *ah-kines* gave a sermon telling them that it was good and what they must do, and that through adoring those gods they would be saved, and that they should not believe that which the friars used to say to them.[28]

The chief, the schoolmaster, and all the other notables of the village had been present. The body, still nailed to the cross which was weighted with great stones, was thrown into a *cenote*.

Further testimonies of 17 and 18 August further clarified the pattern. It seemed that in other villages victims had been subjected to crucifixion as a preliminary to the excision of the heart, and that some of these macabre sacrifices had been carried out during Holy Week and Easter. Schoolmasters were frequently named and some confessed to having played a major part in these vile parodies.

On 19 August Landa recorded the last testimonies of the enquiry. These came from two men from Sotuta, one a schoolmaster, the other a student at the school. They revealed that the practice of crucifixion had originated in Sotuta village, and had been introduced five years before. They identified its originator as Landa's old intimate, Juan Nachi Cocom. According to their testimony, the old chief had organised and attended at least four sacrifices in which children had been tied to crosses before having their hearts cut out. The witnesses recalled that at the first sacrifice of five years before, when two little girls had been placed on crosses made especially for the ceremony, Juan Nachi Cocom had said, 'Let these girls die crucified as did Jesus Christ, they who they say was our Lord, but we do not know if this is so . . .' The crosses had been preserved to be used again and again in later sacrifices. The ceremonies had stopped, they said, during the three years of Monterroso's curacy, but they resumed when he left the district. Lorenzo Cocom had continued to organise similar sacrifices after his brother's death. One double sacrifice had taken place only four months before. Great care had been taken over the disposal of the bodies, which were carried to remote *cenotes*.[29]

With the knowledge of the source of the resurgence of human sacrifice and its blasphemous embellishments, and of the extent of the conspiratorial network of chiefs, schoolmasters and *ah-kines* of the villages of the province, Landa was ready to halt the enquiry, at least for the moment. Immediately after taking those last crucial confessions he extorted indictment and confessions from the unwilling notary (required by law to keep them in his own custody) and left Sotuta on the same day for Mérida. The appalling material he had collected over those few days demonstrated the depravity of the Maya and the obstinacy of their attachment to their old ways and their old leaders, an attachment which had only been broken by extreme physical anguish. The suspiciously dilapidated state of the 'idols' offered to the friars was explained; and the lies, evasions, and omissions of the confessions, so often gratuitous on any rational analysis, proved the Maya to be not only strangers to truth, but its enemies. If the Maya had crucified and killed human victims, if they had lied so obsessively, if they worked to deny and corrupt Christian teachings, then all the actions of the Provincial and his friars had been justified, and their dark reading of the Mayan character, of its infinite capacity for deception, had been vindicated. Further, Landa's week of furious work had only sketched the general shape of the conspiracy. Faced with a crisis of such dimensions, the bishop could scarcely remove Landa from his commanding role as director of the enquiry. Armed with the confessions, which so magnificently justified Franciscan actions, Landa was ready at last to meet his bishop.

7

Attrition

No report survives of the first meeting between the bishop and the Provincial. It must have had some of the quality of a tidal wave meeting a rocky coast. Toral, entering a situation charged with malice and close to hysteria, was determined to slow the onward plunge of events by introducing the bridle of legal process. That determination must have indicated to Landa the bishop's essential identification with the settlers' reading of events. Having examined the Sotuta confessions Toral confirmed Landa and his friars in their inquisitorial authority. But he absolutely prohibited any further use of torture.

The prohibition implies a degree of scepticism, even at that very early date, as to the veracity of the Sotuta confessions. Clearly the reckless use of torture could not be permitted, but under proper regulation it was a permitted instrument in the inquisitorial armoury. Toral might have hesitated to authorise its employment against neophyte Indians fallen back into idolatry, but deliberate acts of blasphemous human sacrifice would have required the sternest measures. It would seem that Toral had made an early judgment not so much from the content of the confessions, which were compelling enough, but on the man who had secured them. His prohibition, despite Landa's furious protests, remained absolute. Landa and his friars for their part refused to participate any further in the enquiry.[1]

There began a long contest between the two men, reminiscent in its wary intensity of the Hernández affair; although here the players were more evenly matched. Within a fortnight they communicated only through notaries. Toral's strategy was to focus on the legal inadequacies of the friars' procedures; on the paucity of records, the excessive penalties imposed, the injuries and deaths inflicted during the interrogations; while Landa struggled to hold attention on the vileness of Indian crimes, and the bishop's clear duty to extirpate them. Late in August the bishop turned to the colonists for advice as to how the enquiry should proceed. Ten leading men made their recommendations. They had been shaken by the horror of the Sotuta discoveries, but only one advocated the extension of the investigation. The rest urged a slow and cautious enquiry to identify the most guilty of the chiefs, and then their swift collective punishment, these being the strategies best designed to avoid what the colonists most feared: a full native insurrection.[2] Accordingly, Toral began to review the cases of the imprisoned chiefs, examining both the chiefs and those Indians who had testified as to their guilt.

The procedure he followed was an implied rebuke to the friars, for he was careful to question each witness in private, and to keep each individual segregated to prevent the possibility of collusion. He selected for his interpreter Gaspar Antonio Chi. It was a courageous choice, given Toral's total ignorance of the native tongue, for if Chi was the best interpreter in the province he had also long been a servant and intimate of the friars, most particularly of Diego de Landa himself. Chi's acceptance of the office also took courage, for it was to cost him Landa's friendship.

Toral found that every Indian offered the same explanation for the incriminating testimonies. They claimed:

they had been speaking the truth honestly before the fathers and because when they did not believe them they ordered them hoisted for the torture, they had decided and agreed among themselves that all should speak of deaths and sacrifices lyingly, as soon as they were asked about it, counselling one another and understanding that by this method they would escape the said torments and prison. And that many of those who went to make their confession came back to the prison they had left and told their imprisoned companions how they had told of many deaths and sacrifices . . . and that they should do the same . . .[3]

The story was plausible: the Indians had been kept in a common jail in Sotuta, and there had been no attempt to keep those already questioned and those awaiting questioning separate. But the bishop was not satisfied. He made another approach to Landa: that the friars Brusselas and de la Puebla – those two friars who had so effectively terrorised the province of Hocaba-Homun – should return there to take formal written statements from the Indians they had already interrogated. The statements were to be voluntary; the prohibition of torture was to stand.

Perhaps the Provincial believed the psychological domination the friars had already established would be enough to get at the truth, because he agreed to Toral's terms. Between 3 and 9 September the two friars took down fifteen sworn statements, and in those statements the Indians admitted to having performed human sacrifices over the last ten years in which perhaps thirty-five children had died. Vivid pictures of the sacrifices emerged from the testimonies. Oddly, despite the claimed involvement of Juan Nachi Cocom, the confessions made no reference to the burning of crosses or the preliminary crucifixion of victims: there was no tincture of 'Christianity' about these performances. They had been carried through not within the churches, but in secret ceremonies in out-of-the-way places, the bodies being buried in the bush, or thrown into *cenotes*. Some of the sacrifices appeared to recall pre-conquest practices, untouched by the teachings of the friars or the passage of the years. One suggested the reenactment of an ancient and gruesome legend. At Yasleuea, three years before, at a sacrifice in which two other children had been dispatched by the usual method of excision of the heart, a little girl was tied to a stake, and beaten on the breast with a thorny club until she died. There had been two offerings at the Sacred Cenote at Chichen Itza. In one, the victim was said to have been killed before his body was flung into the *cenote*, but in the other, a living child was reported to have been thrown into the water, 'to consult the oracle', and his escort had lingered for a day awaiting his reappearance before they returned to report to the chiefs. The latter sacrifice had been ordered by Nachi Cocom of Sotuta. Indeed, the Hocaba-Homun testimony suggested an even higher degree of cohesion and cooperation among the chiefs in organising their foul rituals than had the Sotuta confessions, all the chiefs and nobles of the whole province being said to have been in attendance at some sacrifices. At one, the six little girls who were immolated were reportedly supplied as a courtesy by one chief to another in accordance with ancient custom.[4]

The friars' findings unleashed a new round of tension and debate, especially as they claimed the Hocaba-Homun Indians had taken much comfort from the bishop's intervention, and were telling their followers that he approved the old ways. But most of the colonists were waiting for another report, from one of their own. Toral had commissioned Juan de Magaña, *encomendero* of Sotuta village, to carry out an intensive enquiry through the province. His instructions were highly specific. Magaña was to search out corpses said to have been disposed of in identifiable locations, and to question individual Indians closely as to the whereabouts of children named as victims; for example:

One Francisco Pot, villager of Mopila, a rich man, must be questioned about a boy called Ah Couoh he either had brought up in his house or had purchased, and another called Ah Chable [to establish] if he has them or if they are alive, or whether it is true that he had them at some other time. And if he should say that he had them, then he must say where they are, and if he should say they are dead, [he must say] where they died and how they saw them die and be buried. At the same time, verification must be sought by enquiring among some of the villagers, by way of the women and children, to discover if there were some bearing those names, or what became of them . . .[5]

Magaña, who had set off for Sotuta on 9 September, returned to submit his report on 23 September. He apparently failed to carry out Toral's instructions to search for the bodies of those claimed to have been sacrificed, and no explanation or comment on that failure survives in the records. His questioning of villagers regarding identifiable victims produced inconclusive results – unsurprisingly, given the widespread distribution of a relatively few lineage names, the mobility of populations, and the social anonymity of lowly dependants. For example, Yaxcaba Indians triumphantly produced one 'Francisco Cauich', who was originally from Tekax and who lived with his wife in the house of Juan Cauich, and they told Magaña of another 'Francisco Cauich', Juan's brother, who had died nine months before of fever, escorting him to inspect the grave. In his own *encomienda* village of Sotuta Magaña found no crosses in the house once occupied by the dead chief Lorenzo Cocom. And everywhere, again as we might expect, Indians repudiated their confessions as complete fictions. In each village Magaña heard painful accounts of particular Indians driven to desperate lying by the anguish of repeated hoistings, and then to despair through guilt and shame for the lies and for the other men tortured because of them.[6]

The problem was that both reports spoke only to the converted. They settled nothing. Innocent Indians in Hocaba-Homun could have falsely 'confessed' to the friars who had terrorised them only a month before, and who had then returned under the aegis of the bishop. Guilty Indians of Sotuta could have lied to Magaña, secure now from the anguish which had fleetingly wrenched the truth from them. Essentially one decided according to one's reading of the men involved, both Franciscans and Indians. Toral's assumption, increasingly clear through the slow legal manoeuvrings of the next months, was that the Indians had been guilty of no more than trivial idolatries – the result of the indolence and inadequacies of the friars' teaching –

and had been the victims of the Provincial's cruelty and anger. Landa's friars were also blameworthy, although their guilt was less, as they had been infected with the passions of their leader.[7]

Meanwhile, Landa worked furiously to strengthen his own position, and to accumulate evidence damaging to the bishop. A beginning had been made with the Hocaba-Homun confessions, most particularly with accounts of the Indians' exploitation of the bishop's leniency. On 16 September there had been an angry encounter between Toral and the friars Juan Pizarro and Francisco de Miranda; on the same day, the friars hastily swore out a statement recording the Bishop's unseemly and imprudent words.[8] And Don Diego Quijada as *alcalde mayor* was again pressed into service. Quijada, understandably anxious to maintain a neutral stance in the developing conflict between Toral and Landa, demurred when Landa required him to seek testimony damaging to the bishop on the reasonable grounds that he was incompetent to judge an ecclesiastic, but Landa knew how to deal with his reluctant collaborator's waverings. He pointed out that if Indians had indeed died under excessive torture, the blame, at least in law, attached not to the friars but to the constables, and so to the man who had signed their appointments. Quijada yielded once again. On 18 September he undertook the unappetising task of recording the statements of three Indians from Mani. They claimed that when one Indian had returned to the village from Mérida, he had told his fellow villagers that the Bishop was grieved that the friars had taken away the Indians' idols, that those who had been involved would be punished, and that the Provincial was hidden in Sotuta, preparing to flee.[9]

Alone, the gossip would appear sorry and trivial nonsense, but Landa's enormous energies sought allies and evidence everywhere. The friars collectively entered the fray with a declaration of 17 September in which they announced that they could not in conscience administer the sacrament of baptism (save to baptise sick children) to any Indian, on the grounds of their 'pertinacious idolatry'. The next day they declared their inability to man more than five monasteries – two of those in Spanish towns, and another in the already 'purified' province of Mani – until the idolatries were remedied.[10] Toral was faced, in effect, with a friars' strike. Landa also persuaded Fray Pedro de Ciudad Rodrigo to make a full statement regarding the incident of the deformed baby born in Hunacti village the year before, for while Fray Pedro, despite the Sotuta revelations, remained persuaded that death at least had been a 'natural thing', Landa had come to believe that the friar had been duped, and that the Indians had crucified the child.

For the colonists the situation was complicated. No Spaniard, whether friar, settler or bishop, could tolerate human sacrifice, with or without Christian embellishments, among Indians living under Spanish rule. But the fact of human sacrifice was far from established, the evidence for it coming as it did very late in the enquiry, and being immediately subjected to challenge. It was the fact of idolatry that the enquiry had established, and on that issue friars and settlers felt very differently. Despite some indulgence towards individual or highly localised idol-worship, the friars saw mass idolatry as a massive offence. Their notion of conversion was a gradualist one: not a transforming individual experience, but a slow, cumulative, collective process, by which whole communities, accepting baptism, would slowly learn to live according to the rhythms of Catholic observances, and slowly grow in understanding through the friars' preaching and their holy example. Collective persistence in idolatry – or reversion to idolatry, as the friars preferred to think of it – destroyed the entire strategy. That humans should be killed, and killed with parodic Christian embellishments, of course darkened Maya depravity, but their obstinacy, their wickedness, had already been all too clearly demonstrated from their idolatry.

For lay Spaniards, who had not so painfully mixed their labour in the missionary enterprise, the persistence of Indians in idolatry was to be expected; it was the friars' reaction to it which was reprehensible, excessive, and dangerous. The September crisis over the human sacrifices stories coincided with a period of tribute collection, always a nervous time of the testing of control over a numerous subject population. *Encomenderos* riding through the villages had noted the empty houses, the absence of the usual bustle, and they worried about the temper of the people. Only those few settlers persuaded of the truth of the human sacrifice confessions shared the friars' conviction of the necessity for continued, vigorous – though legally controlled – action.[11]

For the bulk of the settlers, with the friars shackled, and the human sacrifice stories as open to doubt as the authenticity of some of those 'idols' produced for the enquiry, the most pressing question was a political one: who was the more likely to prevail, the bishop or the Provincial? A wrong choice could have dangerous consequences, and some struggled to remain, for the moment, uncommitted. Three, who testified for Landa on the great numbers of idols collected from the Indians, also testified for the bishop on the cruelties of the tortures inflicted by the friars.[12] Juan de Magaña obviously regretted the clarity of his Sotuta report, given the evidence of the Hocaba-Homun confessions and the growing bitterness of the conflict, for the day after he submitted his findings he wrote a careful letter to Alonso de Zorita, judge of the *audiencia* of Mexico, in which he praised the friars' zeal and lamented the prevalence of idolatry. The hoisting by the wrists, he assured Zorita, merely distressed the Indians without imperilling them. On the question of the reality of human sacrifice he was discreetly vague, although he implied that the Indians had repudiated their testimony because they had a new judge.[13]

Magaña was wise to be cautious. But the balance slowly began to shift in the bishop's favour. When the Yucatan veteran Fray Lorenzo de Bienvenida, now Commissary General of the order, returned to Yucatan in November, he joined the bishop in his denunciation of the local friars. Many waverers must have been persuaded by the political implications of his decision: the Franciscan hierarchy would not support the Provincial.[14] By January, when Toral began handing down his final judgments on the Indians still in custody, the great majority of colonists were ready to applaud his decision to impose light penance on the chiefs and lords for their confessed idolatries, and to return them to their villages and their offices. The settlers were also ready to support him when he turned at last to deal with Landa. Collecting yet more statements to send to the Council of the Indies, Toral presented his witnesses with the usual questions relating to the severity of the tortures and the disruption of Indian life, but the most insistent questions had to do with Landa's character. Had the Provincial been persistently at odds with all authorities, religious and secular? Had he, specifically, rejected the jurisdiction of the Archbishop of Mexico? Had he gained his present eminence by craft, manipulating the friars of the order, and driving from the province those old and learned men who might have opposed him? Did the Provincial recruit ignorant young men into the order, and were those ignorant young men then given extensive powers over both Spaniard and Indian?

Nine leading citizens took their opportunity to give resounding affirmatives to the bishop's questions. They emphasized the Provincial's lust for power, and his impatience of any restriction. They recalled the persecution of Francisco Hernández and others like him, who had been the victims of Landa's captious and relentless spirit. They dared at last to express the hatred and resentment it had been politic to repress over the last years. In response to Toral's offensive, Landa could muster only five Spaniards to make statements on his behalf for transmission to the Crown, and of those five one was the vigorous constable from Hocaba-Homun and another a man who had been in the province for only two years.[15]

The Provincial's concern was to defend his own character and his use of power, to besmirch some of the 'opposition' witnesses, and to demonstrate the vitality of the friars' missionary endeavours. But Landa was on the defensive. He was ready to present a manifestly false picture of the Maya before the coming of the friars – going naked, full of sins, repudiating their wives – and to pretend their living in villages, in a recognisable polity, was a Franciscan achievement. He produced at last the full financial accounts of the inquisition fines and a few receipts of his own expenditures of the monies collected from the penanced Indians. And – more significantly – he was also anxious to modify his position on the severity of the tortures. Whereas he had earlier emphasised the obstinacy of the Indians and so justified the use of harsh methods, his January testimony denied that the friars' methods were harsh at all. The hoistings were not 'tortures' but a 'remedy', merely causing the Indians 'some vexation'. The 'floggings' had been a matter of a few stripes only, 'laid on with great moderation'. If some Indians had committed suicide it was because they wilfully chose to kill themselves rather than yield up their cherished idols.[16] The shift in emphasis was significant. Landa had, for the first time, retreated.

On 11 February Toral freed the last of the imprisoned Indians. Beaten on his home ground, Landa prepared to carry the case to Spain. He took with him the Sotuta confessions and other testimonies he had accumulated, but he lacked the statements from the Indians of Hocaba-Homun, for they remained in Toral's possession. To the last, he strenuously resisted the notion that any man in Yucatan had jurisdiction over him; his Commissary General Bienvenida had said Landa left the peninsula on his orders, but Landa dismissed the claim contemptuously. He had journeyed to Spain because of his ailments, he said, and because he could not bear to watch the way in which Bienvenida and Toral treated his beloved friars.[17]

Those beloved friars offered him an impressive demonstration of their readiness to sustain the cause. After Landa had left the city of Mérida Bishop Toral, perhaps in an attempt to reassert his authority, elected to celebrate the mass in the Franciscan monastery just outside the city walls. Fray Juan Pizarro was to preach the sermon. Pizarro spoke on Jesus going from Galilee to Judea, and his exhortations to those in charge of souls to defend their lambs from ravenous wolves. For the benefit of his attentive audience Pizarro made the analogy explicit; he prayed 'that it would please God that Spanish Christians could hate so much these heretical idolatrous dogs, who are the enemies of God and of our Holy Catholic Faith', and lamented that 'those who were to punish them . . . are defending them, and instead of harassing them, they give them comfort'. The bishop apparently maintained his dignity and his temper within the church, but when Pizarro approached him in the porch, 'with', as Pizarro claimed, 'all the humility and reverence in the world', Toral's anger burst forth; he denounced Pizarro as a fool and a heretic, and addressing the assembled Indians (in the Mexican Indian tongue, which suggests how profoundly he was stirred) instructed them to offer no more services of food, not even a jar of water, to Fray Juan.

The baiting of the bishop had been a magnificent success, as Pizarro gleefully reported to Landa, still lingering at the port. But the aftermath indicates further erosion of support, for when the jubilant friars sought to gather signatures from the large assembly of Spaniards who had witnessed the bishop's outburst, only Landa's notary was prepared to sign.[18]

The friars' love and concern followed Landa back to Spain. Some time during 1567 the Crown received at least seven letters – there could well have been more, but seven survive in the archives – variously dated 11 and 12 February of that year, urging that Franciscan friars be sent to Yucatan; especially 'those who have been in this country, and went back from here to Castile, who know well our language in which to preach and teach us'; and most especially 'Fray Diego de Landa, for he is great, sufficient, worthy and good in the eyes of our Father God, who calls on us much to be Christians'. The signatories of each letter claimed to be native rulers of some of the major provinces of Yucatan.[19]

Scholars who have seen the letters say that the phraseology and even the handwriting are practically identical, which could well have raised doubts as to their spontaneity. Their effectiveness must have been further reduced with the receipt of another letter, this one dated 12 April, and signed by Francisco de Montejo Xiu and three other Xiu chiefs. It ran in part:

The Franciscan friars of this province have written certain letters to Your Majesty and to the head of the order in praise of Fray Diego de Landa and his other companions who were those who tortured, killed and put us to scandal. And they gave certain letters written in the Castilian language to certain Indians of their familiars so they signed them and sent them to Your Majesty. May Your Majesty understand that they are not ours, we who are the chiefs of the land who did not have to write lies and falsehoods and contradictions . . .

As for Diego de Landa, whom they considered the main author of their miseries, 'may he and his companion suffer penance for the evil they have done us . . .'[20]

The friars' intervention can have had no effect on the judgment of Landa's case. Delayed by illness and shipwreck he had arrived in Spain to face the Council of the Indies only in October of 1564. The Council's order of the February of that year, that Landa and his three fellow inquisitors be sent on the first available ship to Spain, suggests how completely the Council had accepted the bishop's version of the events of 1562, and it is likely his reception was hostile. But Landa had brought with him evidence not yet seen by the Council, including the Sotuta confessions and chilling anecdotes provided by Spaniards favourable to his cause. The Council therefore remitted the case to a committee appointed by the Provincial of the Franciscan order in Castile. By May of 1565 the committee had reached its conclusions. Landa had been justified in his assumption of episcopal authority to conduct the inquisition, and justified, given the heinous nature of the Indians' offences, in his procedures. The Indians had not lied when they had made their confessions, but when they later denied them. It had been the bishop, not Landa, who had erred.[21] Exculpated, although still awaiting his formal exoneration, Landa returned to his 'home' monastery of San Juan de Toledo, where he had served his novitiate, to wait on events.

Meanwhile, in the peninsula, the warriors fought wearily on. Landa's most notable secular ally was in a vulnerable position. With Landa out of the way Alcalde Mayor Quijada became the focus of hostility. His early popularity had been short-lived. Apart from his role in the idolatry affair he had exhibited other deficiencies. The long-coveted authority to distribute Indians in *encomienda* proved double-edged: there were too few Indians, too many demanding Spaniards, and accusations of favouritism multiplied. In February 1563 the royal officials of Yucatan requested the Crown to take Quijada's *residencia*, and by March Bishop Toral and the council of Mérida had joined the chorus.[22] Quijada's enemies also brought charges before the *audiencia* of Mexico, and late in 1564 that body commissioned Sebastián Vázquez to investigate the affairs of the province.

Vázquez spent three months in Yucatan, collecting a mass of testimonies which he submitted to the *audiencia* along with his official report on the idolatry trials in April or May of 1565.[23] But the King had already acted. In June 1564 he had appointed Don Luis Céspedes de Oviedo governor of Yucatan and Tabasco and had authorised him to take Quijada's *residencia*.[24] After a brief stay in Mexico where he was provided with the Vázquez findings, Céspedes journeyed to Yucatan, arriving in November 1565.

When Céspedes ordered him to yield up his wand of office, the *alcalde mayor* knew he had lost the post he had valued so highly and struggled so hard to retain. But he did not comprehend the reasons for his dismissal. He later wrote to the Crown seeking to find explanations, for himself as much as for the king, for his disastrous change of fortune. He could only point to the hatred he had won for his work in improving roads and encouraging the breeding of pack animals to free the Indians from the endless task of bearing burdens, and then to the extraordinary and wilful blindness of the bishop in the idolatory affair – that is, to the idiosyncratic, gratuitous malice of men.

Quijada had certainly been unlucky. He knew himself to be a loyal and punctilious servant of the Crown. In a different community he could have lived out his life as a somewhat fussy and dependent but useful agent of the royal will. In Yucatan, he was faced with essentially unmanageable challenges. Frail and immature institutional structures had offered him no protection against Landa's passionate righteousness and ruthless politicking. There was a personal failing, too, at least in that context: Quijada lacked the manner to command deference. Throughout all the conventional range of charges against him in his *residencia* a less conventional note sounds persistently. Joaquín de Leguízamo, after laying thirty-one charges against the *alcalde mayor* in the name of the citizenry of Yucatan, came to what was for him the heart of the matter. He declared:

the principal cause from which all else springs . . . is that the said *alcalde mayor* is a man unsuited and unworthy to the office he holds, and all follows from his lack of prudence and sense . . . and he says and does things like an imprudent, foolish and unstable man.[26]

Quijada's defects, when listed, look trivial enough. He went about the street plumed and bemedalled like a soldier; he strummed a guitar, and had a taste for singing joking songs. In the course of a gay evening, Leguízamo reported, in company with a public prostitute and a group of friends, the *alcalde mayor* exhibited 'shameful parts of his body', boasting that his buttocks were skinny as a rabbit's. (His audience was unimpressed, and said, 'The devil take your buttocks, we don't want to see them.') It was something of an anti-climax when Leguízamo added that Quijada sometimes jiggled about, even in court.

Sebastián Vázquez, after judicious enquiry, drained some of the colour from Quijada's reported exploits. Vázquez found that the *alcalde mayor* did indeed strum the guitar, in the privacy of his own house, and readily sang, being proud of his voice, and that he would sometimes, while strumming, sketch a few dance steps. But Vázquez knew what Leguízamo meant. Such behaviour led people to laugh at the *alcalde mayor*. He was, in Vázquez' judgment, a man lacking in presence.[27] Don Luis Céspedes, Quijada's successor, was able to indulge his passion for masques and dancing parties and to frequent houses of ill-repute without perturbing anyone except Bishop Toral. It was not Quijada's actions but his style, or lack of it, which so irritated the colonists. He was accused, essentially, of being vulgar. His pretensions to rule, however legitimate in law, were ridiculous in a man who lacked the manners of those with a right to rule. His successors were aristocrats, to whom the colonists could more easily and naturally accord the deference they so easily denied Quijada. There is a whiff of contempt, of pleasure in the infliction of humiliation, in Céspedes' treatment of him: when Quijada could not pay certain fines and bonds (amounting to no great sum) Céspedes had him put in the public jail in Mérida, and left him there for eleven months. In February 1567 he was released, and went to Mexico and then to Spain, where the Council of the Indies substantially reduced the penalties Céspedes had imposed on him.[28]

Quijada was to die in Castile, late in 1571 or early in 1572, still bewildered by what had befallen him. The most bitter because the most bewildering experience in the whole bitter affair had been the Vázquez enquiry. Quijada had navigated his way through the difficult waters of colonial administration by an earnest following of official instructions, and a careful scanning of legal implications. He had believed, more totally and passionately than the Spanish settlers, given his professional commitment, that the official investigation conducted through the proper processes of sworn statements, was the way to reason, order, and so to 'truth'. Yet he had been at the centre of an enquiry which though following all the reassuring forms had yet been a triumph of what he could only see as error and wanton distortion, where justice and even sense had departed. He wrote to the Crown:

I know that the poor Indians, whether under oath or not, will say no more than their *encomenderos* and the persons sent with the commissioner by the Bishop order them to say. And indeed I am quite sure that if today the commissioner wanted to prove that the friars tortured to death a thousand men, it will be proven, and [they will] even prove that I have been an idolator . . .[29]

The only explanation left open to him – and this in a man of notably open, even sunny, disposition – was that he had been the unwitting victim of a baffling, unjustified but relentless conspiracy.

The removal of Landa and Quijada did not bring peace to the province. The council of Mérida, which in March 1563 had declared Toral's coming to Yucatan to be an act of Divine Providence, was by May 1566 accusing the bishop of misuse of his authority, 'all in order to oppress, and to hold power over everything . . . in the temporal and the spiritual sphere so' (the sting in the tail) 'following the old custom of the friars of this province'. The issues which divided the one-time allies were the continuing, insoluble problems of the proper demarcation of jurisdiction between temporal and spiritual authorities; of the financing of the Church and of control over Indians, who were at once spiritual beings and material assets.[30]

Toral continued, initially, energetic. He carried out extensive episcopal visits through the diocese, travelling as early as 1564 to Cozumel island, which had seen only one friar for three days since its discovery by those three small ships fifty years before. He confirmed, he said, more than 150,000 Maya in these sorties, an implausibly inflated figure, but more plausible than the 250,000 he was later to claim.[31] But he was growing weary, and oppressed by his social and psychological isolation. His letters to the Crown over those last years make painful reading. At first he made precise recommendations, reflective and carefully evaluated: procedures for somehow financing the necessary work of the Church without burdening the already over-burdened Indians; of setting in order a mission he had found in so deformed and destructive a condition. He had asked for 'Theatines' (by which he almost certainly meant Jesuits) to be sent to the peninsula, but then he thought it better to remove all the existing friars from Yucatan, as lack of discipline had allowed them to slip into a parlous state, and to bring in other Franciscans who had been properly trained, 'who will recoup the loss so that so saintly and heroic an Order does not remain shamed as it is'.[32]

The Crown remained silent, and the bishop became more deeply entangled in the miserable shifts and compromises of a poverty-stricken Church. Even his tours of inspection bore heavily on the Indians. He needed aid from the Crown, and five hundred missionaries, he calculated, if anything was to be effected. (In 150 leagues of populated territory he had fourteen friars, and only three of those preached to the Indians.)[33] But as the years passed, and no friars came, Toral realised the struggle with Landa was not yet over.

In 1564 Toral had sent an emissary to Spain to beg the Franciscan hierarchy meeting in General Chapter for more friars. His agent had met with a very brusque reception because, Toral discovered, Landa had shown the assembled friars one of Toral's letters denouncing the Yucatan friars to the Crown. Toral had also been told that Landa was travelling through all the provinces 'rousing the friars against me so that it is said they are not going to send any friars to help me but that I will have to quit the Bishopric, because I have dealt such a blow to the Order in writing so to Your Majesty about the defects of its friars . . .'. In October of 1566 he formally asked to be relieved of his post, because, he said, his brothers 'both here and in Spain' were so embittered against him that he was rendered impotent.[34]

He was to reiterate that request many times over the next years, in letters increasingly dreary, querulous, and darkened by despair.[35] Within the passage of time he became increasingly, obsessively concerned with the events of 1562. The local Franciscans had not been really 'Franciscan' at all, but men 'of few letters and less charity', lacking proper training and proper discipline. And they had suffered because of defective, indeed, criminal, leadership. Toral never wavered in his conviction of Landa's central culpability, or that Landa's actions had been motivated by those all-too-familiar sins Franciscans had so long struggled against: pride, cruelty, anger, and the passion to dominate.

His attitude to the Indians went through a slow transformation as his social and psychological isolation increased; as he endlessly rehearsed the injustices inflicted on them. In 1562 and 1563 he had believed the Indians to have been brutally abused by the friars, but he also believed them to have been guilty of idolatries, for which he had penanced them. By March 1564 he had transformed them into pure victims, whose idols had lain buried and forgotten until the friars unleashed their murderous rage. These poor victimised creatures were as forgiving as they were innocent:

the best people I have seen in the Indies, very simple, even more obedient, charitable, free of vices, so that even in their paganism they did not eat human flesh or practice the abominable sin [sodomy], friends of the doctrine and of its ministers even though they have killed their fathers, brothers and kinsmen, and taken their goods and put *sanbenitos* on them and enslaved them etc., they love them and come to them and built their monasteries and give them food and hear their masses, without reference to things past . . . even though when I arrived here they fled from the friars, and even though when they knew a [single] friar was going to the village everyone absented themselves from it and ran off to the bush to hide, and others hanged themselves from fear of the friars, saying they did not want to fall into their hands because they were without pity, and recommending themselves to God the poor miserable ones hanged themselves, pitiable as that is to say and to hear.[36]

So Toral constructed the intelligibility of 'history' out of the confusion of experience, making unambiguous shapes out of the threatening ambiguities of Franciscans who did not act as Franciscans; of Indians who were tormented victims and yet who also worshipped idols. That remaking of the past gave him no comfort for the future. He felt himself impotent to tend his flock. After learning two Mexican Indian languages he was 'deaf and dumb' in Yucatan; useless, ineffectual. The required travelling was a miserable hardship. Jolting over the stony wastes he felt the land itself to be impenetrable, perverse; closed against him, and almost against nature: a 'lake of pure stone', as he called it. The heat exhausted him, and he felt within himself a profound weakness. He had travelled to Mexico in 1565 to attend the Second Provincial Council, and he must have found it hard to leave his old friends there, to go back to his thankless and lonely tasks in Yucatan. He petitioned the Crown for permission to return. The Crown refused the request, but Toral had already set out for Mexico, where he died in the Franciscan monastery in Mexico City in April 1571.[37]

By the time of Toral's death the Yucatan mission was in a desperate state. As early as 1566 a Campeche friar had sounded the alarm: for twelve monasteries there were only thirteen friars, and some of the houses had to be closed. Secular priests would have to take over the mission areas.[38] Closed houses could be reopened when times were better, but it would not be easy to shift the priests. By 1569 there were still no reinforcements from Spain, and the local friars joined Toral in petitioning for help, the petition being carried to Spain by one of the brothers.[39] That plea brought a response; a sizeable body of friars was assembled, but their departure was delayed, and it was not until November 1570 that they arrived on the Gulf Coast.

It is probable that Landa had blocked recruitment to Yucatan for as long as he thought necessary, though in that same period even Mexico had difficulty in recruiting friars. He was a builder, but he was always ready to demolish before he built. It is likely, too, that he had never relinquished hope of returning to Yucatan after the inter-regnum of Toral's bishopric. Given his influence in the Spanish Franciscan hierarchy he must have known of Toral's constant pleas for permission to retire. Certainly his friars continued active on his behalf. In February 1570 they requested three things of the Crown. They urged that the peninsula be returned to the jurisdiction of Mexico, Spain being too far away. They asked that more Franciscans be sent. The third matter concerned:

Fray Diego de Landa who was here a great friar and a great servant of God and who knew and taught this tongue and even while there was no bishop he ruled the bishopric and kept it in the best order, with no comparison to how it is now, and who with great zeal and wisdom and holding authority from Your Majesty and the Supreme Pontiff took away innumerable idols, with great labour, from baptized Indians because of which the Devil, with his usual envy and lies and false stories procured an order from Your Majesty that he should be exiled to Spain . . . for no other offence than that of serving Almighty God and Your Majesty . . .

They urged his vindication, and his return, for without him nothing prospered.[40]

Their wish was at last granted. When news of the death of Bishop Toral was received, Diego de Landa was named the new Bishop of Yucatan. Landa arrived in Campeche in October 1573 with thirty handpicked friars to replenish the mission he had so determinedly starved. He immediately set his new friars to learning the native tongue, and ordered all secular priests, save three who were fluent in Mayan and a few needed to serve in the cathedral, out of the province. Addressing the friars assembled in the Mérida monastery the bishop protested his desire to be accepted among them as a son, but the Franciscan Provincial rejected the suggested relationship, and ac-claimed Landa as the beloved father of them all.[41] The old alliance had been renewed.

Perhaps Landa's writing of his *Relación de las cosas de Yucatán* during his Spanish exile had been part and product of his recruiting campaign. Certainly it eloquently set forth the charms of that stony land. Nothing had happened in the intervening year to make Yucatan more, and a great deal to make it less, attractive; and in 1571 the Europe of the Counter-Reformation was itself enough of a frontier to compel an activist spirit. That thirty men were ready to make the tedious, hazardous voyage to so poor an outpost of a New World which had largely lost its glamour reminds us of something the skeletal sources tempt us to forget: Landa's capacity to inspire men to heroic visions.

But Yucatan had changed. It was no longer the malleable place of ten years before. Being informed of some backsliding among the Indians in the Campeche region, Landa delegated Fray Gregorio de Fuente Ovejuna to investigate. The friar, after some enquiries, proceeded to punish the men he judged guilty, including some chiefs. But the Indians were not as submissive, or at least as naive, as they had been in 1562. Don Francisco May, the governor of the province, with the support of leading Indians, immediately lodged a complaint against the friar and the bishop before the *audiencia* of Mexico. The complaint alleged that the punishments had been excessive and some of a humiliating and indecent nature; that the ecclesiastical authorities had no right to administer them as such action was the task of the secular arm; and that Indian lords should not have been so treated. Don Francisco added that a wave of panic was sweeping the area, as the Indians dreaded a repetition of the excesses of 1562. The *audiencia* responded promptly. Landa was instructed to abide by a regulation of September 1570 which forbade the imprisonment, flogging or shearing of Indians by ecclesiastics. (In 1570, when the Holy Office of the Inquisition was established in the Indies, Indians were specifically excluded from its jurisdiction 'because of their simplicity and lack of capacity, and because many of them have not been well instructed in the Faith'.[42] The Yucatan idolatry trials are thought to have influenced the Council of the Indies in reaching that decision.) The Governor of Yucatan was required to enforce the rule and to set at liberty any Indians improperly fined or penanced by the bishop.

Landa's haughty spirit must have found such a limitation hard to bear, but he had long experience in overcoming impediments placed in his way and in bringing secular officials to a proper understanding of their duties. He immediately sent his provisor to the governor requiring him to punish the delinquents.

Governor Velázquez de Gijón was no anxious newcomer to the

responsibilities of office, and, as a Spanish aristocrat, was not to be intimidated by clerics, however elevated. He refused, and when the provisor dared to threaten him with excommunication had him clapped in jail. He took the precaution of sending his prisoner by the next boat to Mexico before heading a solemn procession to the bishop's palace to solicit his forgiveness for his non-cooperation. Landa, unready to be thwarted, set off for Mexico to try his persuasive powers on the *audiencia*. The judges were polite but unhelpful, and although Landa seized the opportunity on his journey home to rout out some 'wizards and sorcerers' in Tabasco, he must have realised at last that other jurisdictions could and would define and restrict his powers; that Yucatan was no longer his for the making, and that the governor would not be manipulated, intimidated or overborne.

Another incident demonstrated just how much that small world had changed. A conflict over jurisdictions, pivoting on the possession of certain papers, had flared between bishop and governor, and the governor had been excommunicated. In the twilight of a June evening, when most of the populace must have been out taking the air, the dean of the cathedral, ambling along on his mule, chanced to meet the governor and his entourage riding along the street, and urged him to make his peace with the Church, and to yield up the disputed papers. The governor answered 'with passion' that he'd be torn to pieces rather than submit. The dean could not bring himself to record the governor's next words, but Landa did not flinch. He discovered from another witness that the governor had shouted, as the dean backed away,

> To hell with the Bishop, I say by God that if he has two balls I've got four; I swear to God that if need be I'll ride the Bishop and his Brother Gregorio . . . and this witness who was near said, 'not Brother Gregorio, Sir, for he is not here, he is away visiting Bacalar, rather Brother Melchor' . . . and the Governor replied, 'Brother Gregorio or Brother Melchor or whoever else it may be' . . .

While Landa reported that the people who clustered around 'stood amazed and scandalised' by the scene, the interjection, and the fact that from all those present Landa could extract statements only from his own dean, his own notary, and the notary of the Mérida *cabildo*, suggests the audience was more gleeful than outraged.[43] No royal action is recorded in the matter.

Those last years must have been difficult for a proud spirit. Landa died on 29 April 1579 at the age of fifty-four, and was buried in the

Franciscan monastery at Mérida; at some later date his bones were returned to his home village of Cifuentes, and interred in the parish church. It is said that as he lay dying in the sullen heat his attendants thought to remove at last his heavy robe. He seemed momentarily refreshed by the coolness, but then urgently asked for the old familiar garment again, for, as he said, 'enemies were drawing nearer, and this was no time to be without the protection of the habit'.[44]

8

Retrospections

It is worth taking some time over Landa and his Franciscans, to see how they had come to make a world in which they could act with so strong a sense of the necessity of their actions. The group was not large – those friars made uncomfortable by Landa's leadership and his vision of things had already left the peninsula – but individual psychologising cannot explain its cohesiveness and its terrible forward momentum. What was it, then, in the shared experience of the Yucatan Franciscans which made such concerted action possible, and continued to power so formidable an engine of conviction?

The classic study of the Mexican missionary enterprise is entitled *The Spiritual Conquest of Mexico*. It is a fine title, catching the military metaphor which mediated the experience of that campaign. In the peninsula too the friars had come to conquer the land; to map and order it in the creation of their 'Yucatan', a very different place from the 'Yucatan' imagined by the lay settlers. I have already discussed how the opposition between Franciscan values and those of their lay compatriots had sharpened dangerously in the New World. These missionaries were not genial towards human frailties. The way of life they celebrated transcended and rebuked ordinary human impulses. Those who lived by the Rule did so in the sure knowledge that the way to virtue lay through the defiance of natural instincts, the more systematic and vigorous the defiance the better. Individual pre-ference, the personal impulse – which we tend to elevate as the authentic voice of morality – was to them merely personal, merely impulse. If they felt compassion for those suffering pain, they had inflicted pain on their own bodies to drive out wickedness, and they did not confuse the human voice of pity with the commandments of God. However earnestly they probed their consciences for dark and impure things, in their relationships with God and with their brothers, the central task of conversion was clearly lit. All others who claimed power over the Indians – government officials, *encomenderos*, the native lords – had other interests, other ends in view. Only the friars had no interest save that of God at heart. They had no material and, as they believed, no personal interest, for they had subdued the self to make themselves instruments of the Lord.

That conviction could have made them ruthless social legislators indeed, but in most areas in the New World the Crown policy of overlapping jurisdictions and the ranging of one administrative hierarchy against another in dynamic tension worked to prevent the dominance of any single group. Mexican missionaries would have resettled their Indians and dominated secular authorities if they could, but they were regularly and forcefully reminded that others also insisted on their right to intervene in Indian affairs. In the radically simplified frontier situation of Yucatan no such complex equipoise was possible. There Franciscans enjoyed a monopoly of the mission field; no other order challenged their account of the Indians, or jealously assessed Franciscan performance. Quijada, head of the secular administration, had been reduced to the status of docile lieutenant. Given that political ascendance, standard Franciscan rhetoric of autonomous control over Indians could appear to be descriptive of reality, and could be made to be so.

There was, of course – despite Franciscan efforts to suppress and deny it – a large personal dimension in the Yucatan affair. The friars had believed the Indians had ratified their own self-definition as the Indians' special protectors and chosen custodians. Landa remembered that from the earliest days of the mission, when the natives 'saw all [the friars] endured, without any private interest, and the freedom which resulted from their efforts . . . they did nothing without informing the friars and taking their advice, and this gave cause for the [lay] Spaniards to be envious, and to say the friars had acted in this way to have the government of the Indies . . .'[1] 'Paternalism' is a comfortably capacious metaphor. We would be mistaken if we saw its content as necessarily or solely benevolent. There are fathers and fathers. Some loving fathers punish most tenaciously; the profound ambivalence of the consciously loving father towards his child-victim is only now beginning to be explored. In the very violence of the response of the Yucatan friars to that first discovery of the 'treachery' of their Indians we see something of the emotion-charged punitive rage of the betrayed parent. The Franciscans had won battles for the Maya: they had forced a reduction of tribute, and some regulation of the *laissez-faire* exploitation of the settlers. Those victories, it is true, had been won in Mérida, remote from immediate native experience, but they were central to the friars' understanding of their role and their relationship with the Indians. To discover that the Maya were idolatrous was to discover them to be wantonly, grossly, ungrateful, as well as deceitful. (The alternative, that they had been too ill-taught to grasp the nature of their offence, was not one we could realistically expect the missionaries to consider, let alone embrace.) The friars also had the impediment, for impediment it was, of being able to use force on their potential converts. Even missionaries who lack that power and who must rely on persuasion have been profoundly shaken when they discovered how their messages have actually been received, and transformed in the receiving. The Franciscans were convinced that their labours would be aided by God Himself. They lacked all recognition of the profound and systematic otherness of others. They had no sense of the intricate interrelationships between different aspects of Indian life, rather seeing here the hand of the Devil, there the tender intervention of Christ, and so they could have no sense of the difficulties in the way of the reception and understanding of their message. Violence against the Indians was not initiated by the Provincial; Ciudad Rodrigo and his brothers at Mani had established the pattern of mass arrest and savage unselective torture before Landa arrived to take command. Throughout the enquiry extreme brutalities were perpetrated equally by Landa and by his lieutenants. The friars' actions declare their anger and outrage, and their bitter determination to make the Indians suffer for their deceptions.

It is possible that fury subdued a touch of guilt at the direction, or misdirection, of their energies. For all their high dedication, the missionary programme must be judged as slipshod. Toral, coming from New Spain, where long years of competition between the orders had bred a tough professionalism, was shocked by what he saw in his new diocese. Very few friars had bothered to become proficient in Mayan; remote areas, like Cozumel, had been entirely neglected; and even where the Spanish presence was well-established the friars appeared content to minister to those Indians living conveniently close to the monasteries. By his standards there was in 1562 no Church in Yucatan.[2]

The friars saw their world very differently, and here the influence of Landa is crucial. It was he who had conceived and laid out the magnificent structures of the monastery at Izamal – the monastery which Toral, judging conventionally, declared 'a splendid thing to see and a scandal to permit, and that certainly St Francis would

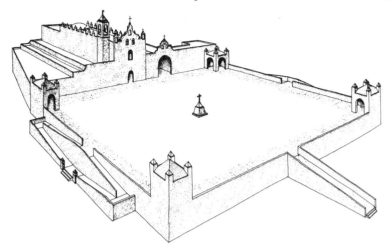

4 The monastery at Izamal.

condemn', especially as it would house at most one or two friars.[3] Landa understood the declamatory power of structures; their capacity to mark and order a landscape. He also knew the power of properly orchestrated ritual action. His formalisation of procedures at Mani allowed his friars to become habituated to the exercise of violent physical domination while distancing their actions from the zone of the personal and the personally culpable. If the elaborately staged *autos de fe* failed to recruit settlers to the Franciscan view of things, they must have carried a powerful message of legitimation for the inquisitors themselves. Ritual can create reality, as well as confirm it. Bound together by their initial repudiation of their 'natural' world and by their oppositional stance to the values of their compatriots; by their shared experience of the novitiate; steeped in the mythology of the Order, and in the vibrant and distinct mythology of the great missionaries of Mexico, who had been splendidly intransigent in the face of secular government and – where need be – of the episcopal hierarchy, and further worked on by the grandeur of Landa's vision; is it surprising that Landa's men responded as they did in Mani, and then moved in ever tighter formation down a narrowing path?

Landa's dynamism, the infectious power of his superb theatrical sense, had transformed a dusty round of duties and the sordid broils which punctuated them into events resonant with significance. The glamour was powerful, and sustained itself even in Landa's absence. Juan Pizarro's letter to Landa in which he describes his successful public baiting of the Bishop through his provocative sermon catches perfectly the surging rhythms and loftiness of Landa's style: a nasty little scene on a church porch is reported in terms appropriate to the cosmic dimensions of a morality play. The friars' political machinations – even the apparent cynicism of the affair of the Indian letters – speaks of their dependence on their leader. They were to remain steadfast despite Toral's blandishments, and despite, or because of, their increasing isolation, and the deterioration of the mission. For those touched by Landa's alchemy, whose lives had been transformed by contact with his magnificent, turbulent spirit, critical reappraisal of past actions could offer only poor rewards.

What of Landa himself, centre and agent of those embittering events? For the Landa of 1562, the revelations of what he identified as the Indians' systematic deceptions had been especially grievous for 'he spoke their tongue and had taught them the doctrine . . . and no-one had a higher opinion of them than he, until they had disillusioned him . . .'. In all outward things they had appeared to be Christian, yet they had secretly cherished the old faith; 'while they seem a simple people, they are up to any mischief, and obstinately attached to the rites and ceremonies of their forefathers . . . He knew the whole land was damned, and that without compulsion they would never speak the truth.' Returned to Spain, he wrestled still with the painful paradox of his own earlier patience and gentleness in rebuking and forgiving his Indians for their backsliding, when all the while they were exploiting his tenderness so as to deceive him further. He had finally come to realise, he said, that only through punishment could such a people be improved.[4]

The administering of that punishment may have helped assuage his anguish: whimpering under the lash, men are made children again. But it is in the pages of his great *Relación*, written in the familiar tranquillity of the monastery of San Juan de los Reyes, that his matured understandings of the whole affair could reasonably be sought. Scholars have taken polar views at Landa's intentions in writing the *Relación*, some seeing it as a work of self-justification; others as an attempt at restitution for his persecution of the Indians.[5] What is most remarkable about the *Relación* (and what makes the polar judgments possible) is that it has so very little to say about the events in which its author had just been embroiled, dealing briskly with Landa's appearance before the council, and with the events of 1562 more briskly still. It could be thought that Landa, keeping in mind his interest in recruiting friars for the renewed mission, and given that the *Relación* was almost certainly written as part of that campaign, deliberately muted past conflicts, but such a strategy is compatible neither with his direct, combative temperament, nor indeed with his understanding of what incites men to commitment.

There is another more troubling possibility. The original *Relación* has been lost: what we have is a copy of parts of the original, 'taken from that which the Fray Diego de Landa of the Order of San Francisco wrote'; written in three different hands, and perhaps made in 1616.[6] It is possible that the unknown copyists not only omitted or abbreviated sections, but also rearranged the order of the original, for there are curious breaks and alternations in tone and subject matter. This makes the *Relación* an awkward source for the workings of the mind of its author. Is the brevity of the account of the idolatry affair indicative not of Landa's state of mind, but of an editing scribe's judgment? I think not. The account flows smoothly, and for all its brevity, contains a coherent and complete explanation of events. It runs:

These people, who after being instructed in religion, and the young boys having advanced in their studies as we have said, were perverted by the priests whom they had at the time of their idolatry and by the chiefs. And they returned to the worship of their idols and to offer them sacrifices not only of incense but also of human blood. The friars made an Inquisition about this and asked the aid of the *alcalde mayor*, and they arrested a great number and put them on trial, after which an *auto de fe* was celebrated, at which they placed many upon the scaffold wearing the *coroza* [the headdress of shame] and scourged and shorn, while others were clothed in the *sanbenito* [the garment of shame] for a time. And some, deceived by the Devil, hanged themselves for grief, and in general they all showed deep repentance and a willingness to become good Christians.

There follows a slightly more elaborate but still laconic account of Landa's examination before the committee of the Council of the Indies, and his ultimate vindication for 'making the *auto de fe* and also in the other things which he had done in punishment of the Indians'.[7]

The account is selective, omitting all reference to the violent preliminary tortures, and the heavy penalties imposed. But it encapsulates what we must accept as Landa's final judgment on the matter. The problem had been one of authority. The common people had indeed been in process of conversion, responding to the friars' tuition, when that process had been interrupted by the intervention of the superseded men of authority, the native chiefs, and the priests of the old religion. The people with their habit of deference had been misled as to where authentic authority lay. So the offences had to be extirpated, and the power of the chiefs and priests broken; a task neglected before, in the interest of the easy management of the country, but now, with their malice exposed, unavoidable. And the commoners had to be taught that the authority of the old regime had gone, and that authority rested with the Franciscans, and only the Franciscans. All those ends could be achieved immediately, economically and indeed only through unrestricted torture, as priests and lords twisted and moaned, as surrendered idols burned, as Indians learnt through their own wincing flesh 'a willingness to become good Christians'.

With that diagnosis made, those days of desperate emotion and confusion shaped and moulded and twisted into the coherent and the rational, which is to say into 'history', could be set aside. The tone of the *Relación* is tranquil; the pervasive mood nostalgic. When he wrote Landa could not have been sure that he would ever return to the country which had consumed his youth and his middle years. No other European knew that country and its people as he knew them: the friars who had preceded him in the peninsula were dead or had, like Bienvenida, been drawn into the affairs of a wider world. The whole spirit and texture of the work suggests that Landa, like so many other great travellers, saw the small lost world of Yucatan the more vividly for being distanced from it, and sought to record its clear bright shapes before they were dimmed by age and failing memory. That dour land is evoked as a place of abundance, its fruits rich, its flowers of incomparable beauty and fragrance. Sixteenth-century reports tend to the encyclopedic, but Landa's tone, partisan to the point of chauvinism, is distinctive. When he tells of creatures unknown to Spaniards, like opossums and armadillos, his images have the freshness and precision of long and fascinated observation. He recognised the Maya as the descendants of the men who had built the magnificent structures of such 'grandeur and beauty' as to make them 'the most remarkable of all the things which up to this day have been discovered in the Indies'[8] and which made Yucatan worthy of a fame at least equal to New Spain or Peru. Their society, as he recreated it, was characterised by justice and good order, its harmony jeopardised only by a few disruptive individuals, and by foreign intruders. In his narrative of the conquest he was persistently sympathetic to the defenders, whose desperate struggles he justified as natural responses to injustice and brutality. It was in the extended passages describing the Maya as he himself had known them that his pen moved most freely. Like other ageing men recalling their past, it was not the most recent years, with their bitterness, rancour, and betrayal, which compelled his attention. The world he evoked was the world which had challenged, absorbed and enchanted him in the heroic days of his youth. The *Relación de la Cosas de Yucatan* is a tender remembrance of beloved things past.

For all that, it is a very odd document. To say a text tells us more than even a candid author (and Landa was candid) had 'in mind' is not to invoke some inaccessible unconscious, but only to acknowledge something we all know, from introspection as much as from observation: men typically act from understandings and intentions which are less than explicit but which can, with effort, sometimes be brought to light. Landa was not a man given to self-analysis. But in the flow of the *Relación*, even in the defective form in which we have it, there may be allusions, omissions and emphases which could reveal something of Landa's tacit response to the terrible events of 1562.

One peculiarity is that the *Relación* has relatively little to say about the early days of the mission, the triumphs of the founding friars, or tales of individual Indian conversions – the stuff and texture of most Franciscan histories, and which no Franciscan copyist would be likely to abridge. A pointer to the scarring of that last year in Yucatan is the omission of any mention of Gaspar Antonio Chi, the Indian brought up from childhood by the friars (if we are to believe one biographer, by Landa himself) and presumably a notable success story of the mission.[9] There can be no doubt that Chi was a major informant on Indian ways, but Landa does not admit his existence, presumably because he judged Chi to have betrayed the friars by accepting service with Bishop Toral. On the whole question of informants Landa suffers from a curiously selective amnesia. He generously acknowledges his debt to Juan Nachi Cocom – but makes no reference to the fact that he had ordered the corpse of his old friend to be exhumed from holy ground and had watched it burn, along with the corpses of other apostates and the idols they had secretly cherished.[10]

Landa's generosity extended to the 'sad priests of the devil' worthy of emulation by the priests of God for the assidity of their mortifications, their prayers, and their vigils for their vicious master. The terrible devotion of the commoners impressed him even more deeply, as they drew forth blood from ears, lips and cheeks to offer before their idols.[11] He told of their tongue laceration, in which they pierced their tongues in a slanting direction from side to side and passed 'straws through the holes with horrible suffering', and in even more detail of the 'obscene and bloody' penis laceration ceremony:

holes were made in the virile member of each obliquely from side to side and through the holes which they had thus made they passed the greatest quantity of thread that they could, and all of them thus being fastened and strung together, they anointed the idol with the blood which flowed from all these parts; and he who did this the most was considered as the bravest; and their sons from the earliest age began to practise it, and it was a horrible thing to see how inclined they were to this ceremony . . .[12]

He noted their offering of the heart, blood and flesh of 'all the [animals] which they could obtain, whether they were birds of the sky, or beasts of the land, or fish of the sea', and also, of course of men. Here indulgence vanished. Landa gave brief descriptions of several modes of human killings – death by arrows, or being cast down on stones – but his most extended account is of death by the cutting out of the heart. Note the darkening modulation of tone, obscured but not quite removed by the translation from the Spanish; and the shift from images of the reassuring formalities of human ceremony to one of unmitigated and purely animal ferocity as the action moves from preparation to the actual killing:

If the heart of the victim was to be taken out, they led him with a great show and company of people into the court of the temple, and having smeared him with blue color and put on a *coroza* [headdress], they brought him up to the round altar, which was the place of sacrifice, and after the priest and his officials had anointed the stone with a blue color, and by purifying the temple drove out the evil spirits, the Chacs [four old men assistants] seized the poor victim, and placed him very quickly on his back upon that stone, and all four held him by the legs and arms, so that they divided him in the middle. At this came the executioner, the *nacom*, with a knife of stone, and struck him with great skill and cruelty a blow between the ribs of his left side under the nipple, and he at once plunged his hand in there and seized the heart like a raging tiger and snatched it out alive and, having placed it on a plate, he gave it to the priest, who sent very quickly and anointed the faces of the idols with that fresh blood . . .

He continued:

sometimes they made this sacrifice on the stone and high altar of the temple, and then they threw the body, now dead, rolling down the steps. The officials below took it and flayed it whole, taking off all the skin with the exception of the feet and hands, and the priest, all bare, covered himself, stripped naked as he was, with that skin, and the others danced with him . . .[13]

Which leads us to the consideration of the most startling characteristic of Landa's *Relación*: nowhere in the text as we have it is there any unequivocal indication that Maya Indians after accepting baptism had reverted to the practice of human sacrifice. So much of the *Relación* is devoted to the reconstruction of the religious rituals of the pre-contact Maya that we could reasonably expect Landa to draw on the rich material of the confessions, as have later scholars, for comparison and verification. There is no reference to it. (It strains credulity to imagine a scribe filleting out all such references had they been made.) In one passage Landa laments that idolators were so enslaved by the devil as to offer him their own blood, and even 'the lives of their neighbours and brothers', but the 'idolators' (not identified with any particular time or place) are, presumably, generalised pagans – not backsliding Christians. We could at least expect an explicit statement of the precise nature of the Indians' crimes in his account of the launching of the 1562 inquisition. Instead we are offered: 'they returned to the worship of their idols and to offer them sacrifices not only of incense but also human blood'.

'Sacrifices . . . of human blood.' The phrase is magnificently ambiguous, for elsewhere in the *Relación*, as we have seen, Landa had given memorable descriptions – those pierced tongues and penises – of self-laceration, and the drawing of blood from different parts of the body as an offering to the gods. The most careful reader of the *Relación* would have no reason to believe the Indians' 'crime' was anything other, anything more sinister, than that. Why does Landa swerve into ambiguity on this essential point? Perhaps that bitter period remained so painful a memory that Landa flinched from rehearsing its events, but is it possible that the threat of an unbearable self-knowledge persistently deflected him from dwelling upon it? Just how far the Indians' testimonies were 'inventions' (as Toral believed them to be) will be explored at a later point, but here I want to consider the evidence for the following hypothesis: that the confessions as we have them reveal more of the shaping power of Landa's imagination than the actual behaviour of Indians.

One of the factors which nudges an incautious reader towards acceptance of the testimonies is that some are so vivid, so rich in compelling detail. A forceful example is the confession of Juan Couoh, the schoolmaster from Yaxcaba. He offers a sustained and detailed narrative, studded with sharp images and incorporating believable dialogue, of the sacrifice of the youth Francisco Cauich in the village church. It is a dramatic, evocative and persuasive account, but is it, for all its realism, a precise description of reality? We know the imperfections of the missionary campaign, and the Mayas' determined adherence to their old gods. Cauich was not known to the friars. His 'Christian education' could therefore be no more than that dispensed by a native schoolmaster. Yet in Couoh's account he is presented as remarkably serene and secure in his new faith. Surrounded by the sinister shapes of his murderers, and by the hideous idols of the old religion, in the certainty of his own imminent and gruesome death, he maintained a demeanour of Christian resignation, and declared, so Couoh informs us, 'Do with me what you wish, for God who is in Heaven will help me.'[14]

Cauich's performance is at least anomalous, given what we know of the missionary enterprise, yet it could accord well with the fantasies of a Spanish missionary friar. The 'crucifixion' stories too are in a sense a compliment, if a perverse one, to the friars' teachings, implying as they do that the symbol of the Cross had bitten deep into the Maya imagination. We know that despite the extravagance of the tortures inflicted in Mani and in Hocaba-Homun Landa was the first of the friars to extract confessions to human sacrifice, and the only inquisitor to wring admissions of blasphemous crucifixions from the Maya. We know that men subjected to the *garrucha* could do little more than affirm or deny propositions put to them, and then, later, when their confessions were taken, to flesh out with details the skeletal account already provided. We know that Landa chose for close interrogation schoolboys and schoolmasters, presumably because they were more responsive under questioning. And we know too well from our own times the terrible intimacy of the relationship between interrogator and interrogated.

Over many years, Landa had served his superiors in the Franciscan order loyally and well, but they were 'superiors' in a very limited sense. For all of that time, he contrived to create situations in which he was effectively independent. Easily provoked to challenge the validity of others' claims to rule – he had on different occasions rejected the authority of the governor of the province, the *audiencia* of Guatemala, and the *audiencia* of Mexico in the secular sphere, and, in the religious, the jurisdiction of his own Commissary General, the General of the Franciscan order, the Bishop of Yucatan, and the Archbishop of Mexico – he was fiercely jealous of his own. Denial or even questioning of the legitimacy and extent of his authority brought swift retribution: Hernández' real offence had been his refusal to recognise Landa as his rightful judge. Those who accepted his own definition of his authority he rewarded with rock-like loyalty; those who contested it he pursued relentlessly, using any method necessary to bring them down.

With the Indians of Yucatan he had a special relationship. His experiences with the Maya in his days as a solitary missionary had been gratifying at the deepest level of his personality, and had set the psychological mood for his later relationship with them. Alone, a stranger, without the external trappings of power or the backing of force, armed only with his righteousness, he had gone among them, and they had recognised him. They had perceived the truth of his authority, and the truth of his message, as he thought. It is possible that his friendship with the old men who were his informants were among the most emotionally rewarding of his life.

With the revelation of their secret persistence in idolatry he concluded that they had betrayed him, and proceeded to punish them, and to strive to wrench the last root of opposition out of them. Then, as the hostility of the lay settlers was threatening to transform itself into legal restraints on his freedom of action, he had news of the bishop's arrival, and the termination of his own independence. Only under Landa's interrogation did Sotuta Indians confess to human sacrifice. Was this because only he, of all the interrogators, had the wide knowledge of traditional Maya rituals necessary to shape his questions and their responses into dramatic accounts which mirrored his inner certainty? He must have known of the Bishop's arrival at the port town of Campeche by 10 or 11 August. The indictment making the first mention of human sacrifice was drawn up on 11 August. Did the news of the bishop's arrival, the imminent abrogation of his own authority by an outsider who would be his direct, his inescapable superior, drive Landa to 'see' that further dimension of Maya depravity, beyond idolatry? On 14 August, Toral arrived in Mérida; then, or very soon after, Landa would know of Toral's increasing impatience. From 14 to 16 August, he took no testimonies. Then, between 17 and 19 August came the 'crucifixion' stories, not from new areas, but elicited from witnesses from villages already examined.

In the midst of the testimonies taken down on 11 August there is a grotesque detail. In the course of his confession the *ak-kin* Francisco Chuc of Sahcaba told how he together with four other village leaders had killed a pig inside the village church. They had then taken a little cross from the altar and set it on fire, along with six of the little sticks used to make barbecue frames. Chuc admitted that he had twice plunged the burning cross and sticks into the opened belly of the pig, so quenching the flames. The scribe, presumably at something of a loss to find a word to describe the macabre exercise with the burning crucifix, referred to the pig as having been 'crucified'. Did intensifying anxiety generate in Landa so powerful a surge of energy and emotion that he was brought to connect the scribe's use of the word 'crucified' with the old story of the deformed baby born in Hunacti village with the strange lesions on its head, hands and feet, and so perceive the 'true' meaning of that episode: that the Maya had blasphemously parodied the central mystery of the Christian faith? Once he had perceived that 'truth', it would not be difficult to extort the evidence. Given that evidence, no-one could criticise the violence of his methods, and, in such a situation of crisis, no newcomer, however elevated his rank, could lightly remove Landa from his directive role.

There is nothing to indicate that Landa had any conscious doubt as to the truth of the confessions his probings had extracted from the Indians. Such cynicism is incompatible with all we know of his lofty and passionate spirit. He had known, and had known with complete certainty, the 'truth': the Indians were idolators, blasphemers and murderers. It had been his task and his duty to lay bare that truth. But he also knew that in performing that task he had been forced into moulding the evidence of their iniquities. He had pointed to mountains of idols as proof of the Indians' idolatry: he knew that some of those 'idols' were not idols at all, but odd fragments and shards collected from abandoned sites by desperate men. He had claimed that the tortures were mild, a matter of 'some vexation only', but he had lived through those days of blood and anguish, and he knew that the confessions had been wrung from men in the extremes of physical agony. He had presented the confessions as true accounts, but he knew their confusions and contradictions, and what sustained pressure it had taken to get even a limited measure of coherence. Perhaps some individuals were not guilty of every charge laid against them, perhaps the *ah-kines* had not said precisely what witnesses had sworn they had said, but these considerations were trivial, and could not be allowed to impede him, for he knew children had died, God had been mocked, and that the Indians had betrayed him.

During the enquiry, the constant lash of opposition and his own compulsion had driven him on. Throughout the subsequent conflict with the bishop, he had been full of affairs, organising his campaign, comforting his friends and assailing his enemies. There had been no time and no cause to reflect on the devices and stratagems he had been forced to employ. Returned to Spain, in the strange suspended world of the accused man waiting judgment, he was deprived of the solace of action. The main charges against him did not relate directly to the question of the validity of the Indian testimony, but we can be sure his judges questioned him closely upon it. They were, finally, convinced, but under their interrogation, was Landa forced towards a partial awareness of the extent of his own manipulations?

Such a hypothesis, given the defective nature of the *Relación* text, and the impossibility of better than circumstantial evidence regarding Landa's knowledge of the bishop's movements and demeanour, must remain tenuous, but another oddity lends it some sinew. About three months after his arrival in Madrid, some time early in 1565, Landa addressed a special *Memorial* to the king. The opinion of the Council of the Indies was at the time still hostile to him, and Landa's intention was to win the king to his side. Yet in that document Landa gave only two sentences to the 'sacrifices and crucifixions' brought to light by his own diligence. He chose rather to direct the king's attention to that earlier episode of the dead baby bearing marks like those of the stigmata upon its hands, feet and head.[15] In 1561, Landa had certainly agreed with Fray Pedro de Ciudad Rodrigo's diagnosis that the Indians of Hunacti had succumbed to superstitious terror when confronted by a very unusual birth. Fray Pedro was almost certainly right. It was the Hunacti chief who had alerted the friar, scarcely the action of a guilty man, and the descriptions of the condition of the child and its mother are compatible with death by natural causes. Did Landa fasten on the episode of the 'crucified' baby in his *Memorial* precisely because he had had no hand in it? Did he find the evidence relating to it, for all its ambivalence, less ambivalent and less potentially threatening than the forced testimony of the confessions?

After the committee had entered its judgment, in the quiet of a Spanish monastery, he wrote his *Relación*. In it, the whole sorry episode, with its troubling, festering doubts, is largely repressed. Landa set about recreating the crystal vision of Yucatan he had once held, before it was shattered by the events of 1562. The mood is one of nostalgic tenderness. The conflicts he records are distant; even his enemies are lightly treated. The Maya are an intelligent, responsive, upright people once more. The dark and sinister images which invaded his imagination in that bitter year are rigorously excluded from the lost paradise. Landa had no desire to seek to identify the serpent which had destroyed it, perhaps because he dared not.

There are, of course, problems with this kind of explanation. If some men at the time suspected something like it, none to my knowledge commented on the fortuitous timing of the confessions, or the centrality of Landa's role as interrogator. Historians, unready to stretch their inferences too far, and properly suspicious of free-wheeling speculation, prefer to stay close to the rational, to the calculated, in their efforts to explain conduct – the conduct of people in the past. (Like the rest of us, they find such notions of little help when it comes to explaining the behaviour of people around them, or, for that matter, their own.) But the obstinate peculiarities remain. At the least it is clear that despite Landa's unchallenged 'honesty', despite his passionate commitment to 'truth', he could recognise or, more precisely, construct only a truth cast in the terms of his own system of understanding. He was prepared to accept the Indians as responsible moral beings, as Toral, reducing them to mere victims, was not. But that acceptance meant nothing about a determination to penetrate their own moral order. It provided only the justification for punishing them for offences against his own.

Epilogue: The hall of mirrors

Colonial situations breed confusion. A favourite metaphor for the tangled miscommunications between native and outsider is a 'confusion of tongues', where the focus falls on the dangerous business of translation from one meaning system to another. There was certainly enough of that in the Yucatan situation, and the exploration of that dimension will be the concern of the next chapters. But colonial situations also spawn multiple realities, and that painful fissuring within the Spanish world is perhaps better caught by a different image: a hall of distorting mirrors in which each individual sees himself, as he thinks, truly reflected, while those about him are disquietingly altered into grotesques, as familiar gestures and expressions are exaggerated, parodied, even inverted. The settler-Franciscan division had always been deep; that it became deeper did not seriously threaten the sense of self of either. The case of Quijada was crueller: he found himself abandoned and left defenceless by that 'law' which had been his guide and shield. But it was the Franciscans themselves, causing suffering, who among the Spaniards suffered most, with the fracturing of that small intensely shared world of meanings painfully constructed through the perfected special tongue which was then used to destroy it. They had easily identified with Villalpando's unforgettable image of the Franciscan clasping the bleeding, befouled Indian in face of the homicidal rage of the Spanish settler. Then Toral had to watch settlers doing their poor best to protect wounded, weeping Indians from his Franciscan brothers' murderous anger. The man who after twenty years' service in Mexico had the moral poise to direct Sahagún to bring to light the Indians' real spiritual state was driven in Yucatan to deny that light, and to transform the Maya into pure victims. He found his terrible 'truth' in these events in Franciscans who were monstrous inversions of the Franciscan ideal; missionaries as brutish as the worst pagans; men enslaved by the passions of anger, pride and cruelty, and their chief's ferocious self-righteousness and lust to dominate.

Landa and his friars saw a fellow Franciscan ally himself with flaccid, careless men and astonishingly, unforgivably, betray his clear duty to his God, his order and his brothers. And there was a worse betrayal with the realisation that the Indians they had so tenderly protected, whose sufferings had roused their pity, whose trust they thought they had won, remained strangers: their faces closed, averted, masked, concealing depthless duplicity.

It is those Indians, for so long the objects and victims of Spanish world-making, who now become the subjects of our enquiry.

PART II

Indians

9

Finding out

This is a record of the things they did. After it had all passed, they told of it in their own words, but its meaning is not plain. Still the course of events was as it is written . . . Still he who comes of our lineage will know it, one of us who are Maya men . . .

The Book of Chilam Balam of Chumayel

Is it possible to discover anything of the views and experience of a people whose voices were hushed to a murmur more than 400 years ago? In the preface of his *The Making of the English Working Class*, E. P. Thompson declared in a splendid phrase his determination to rescue ordinary English working men and women from 'the enormous condescension of posterity,' and proceeded to do so. Rescuing the native peoples so casually appropriated to European uses (symbolic and material) over these last centuries presents essentially the same problems – the necessary dependence on outsider reports, for example – at an even more daunting level of intensity. Alien soldiers rarely make sensitive ethnographers. The Spaniards who conquered the peninsula, from Córdoba's ragged hopefuls to the hard men who fought the last campaigns, were concerned with survival and victory. What they saw they saw well: the shape and size of settlements; the swift obedience of commoners to their chiefs; goods produced and exchanged; how work was distributed. But it was a narrowly instrumental perspective, and one inevitably entailing distortion, as the unfamiliar was wrenched into familiar, and so potentially manipulable, forms.

The missionary friars were initially interested in a wider range of Indian behaviour, and were more concerned with Indian intentions. But they arrived at those 'intentions' less by observation and enquiry than by imputation. Pagan behaviour was unproblematic, precisely because it was pagan. If certain Maya men contrived to be baptised again and again it was because they were foolish, or spiteful. If native lords kept concubines it was to satisfy concupiscence; if they drew blood from their own bodies it was because they were the pathetic dupes of the devil. Later – as I hope I have persuaded the reader – friars and settlers were caught up in the pursuit of Spanish dramas and dreams, and their competing visions of 'Yucatan'. Native contributions to the writings those visions generated, like the contribution of Landa's informants, or the large parts of the settler reports to the Crown of 1579–81 written by the official interpreter Gaspar Antonio Chi, were elicited and controlled by Spanish purposes, and so can reveal little of the distinctive contours of Maya understandings.[1]

Nonetheless, we can know the Maya only from the time of, and through their engagement with, Europeans. The Spanish writings must obviously be used for the 'external' information they provide. They can be exploited further through borrowing the method Thompson used in his pursuit of the English working class. He began with the recognition that most men in all ages have expressed themselves more fully in actions than in words, and in words – sung, chanted or shouted as well as spoken – more fully than in script. Actions and words are conceived, expressed, recognised and understood within a system of shared expectations and meanings – in short, within a precise cultural context. Therefore the trick is to strip away the cocoon of Spanish interpretation to uncover sequences of Indian actions, and then to try to discern the pattern in those actions, as a way of inferring the shared understanding which sustains them.

Assistance in being responsive to unexpected patterns comes from reference to a very different kind of resource: the 'ethnographic present' of Indians living in Yucatan today. The past is of course present in all individuals and all societies – in the names we go by, the patterned behaviour of familiar routines and roles, the physical settings we move through – but it is more complacently and completely present in what we call 'traditional' societies. In modern Yucatan the past is exposed in the present like simultaneously revealed archeological layerings, giving travel in the peninsula a pleasantly hallucinatory quality. Today, a Maya matron intends visiting kin. Her snowy *huipil*, the chemise-like pre-conquest dress, is vivid with embroidered birds and flowers, her long hair smoothly braided: a sleeping baby is swaddled in her shawl. A brace of agitated ducks bob in one of her several baskets. There are blue plastic sandals on the broad brown feet, the *huipil* is store-bought, and she, her baby and her baskets are travelling by plane. On a rackety city street foul with diesel fumes an old man encounters his grandson. Time collapses as the fluent sequence of gestures of submission and release replay a greeting ritual recorded four centuries ago by a Spanish friar. The observer himself can be pulled into the action as the past makes its demands on the present. Nelson Reed, researching his superb study of the Caste War of the mid nineteenth century, when the Maya rose against their white masters and very nearly drove them out of the peninsula, was questioning an old man in territory long held by the rebels when he discovered he had been assigned a part in the drama he had thought past and over. He had been identified as one of the *Chachac-macob*, the 'red men' or Englishmen whose coming had been prophesied, and who would bring guns from Belize so that the Maya – in their own view still unsubdued – could fight once more.[2]

'Upstreaming', as the archeologists call it – arguing from the known to the less certainly known – or argument by analogy from the 'ethnographic present', is obviously seductive. It is also, obviously, risky: we may well impose continuity where no continuity exists. Material forms may remain constant while meanings change; meanings may remain constant but attach themselves to different material forms. A Greek Aphrodite, a Botticelli Madonna and Andy Warhol's Marilyn Monroe are all young blonde human females, but they signify very differently. For me the main utility of reference to the ethnographic present is aid in being alerted to areas of experience, like the ritual uses made of plant-derived drugs or alcohol, or the protocols shaping domestic interactions, scanted in outsider reports. It also provides comfort, giving some reassurance about interpretations finding their grounds elsewhere. Because ultimately, any reconstruction of sixteenth-century Maya understandings must rest on the material traces the Maya themselves happen to have left behind.

The survivals are few enough. Most Maya products, before as after the conquest, were as perishable as the plant substances from which they were made. Those less ephemeral were often destroyed by the Spaniards, or appropriated to their own use. The imperishably beautiful objects labelled 'Maya' in European museums date from earlier times, and were protected by the concealing forests during the Spanish depredations. But for the Maya the most comprehensive and precious concrete expressions of their imaginative universe were the great painted books of hieroglyphs, the repositories of sacred knowledge which were the source and warrant for the authority of the ruling lineages. It was one of these books that the old Cocom chief had revealed to the young friar Diego de Landa, as it was these books

which were later systematically destroyed by the friars: an act of
vandalism which must have been monstrously unintelligible to its
victims, which is I suppose the essential horror of vandalism.

Only three of the pre-conquest books survived the onslaught of
the friars, and those three, now appropriated by the international
scholarly world, present daunting problems in decipherment and
interpretation. But the native lords had taken steps to protect their
threatened treasures. The old books had been 'a quarter of a yard high
and about five fingers broad, made of the bark of trees, folded from
one side to the other like screens', and 'painted on both sides with a
variety of figures and characters', as we are told by a Spanish priest of
the late seventeenth century who had seen some of them.[3] They were
altogether too easily identifiable as the work and wisdom of the devil.
The men trained in their elucidation were ageing, and there was little
hope of their replacement, as the sons of the lords who would once
have been trained in the glyphic mode had been rounded up and
sequestered in the friars' schools. So that new training was turned to
the service of the old ways. Men who had learned in the mission
schools how to write in European script, and had some access to
European writing materials, were brought together with *ah-kines*, and
wrote down as best they could the words softly chanted by the
interpreter-priests as they scanned the painted pages, so translating
both mode and form to produce 'books' of a new, externally
European kind. This was not to be the last time the Maya innovated in
order to remain the same.

How far this was organised and how far an independent response
to Spanish action is not clear, but by the end of the century most
villages had their sacred writings secreted away in their new form.
Over the last century fourteen are known to have fallen into the hands
of outsiders, and some of those then found their way to scholars, who
have given them the generic name of 'the Books of Chilam Balam'.
'Chilam', or more properly 'Chilan', means 'spokesman' or 'prophet'
in Mayan, and 'Balam' 'jaguar', which also carries connotations of
lordly guardianship, so they could be named 'the Books of the
Spokesmen of the Jaguar Lords'.[4] There was a Prophet Balam who is
reputed to have prophesied the coming of the Spaniards at the turn
into the sixteenth century, so the books, so much products of the
colonial encounter, are well-named.

The *Book of Chilam Balam of Chumayel* is the best-known and the
most accessible of the genre through Ralph Roys' fine translation. It
is in Roys' description a small quarto volume, leather-bound, and

with numbered pages. Its line drawings are in a naive European style. It is written in an eighteenth-century hand. The three pre-contact Maya codices are museum pieces; beautiful frozen relics of a long-ago past. The *Books of Chilam Balam* were living things – at least for as long as the villagers held them. Their contents and shape display Maya understandings of what 'knowledge' was, and how it was arrived at. It would seem that the essential model was derived from their enduring dedication to the scrupulous observation and recording of movements in the heavens, which observations and recordings allowed properly attentive men to discern the subtle patternings and complex recurrences in the majestic movements of the stars through time. That elaborate, complex, esoteric but ultimately, when sufficiently refined, simple and elegant patterning patterned in its turn other Maya systems of meaning and modes of expression. Europeans confronted by the superb dynamic exuberance of Maya vase paintings or stone carvings – an exuberance always conceived and controlled within an elegantly austere structure – usually resort to 'baroque' as the nearest, if inadequate, description: Michael Coe, perhaps the most distinguished student of the Classic Maya, has characterised their hieroglyphic writing and their art as 'at the same time elegant, baroque, complex'. (He also characterises it as 'fundamentally weird', which is an issue to which I will return.)[5]

That Maya conviction that all things have pattern, however little obvious that pattern may seem to be, provided the dynamic for the *Books of Chilam Balam*, as it had for the folded bark-paper codices which had preceded them. Knowledge was not a given nor a finite thing: it was arrived at through the patient recording of events in the experienced world, and of any clues as to how to decipher those events, until through accumulation of data the pattern of recurrence behind occurrence could be discerned. So the careful men charged with the keeping of the books also added to them: chronicling events so that the pattern which underlay them would be made manifest in and through time; sometimes recording invocations or fragments of information culled from daily experience and judged to have the power to illuminate it. With constant use the books tattered, to be recopied as necessary, sometimes even by scribes ignorant of precise original meanings, but devoted to the same enterprise. The fragments of history, the echoes of local events, the incantations, the snatches of Spanish prayers or astrological lore they collected, however garbled and dispersed they seem to us, were selected and incorporated exactly because they were seen as apposite to Maya needs and meanings.

That dynamic dimension, their history-in-the-writing quality, makes the *Books of Chilam Balam* recalcitrant sources for our very different notion of history. The initial problem is a formal one of establishing the text. Those first transcribers had no rules to follow as they wrote down Maya sounds in European letters. They guessed at spellings, and then changed the guesses; they ran sentences, even words together. Later copyists emended and added as they saw fit. Translation, too, is difficult. Spoken Mayan did and does contain many words with the same sound, but different meanings, which opens the way for the serious word play and elaborate punnings which so gratified the Maya, but also confronts the translator with bitter imponderables as to which of the several possible meanings was intended to dominate on which particular occasion. And where the dominant meaning is adequately clear, there are still the usual problems of nuance. Consider these alternative translations, by eminently scrupulous and expert translators, of what could seem to be a simple statement from the *Book of Chilam Balam of Chumayel*: 'At that time the course of humanity was orderly', as opposed to 'the course of mankind was ciphered clearly'.[6] Not significantly different? But 'ciphered' carries the notion, not present in the more passive 'orderly', that the order is somehow prescribed – indeed, somewhere inscribed and therefore probably, from what we know from other sources, conveys the Maya meaning more precisely. Many discrepancies are wider, but even where the differences are small they matter, especially in their cumulative effect, for it is only through discriminations of this degree of delicacy that we can hope to identify recurrent and therefore typical patternings – which is to use the Maya method to discover Maya thought.

There is another and deeper dimension of difficulty, which arises directly from the kind of text the *Chilam Balams* are, or rather, what they were for. The original hieroglyphs did not contain a totally fixed and circumscribed meaning: only those skilled in their elucidation could read them, fleshing out the spare shapes with memorised formulae. We also know they were less 'read' than performed, in circumstances where audience response could shape the emphases, even the content, of the performances. The initial transcriptions into European script were deliberately gnomic: this was not knowledge to be read off by anyone who had simply learnt his letters, but the sacred preserve of those selected to be taught the techniques of elucidating and elaborating (within formal rules) the bare text. The hieroglyphs, dramatically condensed statements, had depended for their exposition on skilled performers. Although the fuller 'translation' achieved by the transcription into writing rendered the meanings more restricted, more fixed, and less amenable to adjustment, they remained scripts – written material designed to provide the skeletal structure of dramatic action, and allowing dynamic interaction between performer and audience. These performances certainly continued into the colonial period, as we will see: Spaniards lamented that the Indians contrived to continue to hold their 'secret meetings' where they performed their 'fabulous stories and injurious histories', with chantings, dance and drums.[7] So the written words that we have – even if there were no problems of translation – could catch only a part of the complex and shifting meanings they held (and perhaps still hold) for the Maya. And, finally, being as they are the compendium of Maya knowledge, and constantly added to, we have only vague internal hints as to when any particular entry was made.

They are for all that magnificent, absorbing sources. The sense of 'fundamental weirdness' noted by Michael Coe springs from the dislocating experience of encountering a world conceptualised so differently from our own. It is that strangeness, and then the slow recognition of the order sustaining the final magnificent coherence of Maya imagery, which makes the reading of a *Book of Chilam Balam*, even in English, an adventure in the construction of a new imaginative universe.

Through the muffling of translation it is possible to pick up something of the pulse and rhythm of formal Maya speech. The language owes little to Europe beyond the script: the Maya were notably frugal in their borrowings, preferring to stretch their own concepts to incorporate even the unequivocally new, as when the introduced horse was ingeniously labelled 'the tapir of Castile'. The language also exhibits the characteristic Maya preference for parallel couplets and artfully masked 'kennings', and the metaphors cluster richly about certain dominant and recurrent themes – perhaps most notably because most strange to us, the insistence on the symbiosis, indeed the identification between human and vegetable life. And if historians of the pre-contact period lament the deformation of 'pure' native understandings by what are clearly post-conquest accretions, for us those 'deformations' and 'accretions' are gold, giving access to the autonomous accommodations the Maya made to their new masters.

Then there are the very different resources of inquisition records themselves. They are, superficially, Spanish records; produced in the pursuit of Spanish purposes, preserved for Spanish ends. But they are more than that. They contain a mass of information regarding the physical and social context – location of buildings; objects and gestures in common use, who was likely to be found with whom – that abundance of facts about the mundane world trial records so often incorporate. More important, the interrogations, confessions, accusations and denials are direct manifestations, for all their confusions and partiality, of the bloody and painful struggle between different systems of meaning I want to decipher.

It is from these three kinds of materials – the Indian present, Spanish reportings, and native records advertent and inadvertent – that I have constructed what follows.

10

Connections

Then with the true God, the true Dios, came the beginning of our misery. It was the beginning of tribute, the beginning of church dues, the beginning of strife with purse-snatching, the beginning of strife with blow-guns, the beginning of strife by trampling on people, the beginning of robbery with violence, the beginning of debts enforced by false testimony, the beginning of individual strife, a beginning of vexation, a beginning of robbery with violence. This was the origin of service to the Spaniards and priests, of service to the local chiefs, of service to the teachers, of service to the public prosecutor by the boys, the youths, of the town, while the poor people were oppressed. These were the very poor people who did not depart when oppression was put upon them . . .

But it shall still come to pass that tears shall come to the eyes of our Lord God . . .

Prophecy for *Katun* 11 *Ahau*

If Montejo's Spaniards were disappointed, as they moved in from the coast, with the modest size of Maya settlements, they should perhaps have wondered why there were any substantial settlements at all. The peninsula imposed narrow limits on its human users. Each *milpa* could be cropped only for two or three seasons before too stubborn regrowth forced its relinquishment back to the forest for seven or ten or more years. To live in a group therefore meant to spend time trekking back and forth to the *milpa*, as each household required access to a substantial area of land. Under those circumstances we could expect to find single households evenly scattered through the bush, each working its own territory, instead of towns of four thousand and more people.

The convenience of living close by one's *milpa* was well under-stood. In those seasons when weeds sprang most thickly, or when a maturing crop required special vigilance, the *milpa* work team or even whole households migrated out to the *milpas*, camping in shelters distinguished from their permanent wattle, daub and thatch huts only by their more casual construction. Clusters of households would sometimes coalesce to form temporary hamlets while they exploited an otherwise inaccessible strip of forest, returning to the mother village when the *milpa* cycle had been completed. The Maya's was an eminently portable way of life: a few necessities carried – clay pots, favourite tools, mats – and the rest could be contrived from what they found about them. This was no theoretical possibility: time and again, in famine or the man-made catastrophes of war, whole communities fragmented into the forest, to regroup when the crisis was past.

Yucatan seems to have lacked local markets. The conquerors, so alert for signs of commercial promise, report on none, and the *visita* judge López Medel was moved to try to legislate them into existence. It is true the peninsula lacked the ecological diversity which distinguished Central Mexico and sustained its vigorous local exchange – the small movement of salt and fish from the coast, and of copal and honey, was probably handled by itinerant peddlars – but neither did it develop those regional craft specialisations which further stimulated Mexican trade. There seems rather to have been a choice made for the competence and therefore the potential independence of the individual household, with each man and each woman expected to master the basic repertoire of skills appropriate to the sex. Yet there is clear evidence of an active preference for collective life, even at significant cost. While some Maya withdrew permanently from Spanish-controlled zones, most chose to stay, and to stay in highly visible and therefore vulnerable communities. Of those who withdrew some joined established towns. At the turn of the seventeenth century the remarkable Pablo Paxbolon, the enterprising lord of an area to the south of Campeche, was able to extend his authority well beyond his traditional territory by persuading fugitive Maya scattered through the forest to form new – and taxable – communities under his jurisdiction.[1] Given the obvious costs, what then were the attractions of the collective life?

One probably had something to do with preferred conditions of work and of household size. Most Maya lived in multi-generational households of a father and his sons, married and unmarried, and it was that group of related males which made up the usual *milpa* team. The labour was hard, and human company had its own value as men worked under the silent gaze of the forest spirits, always at risk from snake or scorpion or the sudden twist of an axe as it turned to find flesh. For extended periods the group was strengthened by an outsider: a young man fulfilling his years of bride service and residence in his father-in-law's house. Brides were typically sought among the girls of the home village, so marriage linked the household back into the wider collectivity. The bond between the marrying families was close. The young wife would probably bear at least her first child during the bride-service period, and so in the security of her parents' house. When she moved to her husband's people and the bearing of more children, she did so with her reputation as a wife and mother already established, and with her kin protectively near.[2]

Women also benefited from the larger household. Their tasks were multiple, and not all easily compatible. Weaving the complex fabrics of delicately dyed cotton and spun rabbit fur for which the Yucatan women were famous, working and coiling clay, even the endless grinding of softened maize to smoothness, were tasks best performed uninterrupted. But Maya houseyards were lively places, with their fruit trees, their hand-raised wild birds and marginally tamer ducks cherished for their plumage, the frolicsome coati-mundi cherished, it seems, for the charm of their wicked ways, and above all those 'marvellously pretty and plump' infants who so captivated Landa, and not conducive to steady concentration. Then there was the endless fetching of water, which in the dry season could entail a significant journey to a distant but reliable *cenote*. In such a situation not merely the sharing of work but the distribution of tasks could give the satisfactions of some specialisation, and the uninterrupted time conducive to the development of more sophisticated skills.

The expanded household and the maintenance of desirable work situations did not entail village living: kin could have chosen to walk occasionally to visit kin instead of every day to labour. Here it is as well to remember that 'distance' is a relative thing. An intimately known path is rarely wearisome. It is only to the outsider that the Yucatan bush presents an unvarying spectacle. The *milpa* team always had the chance of picking up some game along the way – a rabbit, even an iguana – or of marking a newly settled bee swarm or the nest of a long-coveted bird. Those dappled paths webbed a landscape thick with individual associations: here the eight-year-old, allowed at last to follow the men, watching his first *milpa* made, nervously attentive to the grandfather's smallest glance or gesture; here the bad burn and an uncle's expert care; there the strip, dense with regrowth, where the young man had first demonstrated his strength and toughness before the men of his new wife's family. In the days after the conquest the friars in charge of the resettlement programme adopted harsh measures, as we have seen, to keep the Maya in their new villages, burning the dwellings in the old, smashing the hives, destroying the fruit trees. But still the people filtered back, obstinate in their attachment to a particular place.

There were more positive attractions. To live in the forest, or only for household and *milpa*, was to live to survive, in exile from the complex enchantments of public ritual life. Even the most modest village had its temple, elevated on its platform, flanked by the storehouse for the masks, plumes, flutes and drums displayed in the performances staged in its wide courtyard. The youths of the village lived together in the long warrior house from puberty to marriage, learning a new ease of relationships with peers after the strict age and gender hierarchy of the household, and the speed and strength in weapon-handling, the chants and the dances which made a Maya man. The house of the village chief, like those of the lesser lords, was more public building than private dwelling, its courtyard sometimes a place of justice; more often the setting for the rounds of feasts which at once forged and celebrated mutual dependence.

These were not exclusively male activities. While only old women, safely past menopause, were permitted to penetrate the dark temples to dance before the gods, women had charge of the household idols, and when those idols were brought out to be clustered on fresh-gathered leaves for collective worship, it was women's handiwork in which they were swaddled, and which glorified the dancers. They were excluded from blood-letting penances, the blood of mature women being unacceptable to the gods, but they too fasted and prayed, and in the feasts which climaxed nearly all public ceremonies they too feasted and drank and danced, though separately from the men, and rather more sedately. (Landa, an admirer of Maya women for their beauty, gentleness and modesty, allowed that they used to perform a few dances with the men, one of them 'not very decent'; given their developed commitment to decorum this was probably more sacred than secular.)[3]

The great lords of the major provinces were responsible for maintaining troops of professional 'comedians', who performed on public occasions for the delectation of the commoners. The Maya appear to have had a taste for what we would call low comedies and satires. The players, while supported by the lords, were under the special protection of a particular deity, no bad situation for daring satirists. The god's festival was celebrated yearly at Mani, with five days of dances and plays for his pleasure, but we may reasonably assume the same kind of theatre flourished at a more local and amateur level. A hundred year after the conquest the players and the genre still survived, and still stood ready to mock their masters: Cogolludo reported that at the close of the seventeenth century the Maya maintained:

comedians who act out legends and ancient stories, which, I am certain, it would be as well to abolish, at least the costumes in which they perform them, because apparently they are like those of their heathen priests . . . they are very witty in the nicknames and jests which they apply to their chiefs and judges, if these are severe, ambitious, or avaricious, acting out the events which occur between them, and even what they notice in their parish priest they say in front of him, sometimes in a single word, but anyone who would understand them must be a good linguist and listen well . . .

Cogolludo's conclusion that such dangerous activities should be forbidden was a very different response from that of the pre-conquest lords, sufficiently secure in their positions and the stability of social categories to tolerate mockery.[4] Montejo and his men had been swift to notice the extreme deference accorded all members of the noble caste, the '*almehenob*'; literally, 'those whose fathers and mothers are known', who monopolised all positions of authority sacred and secular throughout the peninsula. Montejo himself had been torn between mirth and outrage when one ruler, unaccountably unimpressed by the momentous Spanish presence, would deign to address the Spanish captain only through a fine linen veil. Yet despite the superb carriage of the lords the Spaniards were unable to establish just what tributes and services they exacted. They could make no sense of what could appear extravagant and casual taking, but with no rule as to measure and no coercion in the taking. Some lords, they thought, took what they wanted, while others seemed to depend on purely voluntary offerings.[5]

When such interested observers are puzzled, it is as well for later commentators to be tentative. But it is possible that the Spaniards' difficulty sprang from their 'natural' concentration on the transfer of material wealth, which, being material and therefore visible, is most easily identified across cultures, and so too easily identified as the most, or even the sole significant currency between men. What they may have missed seeing in Maya interactions (sensitive to it as they were in their own) was that the Maya were engaged in a traffic in symbols of deference and regard, extravagant in ritual, high in rewards, but economical in products, especially home-produced ones. If the lords were allocated the most favoured land for the making of *milpa*, that land was largely worked not by local retainers, but by war captives. Their domestic state was sustained by the labour of their female slaves and concubines. If they were given the lords' share of the game taken in a communal hunt, or levied from the professional hunters, the hunters knew that the meat would be returned to them with appropriate ceremony in one of the feasts the lords were compelled to offer in their multiple roles as sponsors, impresarios and leading actors in public ceremonies. In these ceremonies the commoners made their contributions: a duck or an iguana, fetching and carrying of supplies; the preparation of the ovens or the slow brewing of the *balche* they would drink to happy insensibility. But it was the lords who provided the venues and the bulk of the provender, and who sustained the specialists who made the drums, the masks, the flutes and trumpets required for effective ceremonial. It was the lords who, monopolising inter-provincial and extra-peninsular trade, secured those prized exotic items – the cacao, the red shells from the Pacific coast, the copper, amber and gold nose plugs, the jade, the brilliant feathers and quetzal plumes – which invested ritual life with a powerful glamour. The elaboration of life in the head town in a province where one was so distinguished rested in part on the tribute sent to the head-chief from the dependent towns, in maize, game, honey, cotton, slaves, and a quota of fighting men when the maize cycle released men from war, but again a substantial part of the costs of maintaining the provincial centre was (at least ideally) displaced on to outsiders, through the seizing and distribution of loot. And should demands bear too heavily, there was always the opportunity for a warning withdrawal of services, either briefly, into the forest, or if the grievance was bitter to another town, and the protection of another lord.[6]

The sacred was not the preserve of priests: for example, the man selected every three years as *nacom* or war-captain practised rigorous sexual continence for all of his term, and all treated his person with careful reverence. But the priests' specialist knowledge was highly, and generally, valued. To understand their unchallenged status we need to understand how the Maya conceptualised the divisions of time, and from that conceptualisation inferred the structures which ordered space.

The Maya conceived of the world as quadrilateral. At each of the cardinal points a Sky-Bearer god sustained his quarter of the world. Each Direction was identified by its own colour – red for the east, white for the north, black for the west, and yellow for the south – and possessed its own deities of wind and rain. At each corner of the world grew a tree, of the appropriate colour, while at the centre, or the Fifth Direction, rose the great green silk-cotton tree, the Tree of the World, whose branches pierced the thirteen layers of the heavens. Below the world lay the nine levels of the Underworld, a chill, bleak, shadowy place, where all Maya, save those fortunate few whose manner of death – in war, childbirth or sacrifice – exempted them, were doomed to wander endlessly.

Round this four-cornered world moved the endlessly changing procession of deities which for the Maya constituted Time. The smallest unit recognised was the day, probably measured from sunset to sunset. The main sacred calendar, used for divination and prognostication, was based on a cycle of twenty named days, interacting with a numbers cycle from one to thirteen and so forming a larger 260-day cycle, known as the Sacred Round. (There was also a 'week' of nine nights, the precise significance of which is lost to us.) The solar year controlled another calendar, which consisted of eighteen months of twenty days, along with a nineteenth 'month' comprising five unnamed and dangerously unlucky days, the *Uayeb*, the whole being designated a *tun*. Given that structure, only four of the twenty named days could begin the 'new year'; they were designated 'Year Bearers', and the influence of the particular Year Bearer was felt throughout his year. During the dangerous *Uayeb* days the gods were pausing, some slipping off their burdens of time, others readying themselves for the slow onward march. Those days were thus in a sense 'out' of time; outside the influence of the gods, beyond the weak ritual control of men: they were days of endings and beginnings.

Given that the Maya recognised each day and each larger time division as a deity, each with its own attributes subtly modified according to the other deities with which it was in association, the problem of sorting out the complex influences working on any particular slice of time in this wheels-within-wheels kind of arrange-ment called for a high level of expertise. But it also allowed for prediction, as the recurrence of the same combination of influences could be expected to produce the same effects. Here, their technique for measuring long periods of time is important. Twenty *tun* equalled one *katun*, or 7,200 days, and a period of thirteen *katunes* was identified by the particular named day and number with which it ended. As the names and numbers identified the gods influencing that particular slice of time, each *katun* was identified with characteristic events, which would occur again with the return of the 'same' *katun*. Thus history was simultaneously prophecy, prophecy becoming history again with the next swing of the cycle.[7]

That sense that the future was fixed, and could be 'read' by those who had the skill to do so, meant that the social utility of the most esoteric knowledge could not be in doubt. If some priests, entranced, spoke with the tongues of the gods, those others who traced the great permutations of the interlocking calendars were equally close to the sacred. All who tended *milpas* waited on their words. Rainfall in Yucatan is notoriously unreliable; while the 'average' annual rainfall is 34.33 inches, records over a thirty-year period reveal a range from 16 to 64 inches.[8] The timing of the rains is also crucial. For maximum 'burn' the cleared scrub must be left to dry as long as possible, but left too long, until the coming of the rains, a man's labour and his *milpa* are lost for that season. The priests could determine the most favourable day for the firing of the fields, as they could then bring the rains to quench the last of those smouldering fires by satiating the Fire God with the hearts and blood of slaughtered animals. Thus time and labour spent in the service of those knowledgeable in the swings of the seasons and the moods of the gods were time and labour sensibly invested. Only the priests could set the day for the communal hunt, or the bending over of the stalks of the drying corncobs to save them from the rot of unseasonably late rains. For aid in individual misfortune or sickness the commoner would turn to the local curer, but for great decisions on which the survival of the group depended the calendar priest was essential. When a child was born, only the calendar priest could plot its prognostications. Four invisible Guardians, the Great Balams, protected each of the four ritual entrances, marked by piled stones, of every human settlement, but priests and lords were also collectively called 'the guardians'. It was for the priests to calculate when it was time to return the image of the deity whose year was passing to the temple, and to carry the image of the god who bore the burden of the incoming year on his back to the appropriate entrance, with appropriate incantations and offerings, so that the town was properly located within the great invisible structures of time and space. And given such a conceptual system the ruler was no mere individual exercising individual power, but he who had been designated responsible for that particular segment of the human order for a designated section of time.[9]

Specific as priestly tasks were, they were not carried out in remote secrecy, but under the gaze and in the company of the villagers. When calamity threatened it was the priests who walked singing through fiery embers, or led the dances which would frame the death of a human victim. But the commoners also fasted, though not so austerely, and had lacerated ears, tongue and thighs to draw forth their blood for the gods, and some followed the priest through the fire. In those experiences, when the life of the whole village was absorbed in the ritual process, men learnt that the differences between priest, lord and commoner were less important than their shared dependence on the gods, and the fragility of their human order. While the man-in-the-village-street could not be privy to the complexities of the Maya pantheon, or the bewildering permutations of the multiple calendars, he was aware that it was the priests' knowledge and the lords' largesse which, by bringing human action into harmony with the cosmos, was indispensable for the orderly and safe functioning of human life.

After the fasting came the feasting, where the abundance of fruits and meats, the richness of garments, the shining bodies confirmed that this was indeed the Land of the Turkey and the Deer. The lords' special magnificence exemplified their knowledge of distant places, and the superiority of their own. Yucatan lords on trading expeditions were preserved from the chastening vision of Aztec Tenochtitlan, massive above its lake waters: the Aztec merchants encountered at the port-of-trade Xicalango were gratifyingly eager for the honey and wax and the sumptuous weavings of the peninsula.

Along with the jade, turquoise and rare feathers which spoke of far places, the lords wore other insignia which pointed to local and shared experience. The jaguar-skin cuffs at wrist and ankle evoked at once the dangers and skills of the hunt, the triumph of the kill, the patient craft which cured the skin to suppleness, and a whole vision of lordly power, flickering between man and animal, investing each with the glamour of the other. The great murals at Bonampak, well to the south, and admittedly the product of the High Classic period, nonetheless allow us a gratefully accessible glimpse of the alchemy by which physical power is transmuted into lordly authority, in the canonicals of rule, the taut curve of muscle and mouth, the superbly balanced stance, of the Maya lord in his lordly state.[10]

The cost of all this (although it is far from clear that the Maya regarded it as a cost) was war. Those painted and plumed warriors ranked before the temple at Campeche, whose terrifying display of disciplined ferocity had sent Córdoba's men scurrying for the boats;

5 Maya lord in judgment.

those others who had killed with such efficiency on the 'coast of the
Disastrous Battle', had learnt their discipline, ferocity and efficiency
within the peninsula. War ran along the disputed boundaries between
provinces, and flared deep within enemy territory in raid or ambush.
Its incomparable excitements were memorialised in the songs and lip-
plugs and tattoos which marked a man a warrior, but also in silent
villages: a major commodity in the lords' extra-peninsular trade was
slaves, taken in internal war. Only noble captives were killed for the
gods: the rest, men, women and children, were enslaved, and the men
sold out of the country.

The lords also conducted inter-provincial trade. We are told that pilgrimage and trade conferred rights of safe passage across normally hostile territory, but the transport of locally taken slaves, given the settled depth of some hostilities and the complexities of other shifting alliances, must have been a dangerous enterprise. The 'great wars' which devasted the peninsula in the period of the Spaniards' withdrawal between 1535 and 1540 were precipitated by Nachi Cocom's killing, in a Cocom town, of all the members of a Xiu embassy *en route* to make offerings at the Sacred Cenote at Chichen Itza. That killing was in long-planned retaliation for the assassination a hundred years before of the Cocom ruler and all his male issue, save one son fortuitously absent on a trading venture, by a conspiracy of nobles led by the Xiu. Nachi Cocom's action clearly violated the furthest bounds of convention, as the eruption of the wars attests, but all trade, or more properly exchange between the lords of the major provinces must have been spiced with risk, as were the great ceremonial performances with which the exchanges were associated. We hear of 800 warriors dancing throughout a day with 'a long war-like step', of dances so significant as to draw thousands of men thirty leagues and more: I suspect these supra-provincial occasions of gift exchange and competitive dance carried much the same message (and were charged with much the same dangerous excitement) as did the alternative and violent medium of war.[11] The heady excitements of those contest occasions must have penetrated deeply back into the sustaining communities.

Montejo, familiar with the linguistic and political patchwork of the islands and Mexico, had been puzzled to encounter such sharp division among people who spoke a single tongue, but it was that shared language, or rather the shared experience it signified, which structured the chronic atomism the Spaniard found so bewildering. The people of the peninsula defined themselves and their relation-ships in terms of a series of invasions and their repercussions. The real events are misty indeed, but it seems that some time towards the end of the tenth century Yucatan was conquered by the first of several groups of intruders of Mexican origin. They called themselves the Itza, and were led by the Captain Kukulcan, the Feathered Serpent. They were remembered as establishing their rule at Chichen Itza, the 'well of the Itza'. Chichen Itza was eclipsed in the thirteenth century by the new city of Mayapan, 'the Banner of the Maya', where native Maya chiefs, acculturated Itza and other later and smaller Mexican groups like those headed by the Canul and the Xiu lineages, contrived to live in harmony, under the acknowledged rule (at least in their own account) of the Cocom. The Cocom asserted their status as 'natural lords', despising the Xiu as late-arriving foreigners, yet simultaneously laid claim to connection with the victorious invaders, an essential for the right to rule, as indicated by the Cupul lord's proud statement to Montejo 'We here are the Itza!'[12]

The fluidity of movements of peoples within and around the peninsula, the ambiguity of the archeological record and the furiously partisan stances of the different noble lineages well into the contact period precludes confident assertion, but what we seem to have here is the logically awkward but not unfamiliar claim to a double legitimacy, grounded at once in autochthonous lordship and the lustre of the stranger bent on conquest.[13] What is clear is that Mayapan was remembered as a place of harmony, the chiefs and lords of the different lineages living together within the walled city in a round of ritual, feasting and hunting, while the commoners worked in their dispersed villages to sustain the exemplary centre. Then, in about 1460, it ended, with the Xiu-led assassination of the Cocom ruler and most of his sons. The lords fled to their respective provinces, and the time of war returned.

The level of supra-provincial organisation after the diaspora remains problematic, but arrangements within any one province are clear enough. The dominant lineage provided the *halach uinic*, the hereditary head-chief of the province, and the chiefs of the dependent towns, the *batabob* (or *caciques*, as the Spaniards chose to call them), were drawn from the head-chief's or an associated lineage. Thus the Chels ruled in Ah Kin Chel, the Cocom in Sotuta, the Xiu in Mani, and so on.

These wars, alliances, betrayals were the sinews of peninsular politics. Given the Maya view of the workings of time, not only 'natural' but some human events – human events recognised by their obvious collective impact, or those more gnomic happenings, prefigured and prefiguring in their happening, which masqueraded as trivial – were held within the *katunes*. The painted books recorded wars along with floods, plagues, hurricanes and famines: one great drought, 'when the hoofs of the animals burned, when the seashore burned, a sea of misery', was manifestation and corollary of a change of rulers, as the change of rulers was corollary of the drought.[14] Thus each recurrent *katun* was identified with characteristic events, and a particular texture of experience. There was probably something of a self-fulfilling prophecy effect here: while later chroniclers may have juggled events to fit them into an appropriate *katun*, men living in a *katun* known to be characterised by conflict would move more easily to war. But its most important effect was the significance it lent to happenings in what we would see as the mundane world. Each ruling lineage cherished its history, enshrined, along with the other careful records of the movements of stars and the pulse of great winds, in the painted books they took with them when they fled from Mayapan. The histories were valued not for the celebration of the individual exploits of individual heroes, but for what those actions signified about the ultimate status of the lineages; where each stood, amidst the confusion of actual experience and the clamour of conflicting claims, in the solemn dance of time.

Throughout the colonial period individual towns jealously guarded their individual histories in their *Books of Chilam Balam*. The actual record of 'events' – if that is not too chill a word for those arcane happenings – allowing for the idiosyncratic elisions and omissions of the copyists, is remarkably similar; a kind of Ur-history lies there to be excavated. The particularity exists in the reading; in the emphasis given to the tracing of the bright thread of a particular lineage through the long tangled skein of obscure but portentous utterances.[15] The Maya view of the world, for all its intense localism, was in no way parochial: they found their particular identity only within the common frame. (It is unsurprising that intricate, subtly patterned weaving was the Maya craft *par excellence*.)

As it was for the great lineages, so it was for the lesser. Landa noted how eager commoners were to know 'the origins of their families . . . and they find this out from the priests, since this is one of their sciences, and they are very proud of the men who have been distinguished in their families'. Those who shared the same patronymic regarded themselves as members of the same family, avoiding marriage and recognising mutual obligations. (How this attitude was reconciled with inter-provincial slaving, given the wide distribution of certain patronymics, is unclear.) Each man and woman traced a double strand, as each child incorporated the mother's patronymic, their '*naal*' or 'woman' name, into their own (as in 'Na Chi' Cocom). Landa commented on what he took to be an extravagant passion for image-making, remarking there was 'not an animal or insect from which they did not make a statue': we now know that many patronymics were derived from plant, animal and insect names, and that the bewildering diversity of representations were almost certainly lineage gods. Their shared histories bound commoner and lord together. If the esoteric dimension of the history of the noble lineage was kept secret as a mark and warrant for the lord's authority, much was celebrated more accessibly in the chants and dances of the warrior house in preparation for the wars and rivalries for which it was the justification, and commoners too were intent to follow the windings and twistings of their own lineages through the great events which structured the peninsular world.[16]

For all its divisions, Maya society was tough in ways not immediately apparent. However impassable the line between noble and commoner, each was bound to the other by a multiplicity of bonds, dense, firmly knotted, and almost impossible to tear. Their shared understanding of history meant that each acted within the same arena of social knowledge, however unlike their actual experience, and saw themselves as participants in the same compelling drama.

Among non-human creatures the Maya had a special tenderness for bees, for their vulnerability (the native bee was stingless), and their symbolic equivalence to men through the ordered harmony of the hive, the idealised local community. The bees had their own god, who tended those crushed or injured should the hive be carelessly robbed. The Bacabs, the Atlas figures who sustained the four corners of the Maya world, were their special patrons, their loincloths ending in the clear oval of a bee's wing. All the gods delighted in *balche*, the mead-like drink brewed from their honey, as did men, for whom it was sacred, purging them to physical cleanliness, and through the catharsis of ritual drunkenness to social and spiritual health. The wax moths which could insinuate themselves into the hive to destroy it from within, turning its ordered vivacity to dusty ruin, haunted Maya imagination, being identified with those men who destroy the town, the human hive, by stealthy means.[17]

That sense of the mutual benefits of inter-dependence, of the enhancement of the individual through membership of a complex of groups, suggests the depth and nature of Maya attachment to collective life. Priests and lords 'ruled' not through the sumptuous remoteness of their estate, nor by coercion, nor by the engrossment of material goods, but through the multitude of small gestures and formalities which suffused Maya interactions between age and youth, male and female, and greater and lesser rank. In the shared understanding of proper precedence, in the nice calculation of the values of gifts exchanged between superior and inferior, in the throatily murmured titles, in the very intonations of speech and deferential turns of phrase, rank – which is order – was coded and celebrated.[18] Those routines were to prove durable when subjugation had swept the external material signs of rank away.

There were also deeper shared understandings, to do with the place of men within the natural order, caught up, exemplified and celebrated in collective ritual action. An outsider is struck by the insistent carnality of Maya metaphors for things vegetable; *balche* was described in the riddling *Books of Chilam Balam* as 'the green blood of my daughter', cassava as 'the thigh of the earth'. The human–vegetable identification is most complete in relation to maize, that man-dependent plant. Its phases of growth and maturation were represented as following the human curve: an ear of green maize baked in a pit was 'the girl with the watery teeth . . . Fragrant is her odour and her hair is twisted into a tuft.' The Maya admired a particular style of facial beauty, where the forehead raked back to extend the curve of the nose in a sleek unbroken line. The effect was achieved at the cost of some suffering, new-born infants' heads being routinely bound between two boards when the soft bones of the skull were at their most malleable. That graceful backward sweep was further extended on ritual occasions by headdresses, most desirably of springing green quetzal plumes. Thus human beauty echoed the elegant tapering curve of the maize cob, and the exuberant lift of its long leaves. This man-as-maize vision is seen at its most exquisite in the images of the young maize god, noble, beautiful, and as fully dependent on man for his existence as was man dependent on maize for his own. After the conquest the Maya were, atypically, to borrow a name for maize from the Spaniards: they called it 'Sacred Grace'; that by which they lived.[19]

It was this complex web of understandings which the Spanish presence was to put to the test.

11

Continuities

They did not wish to join with the foreigners; they did not desire
Christianity. They did not wish to pay tribute, did those whose emblems
were the bird, the precious stone, the flat precious stone and the jaguar, those
with the three magic emblems. Four four-hundreds of years and fifteen score
years was the end of their lives; then came the end of their lives, because they
knew the measure of their days. Complete was the month; complete, the
year; complete, the day; complete, the night; complete, the breath of life as it
passed also; complete, the blood, when they arrived at their beds, their mats,
their thrones. In due measure did they recite the good prayers; in due
measure they sought the lucky days, until they saw the good stars enter into
their reign; then they kept watch while their reign of the good stars began.
Then everything was good.

   Then they adhered to the dictates of their reason. There was no sin; in the
holy faith their lives were passed. There was then no sickness; they had then
no aching bones; they had then no high fever; they had then no smallpox;
they had then no burning chest; they had then no abdominal pains; they had
then no consumption; they had then no headache. At that time the course of
humanity was orderly.

The foreigners made it otherwise when they arrived here. They brought
shameful things when they came . . .

The Book of Chilam Balam of Chumayel

   Much of the Maya world, perilously sustained through the years of
conquest, was to change during the years of defeat. I have already
indicated the necessary effects of the dislocations of war, of
continuing, draining population loss, of the forced resettlements of
the friars. Some patterns endured, or were patiently rewoven. The
sharp division of labour between the sexes, which had borne so
heavily on each in times of war, eased the reestablishment of domestic
routines in the time of peace. The new overlords demanded the old
tribute, so that for Maya men as for Maya women the post-conquest

modes of production – techniques, work groups, work locations –
remained familiar, even if the amount of tribute and its ultimate uses
were novel.[1] For women there was still the old houseyard sociability;
the casual sharing of tasks, the easy visiting of kin: for men the
murmured greeting to familiar shapes on village paths in the chill
dark of dawn, and then the slow warming of the morning walk to the
milpa. What was more directly threatened were the structures and
expressions of the wider collectivity: essentially, the relations
between lords and commoners, and the modes of celebration of the
collective life.

The Spaniards recognised no native authority beyond the local
village or town, but at the local level they readily endorsed those local
arrangements which could be made to fit the imposed forms of
Spanish municipal government. The process of translation went
smoothly, with the *batab* assuming the office of governor, and
drawing on some of his nobles to fill lesser municipal posts. The lords
also monopolised the posts attached to the local church: because some
carried exemption from tribute; because temple service had always
been prestigious; most, because they were public positions, and
therefore at once the right and the obligation of the lords. And, as we
have seen, the friars had taken only the sons of the lords to instruct in
the mysteries of the new religion, which, fortuitously, was as the
Maya lords thought it should be.

While a few of those local offices carried official 'salaries', in the
form of the right to have commoners cultivate particular *milpas*, most
did not. With the abrupt cessation of extra-peninsular trade and intra-
peninsular warfare, the lords could no longer displace the cost of their
maintenance away from the home group, nor impress that home
group with the material trophies of lordly exchange. As early as 1552
the judge López Medel was ready to insist that no village should
support more than its prescribed number of officials: Spaniards
disapproved of indolence in others. The situation was clear. If the
lords were to survive as a group, it would be because the commoners
were willing to sustain them.

That, it seems, the commoners were prepared to do. While the
economic distance between noble and commoner groups shrank,
social distance was maintained: there was no collapse into the
egalitarianism of misery.[2] I know of only one early case in which a
village refused to sustain its governor. In 1610 the people of Tekax,
having unsuccessfully petitioned for the removal of their Spanish-
appointed governor, Pedro Xiu, launched so enthusiastic a collective

assault upon him that they were demolishing the monastery door to get at him when rescue arrived.[3] In that affair Xiu appears to have been rejected because his claim to authority was defective in traditional terms. As we will see, the trial records of 1562 give glimpses of village societies in which the lords and *principales* continued to provide the venues, the (sadly reduced) ritual paraphernalia, and the meagre fare for the ritual feasts, and to be accorded elaborate deference.

It is not immediately clear why that social division should have proved so durable, given its suddenly enhanced costs, its lack of significant institutional support, and the savage buffeting the Maya had suffered over the several decades of the conquest. If the local communities had memorialised the vicissitudes of lineage conflicts, they also celebrated a shared past in a world which held other and greater dangers than men. If war and lineage oppositions defined Maya territories, they knew that in time of famine such boundaries melted away, as social life itself dissolved, and families scattered into the forest to survive as best they could until better times came. Their collective ritual life moved to the pulse of the seasons and the production of maize, beans and squash; war, lineage feasts and other affairs of men took a subordinate place within that great context. For all its brutal enslavings, there was a conservative element in the Maya conduct of war. Only noble war captives died for the gods when the battle was over: there was nothing of Aztec prodigality here. They died for the generative power of their warrior blood, and to mark the human event of their defeat as significant in the movement of the *katun*, so revealing history within the contingent. In times of crisis human victims died, but even then a dog or other animal could sometimes replace a man: Maya deities did not demand extravagance. In war a village would be plundered for its stored food, and those villagers who could not escape into the bush were enslaved, but the dwellings were left intact and the sacred standing maize was left untouched. Attachment to steadfast routine sent many Maya back to their villages in face of the Spanish presence, but attachment to routine need not signal a cosy insulation against change, as anyone who has read John Berger's splendid 'historical afterword' to his *Pig Earth* will know. The Maya were, like Berger's peasants, wily and wary veterans of catastrophe: they knew that human societies, like human individuals, were fragile things, and that a careful frugality, a readiness to jettison the less-than-necessary, was an essential strategy for survival. And yet they were ready to sustain the lords.

The puzzle is of our own making, rooted in the post-industrial inclination to see routine, especially routine earnestly pursued, as unthinking. The Maya could remake their world because among them there were men who had studied the processes of its unmaking. Only through knowledge could the bewildering flux of events be ordered into meaning. In good times offices passed to sons; in bad any male of the noble patriline would serve, but it was essential to preserve the lineage, for their knowledge, esoteric in its restricted possession, was eminently practical in its application. In a deteriorating situation their roles as interpreters of events and devisers of strategies was recognised as crucial. In the chaos which attended the collapse of Mayapan, the lords who fled to their respective provinces carried with them their sacred books of knowledge, which only they could read. In the new crisis the books were maintained. Their 'translation' from painted glyph to European script, and the steady recording of events for the expert scrutiny which would reveal their unobvious patterning, point to the continuity of the lords' role. There we find a major diagnosis: the Spaniards were identified with the Itza, those earlier, ambivalent invaders, and their destructive, fructifying presence. That creative identification rendered the flood of novel experience intelligible in familiar terms, providing a formidable shield against cognitive and emotional demoralization. The foreigners brought disruption; before they came the Maya world was orderly, and 'everything was good'.

Then they adhered to the dictates of their reason. There was no sin; in the holy faith their lives were passed. There was then no sickness, they had then no aching bones; they had then no high fever; they had then no smallpox . . . they had then no headache. At that time the course of humanity was orderly. The foreigners made it otherwise when they arrived here . . .

With the coming of the strangers, and more particularly the strangers' god, came misery:

it was only that these priests of ours were to come to an end when misery was introduced, when Christianity was introduced by the real Christians. Then with the true God, the true *Dios*, came the beginning of our misery. It was the beginning of tribute, the beginning of church dues . . . the beginning of robbery with violence, the beginning of forced debts, the beginning of debts enforced by false testimony . . .[4]

One can see why the *Books of Chilam Balam* were so earnestly concealed from Spanish eyes. But for the Maya the recognition that the Spaniards had indeed brought a new order did not abrogate the rule of the legitimate Maya lords, but merely eclipsed it. They had endured the intrusion of the Itza, and survived through calculated accommodation. In time the strangers would withdraw, as had some of the Itza, or be absorbed as had the rest, or would be driven out: in time the native lords would rule again. Two of the *Books of Chilam Balam* which have come to light contain a set of esoteric questions and answers, called 'the Language of Zuyua'. The Language of Zuyua originated in the pre-conquest period as a sort of examination administered by the head chief to identify and remove those upstarts who had managed to infiltrate the ranks of legitimate chieftainship. The test continued to be applied, secretly, during the colonial period, and was held in reserve as one of the main weapons which would be used in the purge which would follow the return to power of the legitimate chiefs, when 'the offspring of the harlot, the two day occupant of the mat [of authority], the rogues of the reign' would be destroyed.

A distinguished analyst of the Chilam Balam books believes the test came to be seen by the natives as resembling the *residencia*, or formal accounting taken of the conduct of Spanish officials at the end of their term.[5] It certainly appears to be addressed to the Governor of Yucatan. Fifty years after the conquest Indian lords were careful to dress like Spaniards, and even sought authorisation to ride horses, despite the inconvenience of maintaining such water-hungry creatures in so parched a land. What appears to be being implemented here is a Maya strategy to bring their traditional authority structures into parallel with (and so alternative to) the Spanish system, which required some adjustment and some innovation in those traditional forms. Yet the meaning, and I would argue the purpose, of the Language of Zuyua remained obdurately Mayan. Consider the following riddle, clearly, with its reference to a 'lofty cross', a post-conquest addition to the Language. The candidate is instructed:

Bring the sun . . . bring the sun, my son, bear it on the palm of your hand to my plate. A lance is planted, a lofty cross, in the middle of its heart. A green jaguar is seated over the sun to drink its blood.

Hearts, blood, lances, jaguars: for the Maya, resonant symbols indeed, as the Great Tree of the World sustained the steady centre between the eternal power of the sun, the eternal hunger of the earth. What is actually brought? A 'very large fried egg', over which the sign of the cross has been made, with a green chile pepper sitting beside it.[6] To us, there is something a touch pathetic in those grand images being contained in such lowly domestic objects, especially given our general reluctance to endow vegetables with much significance. For the Maya, to handle their daily food was to hold the sacred in the palm of the hand. Given that unbreakable connection between the sacred and the mundane, the reduction of their repertoire of ritual objects through the loss of exotic imports would not bear too heavily. Further, in a society where knowledge was power the concealment of the highly significant in the apparently mundane must have been intensely gratifying to those who held the secret key to understanding. European institutions could also be used more directly for the prosecution of distinctively Maya ends. Disputes between communities over land, settled in the pre-contact period by war, or by intervention of the head-chief, were after the conquest taken to Spanish law. Ralph Roys has traced one such struggle over a strip of (nearly worthless) land which was pursued with much guile over 182 years – from 1638 to 1820 – and which accumulated seventy-nine folios of careful penmanship by puzzled Spanish officials.[7]

Even in performances overtly Christian, complacently watched by Spaniards diverted by their colour and by the unusual vivacity of the Indians, the patterns and rhythms of the old ceremonies seem rather too insistent for their presence to be naive. When the Franciscan Commissary toured Yucatan in 1588 he was gratified by the enthusiastic and uncoerced welcomes he received in village after village; the showers of fruit, of turkeys, of flowers; the dances, both 'in the fashion of Castile and of this country', presented for his delectation. How far did traditional inter-village and inter-provincial rivalries fuel those extravagances? The entertainments, too, were autonomously devised, one 'ancient dance' proving particularly popular:

the Indians brought out to welcome him a strange device and it was: litter-like frames and upon them a tower round and narrow, in the manner of a pulpit, of more than two *varas* in height, covered from top to bottom with pieces of painted cotton, with two flags on top, one on each side. In this pulpit, visible from the waist up, was an Indian very well and nicely dressed, who with rattles of the country in one hand, and with a feather fan in the other, facing the Father Commissary, without ceasing made gestures and whistled to the beat of a *teponastle* [log drum] that another Indian near the litter was playing among many who sang to the same sound, making much noise and giving shrill whistles; six Indians carried this litter and tower on their shoulders, and even these also went dancing and singing, doing steps and the same dancing tricks as the others, to the sound of the same *teponastle*: it was very sightly that tower, very tall and was visible from afar by being so tall and painted. This dance and device in that language is called *ʒono* and is what was used in ancient times . . .

The distance of the account, its careful precision of description, indicates how little sense the recording friar could make of it, but he did note that 'great crowds of Indians came to see that dance as well as to see the Father Commissary'.[8]

In Landa's account of the pre-conquest festival of the month Pax, when the lords and priests of the lesser villages came together with 'those of the more important towns', the *nacom*, or chosen war-captain, was especially venerated, being carried in a plumed litter between his house and the temple, with much offerings of food and drink and incense and a special warrior dance. One part of the ceremony involved a long address delivered by the *nacom* to all the lords and priests of the towns, as he distributed incense and charged them to perform the required festivals to the gods each in their own village, and then, 'with the sermon ended, they all took leave of each other with great affection and hubbub, and each went home to his town and family'. We can't be sure just what the Indian in the tall pulpit was up to, but we may recall Cogolludo's noting of the Indians' audacity (lampooning their parish priest before his face) where they could be reasonably confident that Spaniards would not understand them. (He also records the Indians' continuing veneration for the 'singer' in charge of their traditional songs.)[9] It is easy to romanticise every casual gesture into an act of native resistance, but for the Yucatan Maya we have strong evidence of their taste for riddling messages, and their deliberate and conscious endeavours to sustain their own accounts of things.

They were also intent on making their own selection of what they would incorporate from their new overlords. It is that process of selection and incorporation which must now be examined.

12

Assent

It is most necessary to believe this. These are the precious stones which our Lord, the Father, has abandoned. This was his first repast, this *balche*, with which we, the ruling men revere him here. Very rightly they worshipped as true gods these precious stones, when the true God was established, our Lord God, the Lord of heaven and earth, the true God. Nevertheless, the first gods were perishable gods. Their worship came to its inevitable end. They lost their efficacy by the benediction of the Lord of Heaven, after the redemption of the world was accomplished, after the resurrection of the true God, the true Dios, when he blessed heaven and earth. Then was your worship abolished, Maya men. Turn away your hearts from your old religion.

The Book of Chilam Balam of Chumayel

I have suggested how their shared understanding of the past enabled the Maya to confront a dangerous present and a problematical future with something close to equanimity, and to experience subjugation without relinquishing their sense of autonomy. The *Books of Chilam Balam* were not only products of that stance, but also crucial vehicles for its maintenance. López Medel had noted in 1552 how obstinately the Maya lords continued to call their people together for secret meetings for the worship of their idols and the celebration of their histories, and that same complaint echoed down through the century and beyond. In 1603 a Yucatan-born secular cleric was sufficiently scandalised by what he saw as organised, deliberate idolatry to write a long address to the Crown on the matter. Second-generation 'Christians', he said, pursued their old rituals under cover of night, or even vanished into the bush for 'three and four weeks at a time', drinking *balche*, feasting, adoring their idols, chanting their histories, in company with their friends and neighbours, either in their *milpas* or in any one of the many hidden caves. He was not the first Spaniard to believe that the landscape itself somehow conspired to protect the Maya from proper supervision, proper control. (In fact, he wistfully recalled the vigorous punitive activities of Diego de Landa, who he thought had had the knack of handling Indians.)[1] But it is only in this century that we have really grasped just how tenacious the Maya were in the performance of their 'histories', both through the discovery of those few *Books of Chilam Balam*, and from the work of anthropologists among present-day Indian communities. Here, reference to the ethnographic present produces some very interesting hypotheses indeed. Allen Burns, working in the remote villages of what is now Quintana Roo, in the far south-east of the peninsula, has watched the descendants of the Caste War insurgents continue to celebrate their high sense of separateness and autonomy in great annual ceremonies, at which their shared history is expounded and interpreted in prolonged performances by specially trained and specially respected old men. Burns has brilliantly elucidated the ways in which the histories have been developed into a coherent cultural system, modelling and interpreting the modern world as experienced by the Maya, and providing modes of evaluating past and future action. He also describes the meetings at which the performances take place as 'times of unification and intensification' for the several thousand Maya who attend.[2]

I suspect that the tradition of the celebration of the community through the celebration of its history has very long roots, and that the meetings Burns describes found their origins in the immediate post-conquest period, when the pressures of the conquest situation led to a 'democratization of participation' in what had previously been the rather more private celebrations of the lords. The history of the dominant lineage, always known in outline to the commoners, was transformed into a statement and a developing account of the identity of the local community, while the story of the taming and final incorporation of other earlier invaders provided a mode for the interpretation and the management of Spanish actions. Thus through the histories of the *Chilam Balam* – still after the conquest what they had been before it, scripts for dramatic action – the Maya were able to reflect upon, to annotate, and to make collective sense of their experiences.

The notion that human affairs were cradled in the great swings of the *katunes*, and that the people who belonged to the land would contrive to endure, was attested by the landscape itself. Like all agriculturalists the Maya lived according to the rhythm of the yearly agricultural cycle and the lesser growing cycles it contained. The seasons were strongly marked: during April, the sun burned hotter and more cruelly day after day, until, at last, the flying ants began to swarm, signalling the crashing thunder which announced the coming of the Chacs, with their life-giving rain. But that yearly cycle was embedded in larger cycles. As a *milpa* could be planted for only two or three seasons before the yields grew too light and the scrubby forest regrowth too stubborn, each man tended *milpas* at different stages of their cycle, marking out a careful space in the forest at one place, and beginning the hard labour of felling the larger trees; gathering what he knew to be the last crop in another. All around him were the signs of this endless process: the blackened patch of a *milpa* being created; the dim shapes of *milpas* in the course of reclamation by the forest. Even the tallest forest, he knew, had been *milpa* once, and would be *milpa* again. Those cycles within cycles the priests could discern in the majestic wheelings of the stars could also be read by the commoner, for they were inscribed by his own hands upon the land.

Human settlement told the same story. The little temporary hamlets of the times of peace, when population growth had forced the dispersal of *milpas* beyond the tolerance even of Maya legs, and the more desperate enterprises in times of war, had left their own soft tracings on the landscape. All around were the signs of those brief habitations, in the slowly collapsing wattle-and-daub huts, or the slight elevations which marked the housemounds on which they had once stood. Then there were the great stone structures, thrusting up through the forest, testifying to the grander habitations of the past. Some of the ruins were of cities the Maya knew from their myths, like Mayapan, Chichen Itza, Uxmal; and recalled past conflict, past harmony, past invasions. They spoke also of continuities and relationships which the Maya knew to be eternal: the masks of familiar deities – the squinting glare of Sun-Eye-Lord, the tender grace of the Maize God, the gaping maw of Crocodile House – and the stone representation of a simple commoner's hut, framed in the mighty façade of a palace at Uxmal, marking an earlier recognition by the elevated of its interdependence with the lowly. As Indians under Spanish orders dragged the shaped carved stones from the ruins of Tiho to build the city the Spaniards called Mérida, or destroyed a pyramid to make a monastery, it is likely that the lesson they drew was not that intended, of the singularity and permanence of the new regime, but rather its identification as one in a series of other, similar and transitory episodes.

Much of what seems puzzling in the glimpses we have of Maya behaviour in the early days of colonization is rendered intelligible by this reading. Nachi Cocom, the formidable territorial chief of Sotuta, and long a mighty fighter against the Spaniards, nevertheless was ready to discuss matters of religion with the young friar Diego de Landa: was that as part of an exchange between men of special wisdom versed in high matters? In 1545 Cocom carried out a prudent survey of the borders of his province. Although he and most of his entourage were then unbaptised, he readily utilised crosses as his boundary markers.[3] Maya land maps of the sixteenth century, like that accompanying the Mani land treaty of 1557, retain the distinctive Maya circular form with the significant direction of the east to the top of the page, but crosses identify boundaries, the churches identify villages.[4] Through the landscape itself crosses proliferated; in private houses, in front of churches, at village entrances, along the roads, at the corners of *milpas*. There is little to indicate the Maya were responsive to the specifically Christian resonances of the cross at that early stage: rather, it seems the cross was appropriated to mark out, as idols and images had once done, significant locations and boundaries in the Maya map of the experienced world, just as it had been utilised, under Spanish direction, to designate locations and boundaries in the painted maps of that world. As early as 1560 we find the genealogy of the Xiu represented in the form of the 'Tree of Jesse', springing from the loins of the founder of the dynasty Hun Uitzil Chac. Bearded, he wears the turquoise diadem and bears the fan of office, while his wife kneels behind him as a Maya wife should. The sophistication of the borrowing suggests the hand of Gaspar Antonio Chi, raised from boyhood by the friars, but it also indicates a ready responsiveness to a foreign form for the expression of a Maya passion for genealogy.[5]

López Medel had been as much puzzled as outraged to find that native lords, obstinately persistent in their traditional rituals, also set up illicit schools and churches, where they pretended to teach the Christian doctrine to their followers, and to baptise and marry them with a fine disregard for the friars' monopoly in that area: were those lords doing no more than maintaining their traditional role as custodians and administrators of knowledge and social proprieties? He also complained of others who, while urging commoners to hide their children to protect them from the dangerous rite of baptism, themselves contrived to be baptised time and again: were these men sorcerer–priests, 'men of power' who having recognised on excellent empirical grounds the danger of the rite (for did not the ailing children and adults the friars rushed to baptise usually die?) nevertheless submitted themselves to it again and again, to test and augment their own spiritual force? To penetrate further into how the Maya lords discharged their distinctive responsibilities in the new situation of the Spanish regime, what meanings they discerned in the friars' preachings, and how those meanings were changed in the grasping, we must enter the area of experience briefly, ambiguously revealed in the testimonies of 1562: the incomparably expressive world of ritual action.

Before that world of ritual action can be explored, a ghost needs to be laid. Historians have largely agreed with Landa and the Council of the Indies that the Maya did indeed continue human sacrifice, with Christian embellishments, the Yucatan episode often being cited as a particularly bizarre example of a naive native response to Christian teachings. That is, they accept the human sacrifice confessions as by and large accurate descriptions of actual events.[6] Yet there are at least as many good arguments against that conclusion as for it: indeed rather more, as I hope I can demonstrate. Here I have to engage in a little of that detective work historians find engrossing, but others can find tedious: readers in the latter category might choose to skip the next few pages.

If we accept the testimonies as true, what does that entail regarding the total number of Indians sacrificed? If the Hocaba-Homun confessions are left out of account as suspect, having been collected by men with a strong motive for finding confirmatory evidence for Landa's human sacrifice stories, we are left with thirty-two confessions from seven villages all within Sotuta province. Those thirty-two were only a fraction of the confessions actually heard, and we do not know Landa's criteria for selecting them to be recorded.[7] They are not exhaustive, even for particular villages, the last witness from any one village often revealing sacrifices not previously mentioned. And the men whose confessions we have were small fry, in no position to know the full extent of sacrificial activity even in their own area. There are many discrepancies between the accounts (usually explained by faulty memory or prudent amnesia) but in so far as we can establish particular cases it would seem at a conservative count from those thirty-two confessions alone that at least 101 people died in just those seven villages over a five-year period.[8] Given that the confessions cover only a small area, and that imperfectly, we have to assume that the 'real' figure would be very much higher. Can we believe that so many human sacrifices could take place, and so many individuals vanish, with neither ceremonies nor disappearances coming to the attention of Spaniards or 'loyal' Indians? Then there is the problem of the provenance of victims. With war captives no longer available, the victims were usually said to be children, sometimes purchased but sometimes stolen from neighbouring villages. Ought we to believe Francisco Na of Mopila when he claimed that on three occasions the slaughtered bodies of children sacrificed in Mopila ceremonies were smuggled back to their home village of Sahcaba and flung into the *cenote* – presumably so that the bodies should later be discovered by the horrified villagers?[9] Could the conspiracy of silence have survived such exacerbations with no murmur of complaint or attempted revenge reaching Spanish ears? Could the tensions generated by the large-scale raiding necessary to provide so many child and other victims have failed to re-ignite the profound, historically based antagonisms, as between the Xiu of Mani and the Sotuta Cocom, both of whom were said to have permitted, encouraged and conspired to perform human sacrifices? As late as 1557, five years before the trials, Nachi Cocom prudently found himself too ill to participate in the meeting and the feasting accompanying the formulation of the Mani land treaty, either fearing treachery, having himself killed a Xiu lord in similar circumstances twenty years before, or not wishing to assent to the treaty by taking part in the feast, a more significant act for the Maya than all the Spanish oaths and signings. (The Xiu understood, and set guards along the boundary with Sotuta.)[10] Given that wariness, it is difficult to accept the active cooperation claimed for 1562.

The alternative theory as advanced by the Indians and accepted by Toral, that the testimonies were concocted, has its attractions. It has been challenged on the ground that there are too many discrepancies between accounts for them to have been deliberate and agreed fictions. But even were they totally concocted we could not expect total accord on every or perhaps even most details. Men still covered in the sweat of anguish are not likely to recollect precisely all that has been wrung from them. Nor would it be easy for their listeners, waiting their own turn, to commit to memory all they heard in those stressful circumstances. However, if each piece of information in each confession is tabulated – a tedious process, although made easier by the formulaic sequence of questions put by the interrogator – an intriguing pattern is revealed. (Here the analysis depends on sequence, and assumes the testimonies to have been taken in the order in which we have them, but internal evidence supports that assumption.)[11] To take the confessions of Indians from Sotuta village recorded on the first day of the enquiry: what we find is a high degree of concordance between the first and third confessions, and between the second and the fourth – although the fourth also incorporates some fragments from the first and the third confessions. This pattern is completely compatible with the Indians' claim that each witness when returned to the gaol strove to recollect what he had said, which material was discussed by the others, but which could not benefit the next Indian taken immediately for the recording of his confession. Again, in the Usil testimonies we find the same pool of names of victims being drawn on by different witnesses, although ascribed to different sacrifices, while the last witness from Tibolon drew on the names provided by the witness questioned before him, but distributed them differently.[12]

Another pattern reinforcing the 'concoction' hypothesis becomes increasingly clear when the testimonies collected over the last days of the enquiry are analysed. There was a noticeable simplification, a streamlining, within each individual testimony – even when that simplification entailed reduced conformity between witnesses. For example, each of the last two witnesses from Sotuta village testified that the bodies of all victims had been thrown into one specified *cenote* – but each named a different *cenote*.[13] This patterning at least suggests the possibility that Indians initially anxious to achieve some concordance between largely fabricated testimonies recognised as the enquiry progressed that their interrogator was not concerned with corroboration, so they accordingly simplified their individual accounts.

Finally, what is perhaps the most suggestive of those obscure patternings centres around what we could call the '*cenote* theme'. Before the 1562 material came to light, scholars had agreed that traditionally only the Sacred Cenote at Chichen Itza was offered living victims. The 1562 testimonies mention living victims being cast into the Sacred Cenote, but they also tell of corpses being thrown into its depths, and of other corpses, some still on the crosses on which they had been crucified, being thrown into other *cenotes*: for example, the *cenote* at Tabi, a deserted village, was said to have received ten bodies, five of them on crosses, in the space of one or perhaps two months, while twelve bodies were said to have been thrown into Akula *cenote* over a two-month period.[14] That kind of information has led some scholars to postulate the efflorescence of a '*cenote* cult', and to suggest the reported crucifixions were indeed authentic, and were associated with worship of the rain gods, springing from Maya identification of the Christian cross with their own symbol for the *Yax-cheel-cab*, the First Tree of the World.[15] That identification with at least some forms of the Cross I think was made, but there are immediate difficulties with the '*cenote*-cult' hypothesis.[16] Not all corpses cast into *cenotes* had suffered preliminary crucifixion, while others had been killed in the course of some other ritual exercise. It is not clear why rain gods – especially the great gods of Chichen Itza – should have been gratified by the offering of bodies already dead, whose hearts had been excised and burnt in ceremonies elsewhere. The rejection of such debased offerings could have disastrous consequences.

I acknowledge that in such matters our notion of logic is a treacherous guide. More telling is the actual sequence of the '*cenote*' confessions. On the first day of the recording of the confessions, the first witness to mention a *cenote* other than the Sacred Cenote at Chichen Itza and to claim it had received the body of a victim was Francisco Chuc from Sahcaba. The only other witness from Sahcaba, interrogated immediately after Chuc, gave burial as the mode of disposal. Through the rest of the first day's testimonies there was no further mention of any cenote save that at Chichen Itza. On the next day, 12 August, the first witness testified that corpses of victims were buried. From that point on – for the rest of that day, *and for all the rest of the confessions* – all witnesses who gave information on the disposal of bodies claimed they had been thrown into wells, *cenotes*, or in one case, a 'cave'. Burial was not mentioned again. What are we dealing with here? The forced disclosure of a flourishing *cenote* cult? Or a random invention seized on by desperate Indians, and converted into a convenient formula?

But even if the *cenote* cult appears to be a fiction built on a fiction – a historian's creation built on the inventions of Indians – that is not to say that sacrifices and crucifixions did not occur, or that bodies were never thrown into *cenotes*. Again, the odd variations in the ritual behaviour described in the confessions – that in Sotuta village human sacrifice with preliminary crucifixion was said to have been practised for five years, while Yaxcaba, also under the jurisdiction of the Cocom brothers, got around to human sacrifice only three months before the enquiry, and to crucifixion not at all; that in Sotuta province there was a heavy infusion of 'Christian' elements into ritual performances, while in adjacent Hocaba-Homun traditionalism flourished unchallenged – need not imply that the confessions were false. Perhaps they were simply incomplete, and so failed to reveal actual conformity of behaviour. Or perhaps we ought not to expect conformity at all. In times of such acute stress might we not more reasonably expect ambivalence within groups, ambivalence within individuals; nervous experimentation juxtaposed with anxious conservatism?

Here it is necessary to tread warily. We know that both during and after the conquest the Maya suffered great population losses, with many of the survivors made refugees, and most made subject to foreign overlords.[17] In those circumstances of social and psychological disruption we would expect some transformation of traditional roles, some uneasy and partial accommodations, some exaggerations and deformations of traditional practices. If human sacrifices before the conquest were high and solemn affairs, required only in times of special danger or calamity, and hedged around with elaborate ceremonial, ought we to be surprised to find the exigencies of the post-conquest situation had stripped away much of the ritual, and that sacrificial occasions had multiplied, as the Maya sought desperately to reestablish communication with their silent gods and order in their disordered world? Perhaps the sufferings and dislocations of those years had burnt away old loyalties, old hatreds, the old bases of group identifications. Perhaps imposed churches could replace proscribed temples as sacred places. And perhaps, when warriors could no longer test their prowess in war, they could display their stealth and swiftness in stealing children, to honour the old gods, or, perhaps, to offer them, in confusion and anxiety, to the new.

Perhaps. And there, of course, is the rub. A 'cultural derangement' theory comfortably accommodates any and all variations in behaviour, and projects us through the door into a hall-of-mirrors world of endlessly multiplying possibilities. The job is to restrict those exuberant possibilities down to probabilities.

Let me say now that the testimonies, however strenuously analysed, will not yield firm answers on all questions of fact. But they will reveal what the Maya certainly did on some occasions, and, from that, what they very probably did on other occasions, and what they – probably – meant by what they did.

Idolatry considered

To begin with what is least problematical in the testimonies: the so-called 'idolatry' confessions, with their accounts of the ritual killing of animals, and the offering of food and drink to the idols of the old faith. The Indians confessed to those activities freely – that is, before even being threatened with torture – and never repudiated them, although they complained that under torture they had exaggerated the number of idols they owned. So the idolatry dimension of the confessions remains uncontested, and may be taken as providing reasonably accurate descriptions of at least some of the things Indians were doing.

The descriptions are truncated. The interrogators were little interested in these routine offences, and probably cut short elaborations. But a sufficiently clear composite picture can be reconstructed from the fragments to identify general patterns.[18] Christian churches, church patios and church cemeteries were used as venues for the action. The structures conveniently echoed the traditional spaces of temple and temple courtyard. When the ritual required enclosed space – to dramatise exclusivity and solemnity rather than secrecy, there being little secret in the narrow confines of a village – the chief, *ah-kines* and lords could withdraw into the 'church', a thatched building in the native style, save, perhaps, for a stone chancel. The larger open spaces of patio or cemetery were used for more public ceremonies, and for the feasting which concluded most ritual occasions. For Christians church ground was rendered permanently holy by once-and-for-all consecration. For the Maya the sacred space had to be created, by ritual cleansing, and then by the assembling of sacred objects. We can see that being done, however jerkily, from the odd snapshots of Maya action we have. There is the first process of concentration in the gathering of the lords – including those sons of lords the Spaniards thought of as Christian schoolmasters. To that assemblage were brought the idols, carried in from their dispersed hiding places in the forest to the house of the chief. Then idols and lords together made sacred the church patio, with the idols clustered about the patio cross, or penetrated the dark interior, where the idols would be ranged upon the altar. Then the idols were offered, essentially, food: vegetable food in the form of special breads; drink, whether the sweet fermented *balche* or Spanish wine; most often the bloody heart of an animal, burned to wreathing smoke, or smeared fresh into and around the mouths. Then, the gods fed, the assembled men ate and drank in their turn. Thus right and essential order was at once displayed and celebrated.

While care was taken to conceal these ceremonies from the Spaniards, there seems to have been an assumption of complete security from Indian betrayal. The risk of Spanish intervention clearly increased with time. Juan Couoh, the schoolmaster appointed to Yaxcaba, recalled a ceremony of seven years before, when there would have been no friars in the area, as a very public and uninhibited affair. (What we note is that the villagers were certainly not inhibited by Couoh's own presence, a new teacher only one year out of his mission schooling.) He remembered that 'all the [male] natives of the village brought fifty idols assembled at the chief's house to the church, and there offered them a deer. . . tortoises and other things . . . and they got drunk on the native wine and ate the flesh of the animals they offered there'. By contrast the killing of a dog in the church a mere month before had been stealthy, as the friars' inquisition was already under way in Mani.[19] But still there was no indication that the worshippers feared betrayal from within.

This carries an implication regarding the effective unity of village communities. The Maya had been protected from certain kinds of blandishments from their Spanish overlords. Lay Spaniards neither sought nor found those marginal men so often recruited to serve foreign masters, as they chose to use their own Negro slaves brought from Europe or their Mexican auxiliaries as agents for their dealings with Indians. Maya chiefs were too poor to be seduced by the desire for European goods, scarce enough in that poor land. Still, the solidarity of the communities is unusual. The best evidence for any disaffection comes from the Maya themselves, with the anxiety expressed in the *Books of Chilam Balam* regarding 'upstart' rulers, the 'two-day occupants of the mat'. From the outside, Maya society looks remarkably united. There are chilling examples of the deliberate stimulation of inter-generational hostility in Mexico, where youths were taught by the friars to terrorise their elders, and Landa was later to claim something of the same success in Yucatan, remarking that mission-taught lads notified their masters of 'acts of idolatry or . . . drunken orgies', despite threats from their own people. We lack any other evidence of such activities. Neither the motives nor the status of the youths who initiated the whole enquiry by their discovery and report of the Mani cave can now be retrieved. They may have been pursuing some personal vendetta, without realisation of the possible consequences, or they may have been, at that stage of their lives, most detached from their old loyalties, and therefore, at least for the time, most amenable to co-optation by the friars. (Their claim to have discovered the cave by accident must have been believed, as they were not punished for keeping evil things secret; this suggests their role in native society was peripheral.)[20] Many Indians of course, had assisted the enquiry as interpreters and constables, how voluntarily we do not know, and some Indians under torture had denounced their chiefs. Yet when Bishop Toral returned the chiefs to their offices no hint of retribution or vengeance came to Spanish ears. The villages settled their affairs silently. Was no vengeance taken on the collaborators because the Maya had learnt that torture and the dread of torture can rip confessions from anyone? (I am reminded of a woman member of the French Resistance, interviewed after the war, being asked if she felt contempt for the colleague who had betrayed her under torture. She answered that she felt closer to someone, anyone, who had undergone torture than to someone, anyone, who had not.)

The confessions describe chiefs, *ah-kines* and *principales* fulfilling their traditional roles, though with more interchangeability than our perhaps too simple reconstructions of pre-conquest ceremonies would have us expect. The *ah-kines* were not always local. Nor were they always old men. In several of the ceremonies the role of *ah-kin* was played by the 'Christian' schoolmaster. Indeed, one schoolmaster admitted to have begun his training as an *ah-kin* only after taking charge of his school.[21]

That chiefs and lords should be involved in sacrifices and should direct them is what we would expect, given both the traditional high involvement of what we designate secular authority in matters religious, and the higher survival rate of chiefs over the *ah-kines* in the period of the war, the latter being singled out by the Spanish soldiery both in the military and the later phase of 'pacification'. That the schoolmasters should also be deeply involved is also what we would expect, given Maya understandings of the social order. The friars had taken the sons of lords for special training, and that group was traditionally defined by its custodianship of esoteric knowledge. In Maya eyes it was fitting that the sons of lords and only the sons of lords should have access to the new knowledge, and discretionary control over its dissemination to commoners. The Franciscans' frugality in housing the boys of any one province together and letting them be served by their own retainers was probably a costly economy, as it must have helped sustain the old bonds.

The schoolmasters' role in sustaining the traditional order is made clear by their involvement in the transcription of the *Books of Chilam Balam*, but their recall to old loyalties could not always be achieved without strain. I have already suggested that the Yaxcaba schoolmaster Juan Couoh was probably speaking both less and more than the truth in his confession before Landa: less in that he claimed he had attended only one human sacrifice, and that one under coercion (his fellow-schoolmaster claimed Couoh had been present at two others, in each of which two boys had died); more in that he responded to Landa's emotional and dramatic requirements in producing a reasonable facsimile of a Christian martyr in his description of the victim Francisco Cauich. Nonetheless, Couoh's account of the interchanges between the members of the village elite is compelling. He might not have played the role he claimed on that particular night, but whether a similar scene had occurred on some earlier occasion, or whether it was a composite of scenes which he participated in or observed, the relationships he sketches carry a powerful sense of authenticity.

Couoh reported that he was summoned to attend his chief at his house 'in the middle of the night'. (He added that it was a Tuesday: schoolmasters kept account of the Christian calendar.) He obeyed without demur, which suggests the force of chiefly authority, and found gathered there several notables, including four *ah-kines*, and (as we discover from later testimonies) those other men of the village who could read European script. They had been summoned with what appears to have been deliberate formality to decipher a letter – a letter from the head chief Lorenzo Cocom, urging resistance to the friars and the continued worship of the old gods. Their immediate business was the sacrifice of a youth in the village church.

What follows is a poignant glimpse of a contest of loyalties which must have been played out many times in many villages. The contest was one-sided: the chief, mixing cajolery with threat, reminded Couoh of the obligations he owed his lord, and jeered at his inclination to submit to the friars. In an echo of the Franciscans' habituated idiom, he told the young man 'you cannot be their son, and they do not have to consider you as their son . . .'. The friars stood irretrievably outside and beyond the webs of filial duty and reciprocal obligation which bound Maya to Maya. And Spanish authority was far away. Couoh, not a native of the village, and so bereft of the protection of immediate kin, reminded of the respect due to age and to rank, and moved by a prudent concern for his own skin, yielded – and proceeded with the rest to the church, and to the sacrifice.

If 'Christian' locations and 'Christian' personnel were being reclaimed for Maya use, what is to be made of the 'Christian' objects sometimes integrated in the ritual performance? Candles are often mentioned. Despite the sacred status of bees, and of the *balche* made from their honey, wax seems to have had no ceremonial use before the coming of the Spaniards, but the Maya showed an early and continuing liking for candles. A modern anthropologist reveals that one highland Maya group, impressed by their slow, mysterious, steady self-consumption, have named candles 'the tortillas of the gods', and it was probably the same measured material diminution as much as the light they shed which gratified the sixteenth-century Maya.[22] The *ak-kin* Francisco Chuc of Sahcaba tells us how in one ritual a mixture of Castilian wine, honey and water was offered to four idols brought in from the *milpa* when rain was needed, the men then capping the wells 'in the manner of fasting, so that the idols would provide them with water for the milpas'. Here again, the Maya enjoyed Spanish wine, and probably thought the gods would too. But the next episode Chuc went on to describe involved the use of a more highly charged Christian symbol, in a more deliberately symbolic way. It seems the desired rain had still not fallen, so a few days later a further offering was made. The same small group of village leaders met in the church and killed a pig – probably not a Spanish pig but a peccary, one of the tough local breed the Maya had often used in rituals. No account is given of how the pig was killed, or of what became of its heart or flesh, but Chuc said the men took a small crucifix from the altar and set it to burn, along with six little sticks. Then the *ah-kin* twice thrust the burning cross into the opened belly of the pig so that the flames were quenched in the animal's blood.[23]

What did the men intend by this curious performance? The Maya had responded easily to the spare, simple, quadrilateral shape of the great crosses raised in the church patios and cemeteries, accepting them as markers for their own sacred locations, and as sacred objects in themselves: idols were clustered around them, and many witnesses admitted to making offerings to the patio crosses for rain. The association was almost certainly with their own stylised 'Great Tree of the World', with its Four Directions. (Later, in the great Maya uprising of the mid nineteenth century, crosses emerged as independent deities, gifted with speech, and addressed as 'Lord Saint Cross'.)[24] Few of the patio crosses of the sixteenth century bore any representation of the crucified Christ: in most, a stylised face appeared at the junction of the arms. But one historian of ecclesiastical architecture notes an interesting exception: the large cross now housed inside the church at Mani, and almost certainly its original patio cross, bears the drooping body of the Christ.[25]

I think the Maya initially distinguished sharply between those great 'architectural' crosses, and smaller crosses and crucifixes, understand-

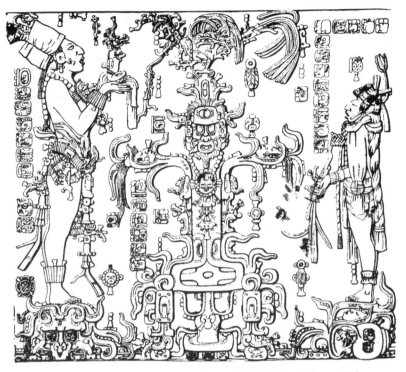

6 The 'Great Tree of the World', Panel of the Foliated Cross, Palenque.

ing them quite differently. Chuc's account is only one of several in which it was admitted that small crosses were 'taken from the altar and burned', probably not so much 'to mock them and hold them in little account', as Landa complained in his general indictment, but to remove an undesired object from ritual space. Were the Maya aware that the altar crosses were sacramental, and so 'belonged' to the friars in a way the architectural crosses outside did not? Probably not, although it would be unwise to underestimate Maya sophistication. But small crosses, most especially crucifixes, were habitually worn and handled by the friars, and so were intimately associated with them. The ritual action Chuc describes appears to be *Tupp Kak*, 'Killing the fire', a rite in which fire was quenched with animal blood as the smouldering *milpa* fires would be quenched by the onset of the rains.[26] If so, the 'cross' is reduced to the status of kindling, or at least to that of redundant wooden object.

Just how the Maya understood the 'Christianity' preached by the friars is an issue for later discussion. But what seems clear is that the traditional offerings described in the 1562 testimonies, whether performed inside churches or not, were made in a mood unequivocally anti-Spanish and anti-friar. The *ah-kin* of Yaxcaba was said to have exhorted his fellow villagers who had gathered to sacrifice the dog, when the inquisition was already well under way, to cling fast to their old ways, for 'what [the friars] preached about was not God nor would they stay in the land and they would leave soon . . . and their gods of clay they had there were true gods . . .'. The priest also urged that they should not yield up their real idols to 'the friars who would come from Mani', but to give them 'only the pieces and broken ones' – on the orders of Lorenzo Cocom, head chief of the province since the death of his brother Nachi Cocom.[27]

The implication is clear: the rulers of the lesser towns of Sotuta were under instruction to sustain the old rituals even under increasing risk, and to resist the incursions of the friars. Here two questions arise. Was part of that instruction that human sacrifices be performed? And did the head-chief of the province, the Cocom, have additional and different obligations in the matter by virtue of his rank?

Human sacrifice considered

Juan Couoh's account of the killing of Francisco Cauich is powerfully persuasive. It also conforms to the patterns already established, in that the church served as the enclosed location, made sacred by the mats, the leaves, the candles, the white cloths, and above all by the physical congregation of the idols. It is also likely that the victim's tears called forth a 'traditional' reassurance from the chief, whose words, allowing for the distortions of translation, faintly echo those of the exhortation traditionally addressed to a warrior victim, garlanded, painted, and awaiting the moment of death. Cauich reports the chief as addressing the bound victim thus: 'Strengthen and console yourself because what we are doing to you now is not an evil thing nor are we casting you into an evil place or into hell, but to heaven and to paradise according to the customs of our ancestors.' The chant runs:

> Make tranquil your spirit, beautiful youth.
> You go to look upon the face of your Father in the high place . . .
> Enspirit yourself, and think only of your Father
> do not be frightened.
> It is not evil which will be done to you . . .[28]

We lack the original Mayan of the testimony, but there is enough concordance to suggest at least a connection. This is not, or not necessarily, to say the report was authentic, but only that Couoh, a mere seventeen years after the conquest, knew the chant as a correct mode of address to a victim, and brought it into play. (The victim's reported response was, of course, notably untraditional.) The method of sacrifice, by excision of the heart, was a traditional procedure. The detail, the dramatic flow of events, the fragments of direct speech, are eminently believable. But was the boy killed, and, if he were, what did that killing signify to the killers? Here we must explore what 'sacrifice' meant to the Maya; what relationship with the gods they assumed and enacted, and, given the admitted continuation of animal sacrifices, how they evaluated human as against other forms of life.

The difficulties in the way of understanding are formidable. We have somehow to detach ourselves from our Christian-drenched notions of 'sacrifice' as the offering up of something of value – comfort, possessions, bodily integrity, life – as a token of submission or propitiation before a notably jealous and watchful personal god. Even more difficult, we must reconsider the clear distinction we (and the Spanish friars) draw between human, and animal and vegetable life. We cannot assume the Maya shared in those notions so 'natural' to us. For the friars, the killing of a human was a supreme offence. (Though for them, as in all cultures, there were killings and killings: they had killed with sufficient deliberation close to 160 people merely in the interests of determining the precise extent of their already admitted idolatry.) The killing of a human for a god, despite or because of the 'sacrifice' of Christ, was blasphemous in the deepest sense. Further, in their interrogations, and in their translations and recording of the confessions – as in their whole endeavour to understand Indian behaviour – the friars had only their own language, formulated out of their own cultural concepts, through which to express Indian actions. So they spoke of 'offering sacrifices to the idols', and they unreflectively identified the moment of killing as the climactic point in their highly selective reporting of the sequence of Indian actions. All the rest of the action they 'knew' to be a mere prelude or sequel to that consummatory act.

The problem of grasping, or even imagining radically alternative meanings might be clearer if we consider an apparently very simple little slice of ritual. An Indian from the village of Tibolon casually mentioned that 'every Sunday [the Indians] burned copal in the village church to the idols that were there'.[29] What do we make of this routine action? The 'every Sunday' is interesting: in this activity at least they follow the Christian calendar. But what do they intend? Is it an offering to the idols? A purification? A prelude to a 'Christian' performance? Is it an act of exorcism? Or is it (and this is the most disquieting possibility) a gesture containing a meaning quite outside the range of our cultural knowledge? So simple an action, yet it could sustain so many different interpretations. Here, as always, the only procedure is to recover as well as we are able from a wider range of Maya actions the conceptual understandings which informed them.

Eric Thompson, whose voice on things Maya must be heard with respect, has characterised Maya relationships with their gods as profoundly contractual; a sharply drawn balance sheet of payments and returns, with credit very tight.[30] While he would emphasise the continuity of the attitude, his most telling evidence for that view is drawn from the modern period. But however true that may be of other places and other periods of the Maya past, it is not true for Yucatan in the sixteenth century. There we see some actions which support the narrowly 'contractual' notion, in the small levies routinely offered to the familiar gods of the forest and *milpa*, but a different understanding informs the collective performances of village and provincial town.

Nowadays we have muffled away the recognition of the elevating power of physical anguish, of pain as a path to ecstasy; of deprivation of food and sleep, and then the cumulative exhaustion of repetitive dance, or the measured ingestion of drugs as ways to the transcendental; of the possibility that in this life we may be brought briefly into harmonious participation with the rhythm and pulse of the gods. Christian emphasis on the post-mortem salvation of the individual can obscure from us an existential and collective notion of what 'religion' is about, but it is in that direction that the Maya fire-walking dramas, the self-lacerations, the testing preliminary fasting and the great day-long warrior dances point. 'Propitiation' suggests something too personal to catch the sense of Maya action. The general Yucatec Maya term translated as 'sacrifice' was *p'a chi*, 'to open the mouth'. In the (relatively uncoerced) accounts of animal sacrifices we have, it is the flowing of the blood, the smearing of that blood on the masks of the idols, and the burning of the heart or its pulping in the idol's mouth which are the focal points of the ceremony. The act or moment of killing is incidental.

Before the conquest human victims, apart from those noble war captives killed according to the protocols of war, were required only

7 Heart excision, Temple of the Jaguars, Chichen Itza.

on specific occasions, 'called for by the priests', as Landa puts it, 'only on account of some misfortune or necessity', and even here a dog could sometimes substitute for a man. Men and women were cast living into the *cenote* at Chichen Itza to carry messages to the rain god and – rarely – to return to carry prophecies to those who waited at the *cenote*'s rim. In other rituals the most common form of killing was the cutting out of the heart, and again it was the performance with the heart and the blood which seems to have been central, as in the animal 'sacrifices'. The meaning of some performances must escape us. We know too little of Yucatan myths to recognise all reenactments of events of high significance, especially as such enactments are typically highly condensed: who after all could reconstruct the Passion solely from observation of the Mass? But Landa gives a skeletal account of one form of killing which appears to have been borrowed from earlier Mexican invaders, as it followed the same shape as the Mexican festival of Tlacaxipeualiztli, the 'Feast of the Flaying of Men' which honoured the Flayed Lord of the spring growth. I have analysed elsewhere the probable meaning of the Mexican festival. In the Yucatan version warrior captives had their hearts cut out, and the corpses were then flayed, the flayed skins being worn by the priests until they were cast off, as the springing seed cast off its integument, and as the fresh spring growth replaced the old dead skin of the earth.

The bodies of the victims were dismembered and the flesh divided between the priests and lords and warriors, and ritually eaten.[31] This flesh-eating was not, as is commonly said, to incorporate the dead man's valour; that, embodied in the warrior scalp lock and thigh bone, was separately dealt with, being awarded to the captor as permanent trophy and token. The intention was rather to draw an equivalence between human flesh, and the vegetable sustenance which had nourished that flesh. I have already noted the insistent carnality of Maya metaphors for things vegetable – the 'green blood of my daughter' for the sacred *balche*, for example. Certainly Maya killings, even of warrior victims, were locked into the agricultural cycle, and drew their meaning from it.

It is dangerous to move too briskly from actions to assertions about intentions, but the strong emphasis on blood and the letting of blood is sustained in the one pre-contact ritual involving the killing of a man for which we have a reasonably full external brief description, and from the chance survival of a magnificent warrior chant which probably accompanied the action. The time of the year is not specified, but I would place it close to the beginning of the planting season. A noble war captive, naked and painted blue, the colour of the sacred, was brought with procession and dance to an open space, and tied to a column. An *ah-kin* then wounded him in the genital area, so that the genital blood began to flow – as it did in the many penis-laceration rituals of the Maya – while circling, dancing warriors shot arrows at him in controlled sequence. Landa claims they aimed for the heart, implying a test of markmanship, 'to make his chest one point like a hedgehog of arrows', but the chant suggests rather different actions and intention:

> make three fast turns
> around the column of painted stone
> there where the virile youth,
> unstained, undefiled, a man, is bound.
> Make the first, and on the second turn
> take up your bow, fit the arrow to the string.
> Aim at his breast. It is not necessary
> to use all your force
> when you let fly, so that his flesh
> will not be too deeply wounded.
> Let him suffer little by little
> as the beautiful Lord God wished . . .[32]

The victim will not only suffer. He will bleed. The intention was not to kill, but to wound delicately, to pierce the skin and flesh so that the blood springs forth. It is likely the Maya understood the whole action not so much as the offering of a human 'life', but as the presentation of a noble spectacle; of a substance of great fertilising power, as blood, especially genital blood, was understood to be.[33]

Such a reading squares with what we know of Maya cosmology, and of man's place in that cosmos. Men reverenced the great dead of their lineages, celebrated their histories and competed to bring more honour to them, but that, compelling as it was, was essentially a human matter. They acknowledged their intimate dependence on the familiar gods of the forests by the small regular offerings they made in return for what necessity forced them to take. But the great gods whose slow march moved the seasons were of a different order. It was through the disciplined acquisition of knowledge that the priests were able to map those movements, and so to discern the regularity behind the apparent capriciousness of events. Then it was for men so to order their lives to allow their survival through an achieved harmony. The gods were aloof and (were it not so anachronistic a word) mechanical in their functions. Men's ritual actions could do no more than invoke those functions through mimicry, and do something to regularise them when the movement faltered. Thus the drawing forth of blood, from oneself or, in times of crisis, from a human victim, could well have been understood as the introduction of a potent fuel to aid the workings of the great cycles of the universe.

The confessions rarely indicate the occasions which elicited the response of a human killing, or, rather, as I would suggest, of a human blood-letting, but those few are compatible with the proposed pattern. We are told that one sacrifice took place when Juan Nachi Cocom was close to death. The impending death of the head-chief. especially in such hard times, especially a chief who had played so vigorous a part in sustaining the rhythm of traditional observances, marked a crisis. (That his brother and not his son succeeded the Cocom is another indicator of a high sense of threat.) Other human sacrifices were dated as occurring at the time of 'the hurricane', which was probably also their occasion. Hurricanes troubled the Maya, not only because of their destructive power, but because of their apparent capriciousness, and so the difficulty of discerning their temporal pattern – though the Maya never doubted that such a pattern existed, and could, with patience, be identified. The reported presentation by one lord to another of six small children for ritual killing could also well be true, the gesture echoing in more modest terms traditional rivalrous exchanges between chiefs rich in slaves and lowly dependants.[34]

While such hints are far from decisive, my own view is that given the ineffectiveness of Spanish surveillance, the resilience of the old social order, and the determination of its custodians to sustain the old ways, some human killings persisted into the post-conquest period, although with nothing like the frequency asserted in the confessions. As for the 'blasphemous' details the friars found so appalling, I have already suggested that the *'cenote* cult' is a historian's fiction built on an Indian invention. Its acceptance involves altogether too much lugging of bodies – some with crosses still attached – around the countryside; too casual a pollution of drinking water; too relaxed a response to insult both by the humans whose slaughtered children were tossed back into the home *cenote* as by the rain gods offered corpses whose bloods and hearts had been consumed elsewhere. The most powerful, if least 'empirical' argument against the reality of the *cenote* cult is its too exuberantly innovatory style. All we know of the Maya points to their caution, the wariness with which they responded to 'change', usually by webbing it into the familiar. They sought to combat the furious instability of their lives by adherence to routines, to practised procedures. Extravagance, in that dour landscape, was not a plausible posture. The wantonness of the *'cenote* cult' is the most persuasive evidence against it.

Crucifixions considered

What, then, of the crucifixion accusations? We know that the Maya early accepted the crosses raised outside the churches and in-corporated them into their own rituals. In that acceptance there appeared to be no hint of responsiveness to or association with the crucifixion story: the great crosses were adopted on purely Maya terms. At the same time they burned small crosses and crucifixes, more closely associated with the friars and (probably) with the crucifixion. At some later time the great cross came to be identified with the 'Lord Dios', the supreme deity of the new order. (The 'Lord Jesus Christ' was very much his deputy, although an active one.) How and when did that identification come about? Did the events of 1562 play any part in it? And just what understanding of the crucifixion did that first generation of baptised Maya have?

Here the first task is to separate out three things: the official

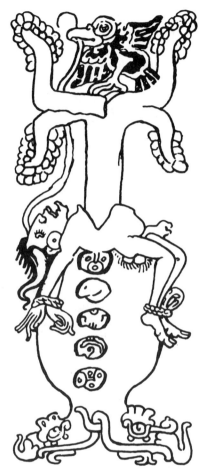

8 Heart excision with cruciform Tree of Life springing from chest cavity.

requirements of the missionary programme; the friars' actual intentions and adjusted objectives; and what 'messages' the Indians actually received. There is a great gulf between the proclaimed aims and the realistic goals of education programmes, as any teacher knows, and the friars were sensitive to it. Officially they were committed to teaching their Indian charges the catechism: the four essential prayers – the Ave Maria, the Pater Noster, the Salve Regina, the Credo; the Fourteen Articles of the Faith; the Ten Commandments of the Lord; the Five Commandments of the Church; the Seven Sacraments; the Seven Virtues and the Seven Sins; the Fourteen

Works of Mercy – and so on.[35] Indians were meant to be able to recite
the catechism before they were admitted to baptism, at marriage, and
at the required annual confession. In practice, the friars settled for
very much less. Toral was ready to baptise Indians who knew how to
cross themselves, and could say the Pater Noster, the Ave Maria, and
the Articles of the Faith. Even this modest aim seems to have been
rarely achieved, at least among the commoners: few of those brought
before the inquisition could stumble through the prayers, and crossed
themselves only awkwardly.[36]

But how commoners conducted themselves was of little account.
The implicit egalitarianism of Christianity was of no interest to the
Maya lords. What mattered was how they themselves assessed the
teachings brought by the foreigners, not as mediated by the friars, but
by the mission-trained sons of those same lords. And here not what
was public and obligatory, but what was apparently secret and
privileged, would have the most appeal. That which was promiscuously given was devalued by the promiscuous giving: what was
restricted was desired because of the restriction.

Indians had access to the sacraments of baptism and marriage, and
if only rarely to extreme unction, there being too few priests and too
many dying Indians, at least the baptised dead were buried in
consecrated ground. They seem to have confessed very rarely, in part
because of the paucity of friars versed in Mayan, in part because of
their own lack of enthusiasm for the exercise. Few if any Indians were
admitted to communion. Ecclesiastical structures in Yucatan were
designed so that Indians could watch the Mass while being physically
segregated from the participants.[37] The Mass would remain something of a mystery even to those Indians – schoolmasters and boys
from the village school – who helped to serve it: all they would see at
certain moments would be the back of the priest as he muttered over
the chalice. The friars kept the Holy Sacrament in their own quarters,
although the schoolmasters were permitted to care for the rest of the
ritual paraphernalia. Nor were Indians admitted to Holy Orders.

Just how little the Maya acquiesced in those exclusions is signalled
by bursts of Spanish outrage as they stumbled on evidence of Maya
activities through the rest of the sixteenth century and beyond. We
have already noted the chiefs' bland intrusion into zones of action the
friars reserved for themselves. The Franciscan chronicler Cogolludo
tells of an Indian lord – from Sotuta, and a Cocom – who was
convicted not only of idolatry but of 'perverse dogmatising' in 1585;
of another Sotuta Indian who in 1579 declared himself to be Moses in

direct communication with the Holy Spirit; and of another pair who proclaimed themselves Pope and Bishop in 1610:

> they said mass at night dressed in the sacred vestments of the church which no doubt the sacristans [schoolmasters] had given them. They profaned the holy chalices and consecrated oils, baptised boys, confessed adults and gave them communion, while they worshipped the idols they put there on the altar. They ordained priests for service, anointing their hands with the oil and the holy chrism, and when they ordained them they put on a mitre and took a crozier in their hands . . .[38]

A most thorough expropriation of reserved authority. What we also note is that the chosen identities were at once priests and lawgivers.

Robert Redfield, in his *The Primitive World and its Transformations*, drew a distinction between the 'literati' of a simple society, those with a high concern for the preservation of the indigenous sophisticated tradition, the protectors and interpreters of the art, religion and the manners of the inherited pattern of aristocratic life; and the 'intelligentsia', primarily mediators of an intrusive civilization in their own society, cultural middle men, marginal both to their own culture and to the foreign one they seek to interpret to their fellows. The Maya ruling elite would have denied the distinction: their traditional role as custodians and mediators of true knowledge incorporated both. Military defeat did not abrogate their responsibility: rather, it made its discharge even more crucial. I suspect it was that conviction of the continued necessity and efficacy of their actions which preserved at both the social and the psychological level a sense of autonomy; a sense which I think lies at the heart of Maya or any other people's 'cultural resilience'. The Maya lords did not have to effect change to demonstrate their authority: they had to understand it. It was that understanding and the confidence in its continued utility which allowed the Maya to remain obstinate pragmatists in a time of desolation; adjusting roles and expectations where they must, clinging to routine where they could.

For Nachi Cocom, head-chief of Sotuta and leader of all the eastern provinces, the duties of office were particularly clear. The men of the lesser towns could be instructed to continue in the old ways for what still appeared to be an insignificant and temporary intrusion; a mere affair of men. His task, once physical resistance was no longer practicable, was to assay the teachings of the intruders for what was worthy of being added to the Maya store of accumulated wisdom.

Given the assumption of responsibility, it is plausible that Nachi Cocom should have experimented with crucifixions. But again the problem is to establish just what notion of the crucifixion would have been communicated to him by the friars, and more importantly by those key men in the whole Franciscan strategy for conversion, the schoolmasters.

The crucifixion did not figure as centrally in the friars' general teachings as we might expect. Their emphasis fell rather on the legitimacy of the hierarchy of Christian authority, with its corollary of the necessity of Indian submission. Ritual life certainly intensified around Easter, but the Yucatan friars were not able to present the elaborate reenactments of the Passion staged by their brothers in Mexico. Given the Maya lords' determination to select out of the multiple assertions of the new religion those they identified as authentically illuminating of the nature of things, and their special taste for 'knowledge' which appeared to be deliberately hidden or obscured, it is unlikely they would ignore the myth of the central symbol and mystery of the incoming faith. The incident of the 'crucified baby' which so exercised Landa was probably innocent, but it is interesting that it was Indians who noted the strange lesions on the head, hands and feet of the dead child, and identified them – perhaps – as the stigmata. Then there is that anomalous, distinctive patio cross at Mani, with its hanging body. This suggests the story of the crucifixion could indeed have penetrated the Maya imagination. Yet the extraordinary sequence of connections implied by the cross and lance metaphors in the Language of Zuyua riddle – the sign of the cross sketched in the air standing for the lance of wood which, piercing the heart of the sun, is identified as the Tree of the World piercing the heavens and the underworlds – points back to purely Maya meanings, providing another elegant example of the economy with which Christian gestures and Christian objects were assimilated into a Maya imaginative universe. At some point in time it seems a crucial recognition had been made: certain Christian teachings were true. Therefore they must be accepted, and so incorporated into a Maya scheme of things.

The *Books of Chilam Balam* present accounts of the death of Christ which are resolutely Maya: the crucifixion has been transformed into a Maya event, and partly assimilated to the arrow sacrifice. The following passage from the *Chumayel* is lengthy, but its sense depends on the completion of the full pattern:

In the middle of the town of Tiho [Mérida] is the cathedral, the fiery house, the mountainous house, the dark house, for the benefit of God the Father, God the Son and God the Holy Spirit.

Who enters into the house of God? Father, it is the one named Ix-Kalem [the 'Holy One'].

What day did the Virgin conceive? Father, 4 *Oc* was the day when she conceived.

What day did he come forth from her womb? On 3 *Oc* he came forth.

What day did he die? On 1 *Cimi* he died. Then he entered the tomb on 1 *Cimi*.

What entered his tomb? Father, a coffer of stone entered his tomb.

What entered in into his thigh? Father, it was the red arrow-stone. It entered into the precious stone of the world, there in heaven.

And his arm? Father, the arrow-stone; and that it might be commemorated, it entered into the red living rock in the east. Then it came to the north and entered into the white living rock. After that it entered the black living rock in the west. Thus also it entered the yellow living rock in the south . . .[39]

And so on, into even more purely Maya symbolism.

Most of the 'sermons' reported as having been preached at the 'crucifixion' sacrifices were unequivocally oppositional, and are essentially presented as acts of defiance. However there was a more ambivalent tone to the sermon preached at the earliest of the reputed crucifixions, five years before the trials, in the presence and under the aegis of Nachi Cocom and his brother Lorenzo, where the priest is claimed to have said: 'Let these girls die crucified as did Jesus Christ, he who they say was our Lord, but we do not know if this is so.'[40] Is this a first experiment, an exploration of the relevance of the new mysteries to the Maya understanding of the sacred? Did the experience of the next years clarify the Maya position, and harden their resolution to sustain their traditional account of the world? Nachi Cocom had led a determined resistance to the Spaniards through war, and through guile when the time for war was past. He was an innovator and a planner, organising the federation of provinces which so nearly defeated the Spaniards at Tiho, involved in the formidable planning which led to the beautifully synchronised uprising of 1546. After the 'peace' he was swift to utilise Spanish forms, Spanish institutions, for Maya ends. In his early relationship with Landa it is possible, indeed probable, that the old chief was at least as manipulative as the young friar. And he too knew how to bind waverers to a cause, how to build an alliance, by enticement into involvement in dangerous action. The maintenance of his traditional role required that he penetrate the mysteries of the invaders' learning. It is possible, too, that he was moved by the knowledge of that distinctive patio cross at Mani to incorporate the hanging of bodies on a cross into his own repertoire, so asserting the priority of his authority over the upstart Xiu. Did he therefore order children to be crucified? Did he watch in the silent church as their hearts were torn out, as their blood wet the masks of his idols, as he strove to decipher what these things meant?

I think it possible, even probable, that he did. The mode of the doing indicates how little a distinctively Christian understanding informed it. In that reported early 'crucifixion' (as in reported later ones) the victims were not mature males, but small children, often female, and killed in pairs. Spaniards read the rituals as deliberate blasphemies and parodies, but they do not conform to the sequence of Christ's crucifixion at all. The children were simply tied to the cross, raised up, perhaps 'named' as Jesus Christ, and then lowered and dispatched in the usual way by excision of the heart. It is possible the 'naming' is a confused echo of the mockery of Jesus, but there is no hint in the brisk sequence of action of any attempt to evoke the long suffering on the cross in its various stages, or the painful way to it. It is likely that Nachi Cocom did indeed experiment with the use of the cross as a ritual preliminary to blood-letting and the taking of the heart, but it is scarcely appropriate to name this selective borrowing 'crucifixion'. Then, it seems, it was rejected as adding nothing of worth, so that the chiefs of Hocaba-Homun, for example, were never urged to incorporate it. The implication is that the bulk of the later 'crucifixion' confessions were – as the Indians insisted – inventions, exacted by torments inflicted by the friars, just as the 'human sacrifice' accounts as given in the testimonies were not only multiplied but distortions, transformed in their meaning by being forced into a vocabulary the friars could recognise. The confessional texts as we have them rarely present descriptions of actual events. They are rather the product of the miserable confusion which besets men when they do not understand the speech of others, and find it easier to make of them familiar monsters than to acknowledge them to be different.

If my admittedly extended inferences are valid, there is a last irony. Intermittently, in the proliferating confusions, and as they struggled with the exigencies of their own realities, the Spaniard Diego de Landa and the Maya Nachi Cocom had been attentive to the speech of the strangers. The Cocom, awkwardly manipulating the cross in his own most solemn ceremonies, had attempted to fathom the meaning of what he thought he had heard, but could make nothing of it. The friar, somehow catching the distorted echo of that fumbling experiment, interpreted it in accordance with his own deepest needs and darkest fears, first developing it to a terrible coherence; then muting it to a dusty whisper. That early moment of intrepid but most imperfect communication was to make division absolute.

Epilogue: Confusion of tongues

The events of 1562 probably marked a major shift in Maya evaluation of the status of the Spanish religion. Until that point, the Spanish presence was seen as temporary, and Christian teachings as little more than interesting novelties to be scanned for useful notions. That attitude changed, I think with the trials. In that three-month-long reign of terror the priests of the new religion, until then peripheral or intermittent factors in Indian awareness, came and sat down in the villages. The idols and the jewelled skulls of the ancestors were burned at their command. The violence, the sufferings inflicted by the friars, the destruction of the idols, signalled that the time of the old gods was indeed over, and the rule of the new gods had begun; when 'the descendants of the former rulers are brought to misery; we are christianised, while they treat us like animals'. The *Chumayel* characterises 9 *Ahau* as the *katun* 'when Christianity began, when baptism occurred. It was in this *katun* that Bishop Toral arrived here also. It was when the hangings ceased in the year of Our Lord 1546. And 7 *Ahau* was when Bishop Landa died . . .'[1]

Given the 'bundle of equivalent events' notion of the *katun*, I would argue that the 'hanging' does not refer to the executions of the leaders of the Great Maya Revolt of 1546 (who were burned, not hanged) but to the hoistings of 1562, so closely associated with the coming of Toral, and with Diego de Landa; and that 'Christianity' – the rule of the Lord Dios – was accepted by the Maya in response to the experiences of that terrible year. That acceptance meant nothing about acceptance of Spanish claims to exclusive rights over the interpretation and administration of the new faith, as constant Maya claims to that authority make clear. In face of Spanish 'religious' expectations and demands they remained lethargic and recalcitrant. A seventeenth-century cleric lamented the sullen unwillingness or incapacity of Yucatan Maya to learn the basic doctrines of Christianity. Despite being flogged into church for weekly instructions; despite all the care taken in their teaching; despite being examined in the doctrines at marriage and at the obligatory yearly confessions, and despite generations having been brought up in this way, 'they have. . . little affection for the church, mass and holy sacrifice'. In Yucatan there was almost a complete lack of the apparatus of popular piety – the rosaries, the shrines, the images – so abundant in Mexico. Yet in the midst of that obstinate lethargy, he was puzzled to notice, the Maya lavished care on their village churches, keeping them filled with flowers and with the songs and hymns in their own tongue that they never tired of singing.[2]

The distinctiveness of the Maya vision of Christianity was revealed to the Europeans only with the great uprising of the Caste War of 1847, when the Maya rose to drive the evil and blaspheming whites from the land. But the millenial theme had been present from at least the last decades of the sixteenth century, and most probably was concomitant with that coerced recognition of and submission to the rule of the 'Lord Dios'. One creation narrative from the *Chilam Balam of Chumayel* begins in a Christian mode, with a reference to 'the resurrection of the true God, the true Dios, when he blessed heaven and earth'; when 'the worship of Maya men' came to an end. The story which follows has no Christian content at all, describing rather the setting-up of the familiar four-cornered Maya cosmos. Then comes a long series of purely Maya episodes recounting the events of the *katunes*. But at the last a Christian theme emerges, and the theme is millenial:

But when the law of the *katun* shall have run its course, then God will bring about a great deluge which will be the end of the world. When this is over, then our Lord Jesus Christ shall descend over the valley of Jehosaphat beside the town of Jerusalem where he redeemed us with his holy blood. He shall descend in a great cloud to bear true testimony that he was once obliged to suffer stretched out on a cross of wood. Then shall descend in his great power and glory the true God who created heaven and earth and everything else on earth. He shall descend to level off the world for the good and the bad, the conquerors and the captives . . .[3]

In those days of justice, when the *katun* would come to an end,

those who are of the lineage shall come forth before their lord on bended knee so that their wisdom may be made known . . . those of the lineage of the first head chief here in the land are viewed with favour. They shall live on that day, and they shall also receive their first wand of office. Thus are those of the lineage of Maya men established again in the Province of Yucatan. God shall be first, when all things are accomplished here on earth. He is the true ruler, he shall come to demand of us our government, those things which we hold sacred, precious stones, precious beads, and he shall demand the planted wine, the *balche*.[4]

For the Maya there was no tension between their repudiation of the Spanish claim to rule and to the monopolistic control of Christian truth, and their acceptance of the Christian gods as deities whose time had come: when the Lord Jesus Christ descends in 'the Province of Yucatan', then at last there will be an end to the domination of the foreigners and of submission to their exactions. Then the rule of the Lord Jesus Christ, and of his Maya lords, will begin.

———————

Then, I tell you, justice shall descend to the end that Christianity and salvation may arise. Thus shall end the men of the Plumeria flower. Then the rulers of the towns shall be asked for their proofs and titles of ownership, if they know of them. Then they shall come forth from the forests and from among the rocks and live like men; then towns shall be established again. There shall be no fox to bite them. This shall be in *Katun 9 Ahua*. Five years shall run until the end of my prophecy, and then shall come the time for the tribute to come down. Then there shall be an end to the paying for the wars which our fathers raised against the Spaniards. You shall not call the *katun* which is to come a hostile one, when Jesus Christ, the guardian of our souls, shall come. Just as we are saved here on earth, so shall he bear our souls to his holy heaven also.

> You are sons of the true God.
> Amen.

The Book of Chilam Balam of Chumayel

Appendix: A sampler of documents

It is impossible to give a 'representative' array of documents. As any reader of documents knows, each one both expands and modifies understanding. The reader will have reasonably easy access to some Spanish conquistador reports, to Landa's *Relación*, and to the scholarly translations of two *Books of Chilam Balam*. What follows is a sampler of less accessible documents which have figured significantly in the text, drawn from the trial records of 1562.

Diego de Landa's indictment of the Sotuta Indians, 11 August 1562

In the village and *advocacion* St Peter, head village of this province of Sotuta, which is held in *encomienda* by Juan de Magaña, citizen of the city of Mérida, the which said village is in the boundaries and jurisdiction of the said city, on the eleventh day of the month of August, the year of our Lord one thousand five hundred and sixty-two years, the very magnificent and reverend Lord Fray Diego de Landa, first Provincial of these provinces of the Order of the monasteries of the lord St Francis that are founded in this province, and Apostolic Judge of the Holy Office by bulls of His Holiness conceded and secured at the request of His Majesty, before me, Juan de Villagomez, his notary and apostolic notary in all the kingdoms and lordships of His Majesty through nomination by Luis Sanchez, Palatine Count, by bulls of His Holiness conceded to him in order to nominate notaries and other things: he said that in so far as His Grace being in this village and province punishing the idolatries which have been and are now in it, he has been informed and thus it is that among the chiefs and *principales* of this said village and province and the rest of the common people there have been great sacrifices and heresies within the churches, and not fearing the fear of God our Lord, holding as they have held for little the things of our Holy Catholic Faith, they have gone against it preaching within the churches the false sect of the devil and things of idolatries as they were used and accustomed to do in the time of their heathen past, bringing to the church for the said preaching the idols and devils they have, that they adore and have adored until now, and besides this they have brought back and perverted the rest who already have and who will come to the said idolatries, threatening the masters and boys of the school and forcing them to consent without delay to the performance of the said sacrifices and ceremonies within the church. And that besides this the principal lords and *ah-kines* and schoolmasters have made human sacrifices to god [*sic*] within the church of this village and in other places in homage to the devils, killing infants and boys and girls, Indian men and women, offering the hearts ripped living from them to the devils. And likewise they have made many other idolatries and ceremonies in accordance with their ancient customs and have burnt crosses, taken from the altar to burn them, mocking them, holding them in little account, and holding in little account the preachings of the religious, and they themselves have become priests, and have preached falsely, claiming that which the priests, friars and clerics were teaching them was not true or good, and that what they [the *ah-kines*] were telling them were things for their salvation and that by doing that which they were advising, sacrificing, worshipping and venerating the idols and devils, they will be saved. And in order to know and to discover the truth and to identify the guilty ones so that they might be punished and castigated each one according to the guilt of his transgressions, and likewise in order to establish who have been the prophets and priests *ah-kines* [*sic*] who have preached the said heresies and things against our holy faith in order to punish all of them which is the province of His Grace, because it is for His Grace to decide whether to use mercy towards them, and in the case of crimes and serious offences whether they should be handed over to the secular arm, always in accordance with the judicial enquiry His Grace would make and other enquiries which the secular justice might further wish to make in order to punish them in accordance with the transgressions they have committed, and in order that the truth of all should be known and verified and explored, His Grace the said Lord Judge wishes to proceed in the case and to have the judicial enquiries and verifications concerning the case. [Here follows the name of Juan Bautista de Campo as interpreter.] *Source*: Scholes and Adams, *Don Diego Quijada*, I, 71–2.

The confessions

Ideally, of course, translations of all the confessions ought to be provided, but that would produce a volume rather more substantial than the text it was designed to illuminate, so I have chosen only confessions of peculiar interest.

Juan Couoh, schoolmaster, from Yaxcaba village, provided probably the most vivid and circumstantial account of a human sacrifice.

Juan Couoh, schoolmaster of Yaxcaba village, 11 August 1562

For information of the aforesaid, on the eleventh day of the month of August of the said year of one thousand five hundred and sixty-two, the very magnificent and reverend father Fray Diego de Landa, Provincial and Apostolic Judge of the Holy Office by virtue of bulls of His Holiness, before me, Juan de Villagomez, apostolic notary, had appear before him Juan Couoh, native of the village of Yaxcaba in this province of Sotuta, within the boundaries and jurisdiction of the city of Mérida, and being questioned through the interpreter Juan Bautista de Campo according to the content of the said indictment, said that which the witness knows and happened in the case is the following:

He was asked his place of birth and whether he is a schoolmaster or holds another office or responsibility in the church. He said that this witness is a native of the village of Tanuz and that he lives at present in the village of Yaxcaba, which is held in *encomienda* by Joaquín de Leguízamo, and that there he holds the office of teaching the boys of the church for the last eight years, during which period he has resided in Yaxcaba. He was asked if he had seen or has known if in the said village of Yaxcaba the native chiefs and *principales* and the rest of the people might have had or might have had idols which they worship and if he has seen them worshipping the idols or if he had worshipped idols himself in their company. He said that this witness knows that the chiefs and *principales* and old men and the rest of the ordinary people of the village have had and still have idols, and have worshipped them with the rest of the said village and that this witness possesses idols, which numbered sixty, and were his father's, and he has them hidden in a cave where he had burnt copal before them. And that the last time he had burnt copal before them was two months ago. And that the said cave where he has the said idols is close to Tanuz. And that in the same way he has made other sacrifices to the said idols in accordance with what they used to do for them in the time of their paganism. He was asked if he had seen or has acquiesced in the making of sacrifices and adoring of the said idols within the said church of the said village of Yaxcaba and Tanuz, putting them on the altar and making sacrifices to them within the said church, and who were the people or leading chiefs who have attended the said sacrifice, and that he should declare the names of those who thus attended the said sacrifice and whether in the said sacrifice they had killed some children to offer to the said idols. He said that what this witness knows is that within a year after having gone to [*sic*] the said village of Tanuz to take charge of the boys of the church he saw how a sacrifice was performed inside the church, and that in order to make the said sacrifice all the natives of the said village one night brought fifty idols that were in the house of Lorenzo Pech, chief of the said village and now dead, and put them in the church, and with [the idols] so placed in the middle of the church they made a sacrifice to the idols of a deer they had brought there and tortoises and other things according to the ancient custom. And after having carried out the said sacrifice they got drunk on the native wine and ate the flesh of the animals they had offered there, at which sacrifice this witness was present and saw all that happened because he was present. Similarly the other chiefs and *principales* of the said village were present. And the said Lorenzo Pech, now dead, preached to all the Indians who were there, saying to them that they should keep it secret and divulge no part of it to the friars because the idols were appropriate to the gods, which they had to worship because they were their gods. And that about six years after this sacrifice more or less, which this witness saw, another sacrifice the same as the first was made in the said village of Yaxcaba, at which this witness was present. And that about three months ago more or less, after these two sacrifices, this witness, being in his house one Tuesday in the middle of the night, the chief of the said village of Yaxcaba, called Diego Pech, summoned this witness by sending an Indian called Diego Couoh to read a letter, and this witness on the summons of the chief was walking past the church where he saw Pedro Euan, *principal* of the said village of Yaxcaba, who in the old days held the office of sacrificing men and boys to the idols. [He] had got hold of a youth, with his hands behind his back. [The youth] was a native of the village of Tekax, province of Mani, called Francisco Cauich, who had come to stay in the said village of Yaxcaba with some of his relations he had in the said village called Juan Cauich [*sic*] and the said

Francisco Cauich was sitting close to the altar of the said church with his hands tied as was said before, and a big candle was burning. And this witness spoke to them and said, 'What are you doing there?' And the said Pedro Euan replied, 'Why do you want to know? Go and read the letter at the chief's house and then come back, and you'll find out what we are doing.' And this witness went straight on without stopping and went to the chief's house where he found the chief Diego Pech, and Juan Ku, chief and Juan Tzek, *principal*, and Francisco Pot, *ah-kin*, and Gaspar Chan, *ah-kin*, and Juan Canbal, *ah-kin*, and Pedro Pech, *ah kin*, and Lorenzo Ku, constable of the mission school, and his father, Diego Ku, all gathered together, and those he knew to be there and he cannot now remember if there were people there other than those he has mentioned. And when this witness arrived the said chief Diego Pech said to him, 'What's on your mind? I feel you want to go back to being a stone, or to eat dirt.[1] Don't you know I am engaged with something, and that you owe me a great deal, and when you were [illegible] I supported you.' This witness answered these remarks saying that it was true that he had done all that for this witness and he knew it. And the said chief said to him, 'Why is it that you repay me so badly for they've told me you wish to help us and yet you go around stirring up trouble for us with the friars, don't believe in them, because you cannot be their son, and they don't have to consider you their son. Therefore agree with what I want to tell you, and that is that we have a boy to sacrifice and it is necessary for you to be present.' And this witness answered him that it was a serious matter and that it was not a proper thing because it was not Christian. And the aforesaid Diego Pech replied that indeed he had to do what he was commanding him to do, and that if he didn't, then he'd [illegible]. At this point he sent Diego Couoh, who had brought this witness along with Pedro Puc to fetch Pedro Euan who was in the church guarding the youth they were going to sacrifice, and that he [Diego Couoh?] should stay there guarding the said youth. And so the said Pedro Euan came, and when he had come the chief in front of the others, told him how this witness was opposing the carrying out of the sacrifice. And the said Pedro Euan reproached this witness saying: 'What's this, brother, is it possible that you are refusing, as the chief says?' And this witness said it was true that he was opposed to it and that they could do as they chose and that this witness did not want to be involved in it. And at this the said

---

[1] The 'dirt eating' refers to a traditional way of indicating submission. See Landa, *Relación*, 35–6, n. 175.

Pedro Euan seized hold of this witness's hair and said to him, 'If you stand against us and refuse to take part in it we'll do to you what we are going to do to the boy.' And when this witness saw this through fear he said that they should do what they wished, and this said, all those present there, who were named earlier, rose and took ten idols which they had brought from the *milpa* of the said Diego Pech, chief, and the other appurtenances used in sacrifice, and took them with them to the church. And arriving there, without offering a prayer or bowing to the altar, they put the idols in a row, each on the leaves of the castor oil plant, and spread out before them a long mat and upon the mat they placed a large flint knife with the handle wrapped in a white cloth. And the two *ah-kines* among those present took two large candles and the *ah-kines* who took the candles were Gaspar Chim and Pedro Pech. And all sat down on some little benches, and they ordered the Indian who was seated near the altar to come, and he came, his hands tied behind him, without a shirt, wearing *zaraguelles*[2] and his eyes covered by a white cloth, and when he came they sat him down in their midst, and Gaspar Chim, *ah-kin*, spoke and said, 'Comrades, this [illegible] this lad is bound to tell about it and he'd write to the friars', which he was saying about this witness. And at this point Pedro Euan helped by speaking with this witness, saying to him, 'Are you going to tell? Speak the truth.' And this witness replied that he didn't know, and the said Pedro Euan spoke and replied, 'Speak up, because if you were to do such a thing I'm the one who will kill you, because it was my office in the old days.' And this witness said that he would not tell. And this finished, Diego Pech, chief, spoke to the one they wanted to kill, who was weeping, 'Strengthen and console yourself because what we are doing to you now is not an evil thing nor are we casting you into an evil place or into hell, but to heaven and to paradise according to the customs of our ancestors.' And to this the boy they wanted to kill replied, 'Do what you wish, for God who is in heaven will help me.' And to this Gaspar Chim, *ah-kin*, said 'untie him before dawn comes so that no people come, let what must be done be done . . .' And so they untied the youth and threw him down to the floor on to the mat, and the *ah-kines* put down the candles they were holding and Diego Pech and Juan Coh took the said candles and the *ah-kines* took the youth and threw him on his back and they seized him by the feet and hands, and Pedro Euan came and took up the flint knife and with it struck open his side to the left of the

---

[2] Pyjama-like, baggy trousers.

heart, and when it was opened he seized hold of the heart and with the same knife cut away the entrails [arteries] and gave the heart to the *ah-kin* Gaspar Chim, who lifted it on high having first given it two little cuts in the shape of a cross, and this witness does not know what part it was he took out of it, and put in the mouth of the greatest of the idols there which was called Itzamna. And the said cuts were made at the point of the heart. And after having done this they took the blood of the said boy who they had killed there in a large gourd and then they took the body and the heart and the blood of the said boy they had killed there and the idols and they all went to the house of the chief and took everything there. And this witness went to his house because it seemed to him that what had been done was evil. And the said chiefs and *ah-kines* said to this witness, 'Are you going?' And this witness replied, 'Yes, because there is no more to see.' And they said to him, 'Look here, now, say nothing, because they'll burn the lot of us and even if they were to burn us alive we won't say anything.' And with this the witness went to his house and the said chiefs and *ah-kines* took the body, idols and heart to the house of the said Diego Pech; and he does not know what they did with him [*sic*]. And that as well as this sacrifice, about a month ago more or less, the aforesaid with the rest of the *principales* of the village, except Diego Pech and Juan Hau and some others who were not there, were present at another sacrifice in the church at night. And in it they sacrificed a dog according to the ancient custom, and after taking the heart anointed the devils' faces with it, each one present having brought his own idols. This witness similarly brought his and they gathered them together in the house of Juan Ku for the purpose, and from there they took them to the church. And after taking the said dog's said heart and making the sacrifice Gaspar Chim, *ah-kin*, stood up and began to speak to them and tell them to listen well to what he wished to say to them, and he said that that which they had done was very good and they had made it [the sacrifice] to their true gods and that that which the fathers told them and preached to them was not true and they should not believe it, that it was a mockery, and he they preached about was not God nor would they stay in the land and that they were going to leave soon and they and the rest of the natives would go back to their ancient ways and practise their ceremonies, and in the same way the words the fathers said were words of the devil and hell and that he who the fathers preached about was not God but a devil, and what he did was the right thing, and the thing of heaven, and their gods of clay they had there were their true gods and that they had cared for them and given them being and that they had to believe that. And that same *ah-kin* said that they should reveal nothing to the friars who were going to come from Mani if they should ask about the idols and that they should collect no intact ones but only the pieces and broken ones so that the new and whole ones should remain in which they could go on trusting, that is what was being taught by the natives of the province of Mani. And the fathers and friars were taking those they gave them and were satisfied with the broken ones. And the said *ah-kin* said that those sacrifices which they had made, and the sermon, was ordered by Lorenzo Cocom, chief and governor of the village of Sotuta, who himself did it this way in the said village, and that he was his father and lord and *halach uinic*, that is in our language the great lord, from whom they had to accept counsel, and by his will they did it. And that this which is said he holds is the truth and that which he knows and made under the oath and he swore it as the interpreter stated it. And the said Juan Couoh signed his name together with the said interpreter and the said lord judge of the Holy Office. His statement was read to him . . . He said it was the truth and that he confirmed it . . . and if it were necessary he would say it again. Juan Couoh. Fray Diego de Landa. Juan Bautista de Campo. Drawn up before me, Juan de Villagomez, apostolic notary. *Source*: Scholes and Adams, *Don Diego Quijada*, I, 103–8.

Francisco Chuc of Sahcaba, 11 August 1562

Chuc's confession contains a reasonably full account of animal offerings, and the first reference to the burning of small crosses and their quenching in the blood of a sacrificed animal.

. . . On 11 August, Francisco Chuc, *ah-kin*, priest as they called [him] . . . native of the said village of Sahcaba, . . . having been [*ah-kin*] in the village [of Sahcaba] as *ah-kin* he had been present at some sacrifices made to the idols in the said village, and especially he remembered being at a sacrifice and ceremony they had made three years before through some *cuentas* [beads] one Baltasar Cocom had given to the witness so that through them they would remember to make reverence to the idols. They made a sacrifice of some birds and a pig[3] and other animals and this witness was present at it. And perhaps

---

[3] Would the interpreter or scribe have differentiated between the local peccary and the Spanish pig? Probably not: Landa in his *Relación* is content to call peccaries '*puercos*' – 'small animals who have their navel on their backs and they stink badly' (204). The use of an animal of Spanish provenance is unlikely, while peccaries were significant animals in pre-contact rituals.

three months later four idols were brought in from the forest, which they carried into the church, and they also took in wine from Castille mixed with honey and water and they offered the wine to the idols, and after having offered the wine and prayed to the idols they capped the village wells in reverence and worship for the idols in the manner of fasting so that the idols should provide them with water for the milpas. And that then a few days after they had made that sacrifice this witness and Gaspar Xeque and Baltasar Cocom and Juan Coyi, *principales*, and Juan Yah, all natives of the village gathered together to make another sacrifice in the said church and they killed a pig [peccary?] and took a small cross that was on the altar and with six . . . little sticks from which they made barbecues they burned the said sticks and the cross that was on the altar before the idols they had put in the church . . . and they quenched the cross and the sticks that were burning in the belly of the pig that had been crucified there, and with the blood of the said pig they put out the said fire of the said cross and sticks. And this witness was he who put the cross and sticks in the belly of the pig to quench them with the blood, which he did twice. And later they made another sacrifice in the church in which they killed a dog and they offered the idols the heart of the dog, and those who were there roasted the said dog and ate it. And they drank [beverage unspecified] there at the sacrifice. And after these sacrifices this witness met together with the rest of the lords and the said chiefs and being together in the house of Baltasar Cocom [a chief] they discussed and agreed together to send two lords called Francisco Xeque and Andres Uc with two lengths of thick beads to purchase children for sacrifice. And so the said lords went to the villages of Quicucche and Pustunish, and in these two villages they bought two little boys who were just beginning to walk, whom they bought from Juan Puc, lord and a powerful person in the village of Pustunich, for one length of beads, and the other they bought in Quicucche from Diego Chan, a rich Indian of the said village. And the said lords brought them to the said village of Sahcaba and this witness knows from the said two lords how they had been bought from the said Juan Puc and Diego Chan and that they were children of slave women belonging to the said lords from whom they had been bought. And having brought the said children to the said village of Sahcaba about ten days after they arrived in the village this witness met with Baltasar Cocom, chief, and Diego Xibe, *principal*, now dead, and Francisco Pot, now dead, and Francisco Be, and so being together in the house of the said Baltasar Cocom, they all went from there to an ancient site a league from the village called Tabi, and they took the two boys they were holding for the said sacrifice. And when they arrived they placed the idols in a ring with the two boys in front of them and they threw them [the two boys] down on to the ground and as they were lying there Diego Xibe came with a stone knife and opened the boys on the left side and took out their hearts and gave them to this witness and this witness received them as *ah-kin* and priest. And after he took them he raised them on high and speaking with the devil [*demonio*] said to him, 'All powerful God, this sacrifice we make to you so that you would provide us with [those things] we have need of.' And then he smeared the snouts of the idols with the blood, and having finished making this sacrifice they took the blood they had from the two boys and the bodies and the heart [*sic*] and threw them all into a *cenote* and returned to their houses in the said village. And they left the idols there. And that when this witness was going to these sacrifices he had there four idols of his own, which he had brought out for the sacrifice of the boys. And that this sacrifice was made at the time of the hurricane a year ago because it seemed to them that their gods were angry and so they would be appeased and there would not be deaths.

He was asked if he knew if they should have made or were accustomed to make sacrifices of men or women or children or other infants in other villages or parts of these provinces and that he state in what parts and what the names were of those present at such sacrifices, he said he did not know [of] it . . . *Source*: Scholes and Adams, *Don Diego Quijada*, I, 100–3.

One Confession from Kanchunup

Pedro Huhul of Kanchunup was the first Indian to testify that he had seen a crucifixion. Huhul, the seventh witness from Kanchunup, had his confession taken on the 17 August. The other six witnesses from Kanchunup had been interrogated on 12 or 13 August. Again, note the reference at the end of the confession to the burning of a cross and its quenching in the blood of a sacrificed animal. Such accounts were frequent in the testimonies taken before 17 August.

Pedro Huhul, 17 August

. . . on 17 day of the month of August [1562] . . . Pedro Huhul, *principal* of the village of Kanchunup. Pedro Huhul said . . . that two years ago more or less this witness had been at a sacrifice made to the idols in the place of Tepopox, in which were killed three boys who were called Ah Kuxeb and Holi Chunlin [*sic*] and Ah May. And that those present at the sacrifice were this witness and Juan Ix, governor of the province now a prisoner in Mérida . . . [here follow nine names] and Francisco Canche, schoolmaster and Juan Can, schoolmaster and two *ah-kines* of the village who hanged themselves and those who cut open the said boys were Pedro May, deceased and Francisco Tuz deceased, and Pablo Ppiste. And they took the hearts and offered them to the demons. And the boys [had been] bought from the Cupules and those named had given the beads and *cuzcas* to buy them, and the deceased *ah-kines* went to buy them. And that at the time of the hurricane, about a year ago more or less, they told this witness that they had made a sacrifice of two boys in Tecon. And this witness was not there, after he had gone to the *milpa* the natives of the village had told him, and that they had been thrown into the *cenote* in Tecon. And they told this witness that the boys were called Ah Chan and Ah Pol, and they told him they had been bought in Tahdziu, and he did not know from whom they had been bought. And about three or four months after this sacrifice, more or less, another sacrifice to the idols was made in the cemetery of the church in front of the big cross which was there. They had their idols around it. And in the said sacrifice they killed and crucified two boys who were called Ah Chable and Ah Xol. The one called Ah Chable they crucified and they nailed him to a great cross made for the purpose, and [that] they put him on the cross alive and nailed his hands with two nails and tied his feet . . . with a thin rope. And [that] those who nailed and crucified the said boy were the *ah-kines* who are now dead, which was done with the consent of all those who were there. And after [he was] crucified they raised the cross on high and the said boy was crying out, and so they held it on high, and then they lowered it, [and] so put on the cross they took out his heart. And in the same way they killed the other boy who was there . . . and [that] the *ah-kines* gave a sermon telling them that it was good and what they must do, and that through adoring those gods they would be saved, and that they should not believe what the friars were saying to them. After the deaths they threw the bodies of the boys into the *cenote* at Tecon, and those who went to throw them in were the deceased *ah-kines*. And at this sacrifice the same people were in attendance as were at the first sacrifice, . . . together with this witness . . . [and] the masters of the school [and] the governor Juan Ix . . . and they threw the cross on which they crucified the boy [*sic*] with him, as he had been crucified, into the said *cenote* with some big stones tied to it so that it should go to the bottom, and this the *ah-kines* who had thrown the said boys into the said *cenote* told them. And he did not know of other sacrifices in which any little children had been killed. And about a month ago . . . another sacrifice was made at the foot of a cross outside the village in which dogs and other animals were killed according to the old custom, and they ate their flesh and drank beverages they brought for it. And in this sacrifice they burnt a cross and quenched it in the blood of the animals that had been killed there, which was done by the deceased *ah-kines* . . . *Source*: Scholes and Adams, *Don Diego Quijada*, I, 93–5.

Two Confessions from Sotuta Village

These two confessions, dated 19 August, from two men from Sotuta village, the schoolmaster and constable Francisco Canche and the schoolboy Antonio Pech, were the last taken in the Sotuta enquiry. They revealed that the practice of crucifixion had been initiated five years before by Juan Nachi Cocom. (Four other witnesses from Sotuta questioned on 11 August had admitted to knowledge of or participation in human sacrifices, but had made no mention of crucifixions.)

Antonio Pech, 19 August

In the village of Sotuta . . . on the nineteenth day of August, 1562 . . . Antonio Pech, schoolboy at this said village of Sotuta . . . said that five years ago more or less he had seen a sacrifice to the idols and demons in the village church in which they killed two little girls. And this witness saw it because on the night the sacrifice was made this witness with the rest of the boys from the school were going to the church to say matins and they found in the said church making the sacrifice . . . Juan Cocom, governor that was of this village of Sotuta and Lorenzo Cocom, also governor, now both dead, and Diego Pech, father of this witness and *principal* of the village and . . . [here follow fourteen names, including the *ah-kines* Luis Ku and Francisco Uicab] . . . And he saw how the said girls were tied to two crosses. And the aforesaid told them to be quiet and that they should say nothing so that the friars should not know anything, and therefore through fear this witness and the rest of his companions had remained silent about what they had seen. And [the girls] being placed on the cross, the *ah-kines* and the deceased ones [Juan and Lorenzo Cocom] said, 'Let these girls die crucified as did Jesus Christ, he who they say was our Lord, but we do not know if this is so.' And afterwards in saying this, they lowered them from the cross, unbound them, cut them open and took out the hearts and the *ah-kines* offered them to the demons as anciently they were accustomed to do. And that the *ah-kin* was Francisco Uicab, he who is alive at present. And that afterwards they took the girls to throw them into a *cenote* called Suitunchen, and that Juan Cime and Francisco Uicab took them . . . And that about a month after this sacrifice this witness going on another night to say matins found the same people . . . sacrificing to the idols and they killed in this sacrifice two girls who they told him were called Ix Chan and Ix Homa. And they crucified them on the same crosses as the first ones because they had kept them for the purpose, and they took the hearts and offered them to the demons the said [*sic*] Francisco Uicab. And afterwards they went to throw the bodies in the said *cenote*. And Juan Cime cut them open and took out the hearts. And they said there that all must be silent and say nothing, Lorenzo Cocom and the rest of the *principales* and *ah-kines* who were there making them fearful. And four years ago more or less this witness saw how they made another sacrifice outside the village at the foot of a cross at which they killed two more girls who were called Ix Ixil and Ix Uicab, and the same people were present who had been at the first sacrifice, . . . and they crucified them like the first ones and the same *ah-kines* who are now living . . . Francesco Uicab and Juan Cime put them on the crosses. And this Juan Cime who is alive at present held the office of cutting open the girls in all the sacrifices. And later they left off making these sacrifices and forgot them for more than three years because the Padre Monterroso came to this province to teach them the doctrine, and that after the padre left, which was about a year ago . . . they went back to making sacrifices and to continue the deaths. And this witness knows that about four months ago a sacrifice was made outside the village on the road to Mani, by order of Lorenzo Cocom, chief, in which they killed two girls and tied them to two crosses like the first. Francisco Cauich, *ah-kin*, offered the hearts of the two girls. And Juan Cime cut the said girls open . . . and they carried the bodies to the said *cenote* at Suitunchen. And they told them to say nothing, not even to their wives and children, because . . . all would die if it should be known by the Spaniards and the fathers . . . And the companions of this witness who went to say matins [were] the master of this witness called Francisco Canche and Martin Tut and Juan Canul and Francisco Cachum, who is the friend of this witness, because they learnt to read together . . .

Francisco Canche, 19 August

On this said day of nineteenth August in the said year 1562 . . . Melchor [*sic*] Canche of the school of this village of Sotuta and constable of the said village . . . said that about five years ago more or less this witness went to the church . . . one night to say matins with the rest of the boys from the school, and entering the church he saw how the chiefs and *principales* of the said village were sacrificing to the idols they had there and were going to kill two girls to offer their hearts to the idols. And this witness saw how they made the said sacrifice and killed the said girls and crucified them and tied them to two crosses they had . . . and he saw that those who put the said girls on the cross were Lorenzo Cocom, chief and governor who hanged himself, and Juan Cime, and putting them on the cross those who tied them said, 'See here the figure of Jesus Christ', and thus they put the name on them. And he saw how saying this they untied the two girls and lowered them, and when they were down Juan Cime and Luis Ku cut open the girls . . . and took the hearts and gave them to the *ah-kines*, which *ah-kines* offered the hearts to the idols. And they told them to be quiet and to say nothing, speaking to the people who were there, so that the Spaniards should not know of it, because if they knew all would die. And . . . Lorenzo Cocom and the *ah-kines* and *principales* threatened this witness and the rest of his companions . . . And those who were present at the said sacrifice were Juan Cocom, governor of the village, and Lorenzo Cocom, both now dead, and [here follow fifteen names], and all were known to this witness because he talked with them and saw them at the said sacrifice. And after making the said sacrifice and the deaths of the two girls the bodies were thrown into a *cenote* called Tilcibichen [Tacchebilchen?] because they told the witness they had thrown them there, which was told him by Martin Ba and Francisco Uicab, *ah-kines* who were those who carried the bodies. And the crosses remained kept there in the house of Lorenzo Cocom for other sacrifices. And further to this sacrifice the witness saw another sacrifice being made in the church and it seems to this witness it was about five months after the first, and he saw how in it they killed two boys and offered their hearts to the demons and idols that were there, and they did not put them on the cross. And the same people were present there as he had declared, and that Lorenzo Cocom, now dead, and Juan Cime cut open these two boys. And then they took the bodies to throw them in the same *cenote*, and that the *ah-kines* were Francisco Uicab and Luis Ku, who are alive now. These offered the hearts to the idols, anointing their snouts with the blood. And that afterwards they forgot the said sacrifice and this witness saw them make no more until a year ago at the time of the hurricane the same people made a sacrifice inside the house of Lorenzo Cocom, and that Juan Cocom was not present because he was already dead. And he saw how they sacrificed two boys and tied them on two crosses and that those who tied them were Lorenzo Cocom and Juan Cime who were saying that such boys were sons of god, and that saying this they cut them open and to cut them open they lowered them from the cross, and the said Lorenzo Cocom and Juan Cime took out the hearts, and the said Lorenzo Cocom offered the hearts to the idols. And this Lorenzo Cocom was an *ah-kin*, and they threw the bodies of these boys into the *cenote* where they had first thrown the others. And that after this sacrifice about six or seven months ago this witness saw another sacrifice made to the idols in the church in which they killed two little girls. And all were present at the said sacrifice who had been present at the first except the said Juan Cocom who was already dead, and they put these girls on the crosses they had for it. And that then the said Lorenzo Cocom and Juan Cime cut them open and they took out the hearts and gave them to Francisco Uicab and Lorenzo Cocom, *ah-kines* and that then they threw the bodies in the *cenote* where the first ones [were]. And always the *ah-kines* and *principales* and the said Lorenzo Cocom were urging those who were there to stay silent, and that they should say nothing and be silent, and therefore through fear no one had dared to say anything because he was a great lord and principal governor and they held [*sic*] him very much. And that after this sacrifice three or four months this witness saw how they made another sacrifice to the idols and demons inside the church of the said village in which they killed dogs and deer and animals and ate them and drank in the manner of the old days, in which sacrifices . . . Lorenzo Cocom and the rest of the *ah-kines* and *principales* warned them all to be silent and that they should say nothing so that the friars should not know, because all would be killed and they would seem to them new things and therefore all said they would keep silent. And the boys of the school and the masters who were there were Francisco Canul, master, and Pedro Can, schoolmasters [*sic*], and Francisco Cocom of the school and Lorenzo Cocom . . .

[The witness signed his name as Francisco, not Melchor, Canche.]
Source: Scholes and Adams, *Don Diego Quijada*, I, 78–82.

Glossary of Spanish and Maya terms

adelantado (Span.) title conferred by Spanish Crown on some conquerors and founders of new colonies – a royal deputy.

ah-kin (Maya) priest.

alcalde (Span.) official of a Spanish town, exercising limited executive and judicial functions within the jurisdiction of the town; in an Indian town, an official under the direction of the governor.

alcalde mayor (Span.) head of a provincial administration in the colonial period.

alguacil (Span.) constable, under the town authorities.

almehen (Maya) noble, known descent in male and female line.

arroba (Span.) 25 lb dry measure.

audiencia (Span.) superior court and administrative commission.

auto de fe (Span.) act of ceremonial ecclesiastical sentencing or the resulting punishment.

balche (Maya) fermented beverage brewed from honey and bark.

barrio (Span.) ward or division of a town.

batab (Maya) in pre-Spanish times, civil head of a town.

cabildo (Span.) town corporation.

cacique (Span./Arawak) an Indian chief; in colonial period the holder of a hereditary office; usually governor of the town.

cenote (Span. from Maya *dzonot*) a natural sink-hole or well, peculiar to the Yucatan peninsula.

congregación (Span.) the policy of resettling Indians in the vicinity of Christian missions.

doctrina (Span.) essential Christian instruction; a village where no regular parish had been established.

encomienda (Span.) a Crown grant of the tribute and labour of a specified number of Indians.

encomendero (Span.) the holder of a grant from the Spanish Crown of the tribute, and in some cases the labour, of a specified number of Indians. The *encomendero* was expected to supply military service to the Crown, and to care for the spiritual and physical well-being of his Indians.

fiscal (Span.) prosecutor.

garrucha (Span.) the 'hoist', a torture device used by the inquisition.

gobernador (Span.) governor; applied to Spanish head of the province of Yucatan, and to the head of each Indian town.

halach uinic (Maya) head-chief or independent ruler of a territory or 'province'.

juez receptor (Span.) official appointed delegate judge.

juez visitador (Span.) judge authorised to carry out an official tour of inspection.

katun (Maya) twenty-year period.

legua (Span.) measure of distance; a league about three and a half miles.

macegual (Nahuatl) common Indian; not a noble.

matrícula (Span.) tax list.

milpa (Maya) field cultivated by the slash-and-burn method, devoted to corn and other vegetables.

monte (Span.) forest, area of scrub or brush; a mountain.

natural (Span.) Native.

oidor (Span.) judge of an *Audiencia*.

peso (Span.) monetary unit of 8 *reales*.

principal —(Span.) an Indian of noble status; sometimes head of a subdivision of a town.

probanza (Span.) a sworn statement of merits and services to the Crown; documentary proof of the nobility of a native family.

receptor (Span.) receiver (of information).

regidor (Span.) member of a *cabildo* or town council.

relación (Span.) account or report.

residencia (Span.) the hearing of charges against an official, and the rendering of a judgment on his activities in office, normally conducted at the end of the term of office.

señor (Span.) lord.

señor natural (Span.) a natural lord; an Indian recognised by Spaniards as having the status of ruler from pre-conquest times.

tamene (Nahuatl) Indian carrier or porter.

vecino (Span.) a citizen of a town.

villa (Span.) a town enjoying certain privileges of local government.

visita (Span.) an official inspection tour by a judge; a town or village with a church but no resident clergy.

visitador (Span.) an inspector-general; a specially appointed commissioner.

Notes

1. Explorers

1 *Vida del Almirante Don Cristóbal Colón escrita por su hijo Hernando Colón*, Edición, prólogo y notas de Ramón Iglesias, Fondo de Cultura Económica, México, 1947, Cap. 89, 274–5.

2 France V. Scholes and Ralph L. Roys, *The Maya Chontal Indians of Acalan-Tixchel: A Contribution to the History of Ethnography of the Yucatan Peninsula* (1948), 2nd edition, Norman, University of Oklahoma Press, 1968, esp. chap. 2; Anne C. Chapman, 'Port of Trade Enclaves in Aztec and Maya Civilizations', in Karl Polanyi, Conrad M. Arensberg, Harry W. Pearson (eds.), *Trade and Market in the Early Empires; Economics in History and Theory*, N.Y., The Free Press, 1957, 144–53; Jeremy A. Sabloff and William L. Rathje, 'The Rise of a Maya Merchant Class', *Scientific American*, 233 (1975), 72–82; J. Eric S. Thompson, *Maya History and Religion*, Norman, University of Oklahoma Press, 1970, 3–47, 124–58.

3 A. M. Tozzer (ed.), *Landa's Relación de las Cosas de Yucatán: a translation*, Cambridge, Peabody Museum, 1941 (hereafter Landa, *Relación*), 42 and ns. 211 and 214; 'Relaciones de Yucatán', in *Colección de documentos inéditos relativos al descubrimiento, conquista y organización de las antiguas posesiones españolas de Ultramar*, 2nd series, vols. 11, 13, Madrid, Real Academia de la Historia, 1898–1900 (hereafter R.Y.1 and R.Y.2); R.Y.1, 44–5; Ralph L. Roys, *The Indian Background of Colonial Yucatan (1943)*, Norman, University of Oklahoma Press, 1972, 15, 77.

4 Bernal Díaz del Castillo, *Historia verdadera de la conquista de la Nueva España*, Introducción y notas de Joaquín Ramiro Cabañas, Editorial Porrua, México, 1966, Caps. 1–6; Henry Raup Wagner (ed.), *The Discovery of Yucatan by Francisco Hernández de Córdoba*, Berkeley, California, Cortés Society, 1942. Wagner offers translations of the relevant Spanish texts. I have largely followed Díaz' participant account.

5 Díaz, *Historia*, Caps. 2, 4–5.

6 Díaz, *Historia*, Cap. 2.

7 Díaz, *Historia*, Cap. 4.

8 Díaz, *Historia*, Cap. 6.

9 Francisco López de Gómara, *Cortés: The Life of the Conqueror by his Secretary* (1552), translated and edited by Lesley Byrd Simpson, Berkeley and Los Angeles, University of California Press, 1966, 58.

10 Christopher Columbus to the King and Queen of Spain, Jamaica, 7 July 1503, *Select Document Illustrating the Four Voyages of Columbus . . . trans. and edited . . . by*

Cecil Jane, Hakluyt Society, 1930–33, 2 vols., Nendeln, Kraus Reprint 1967, 2: 104.

11 Díaz, *Historia*, Cap. 21.

12 Díaz, *Historia*, Cap. 74.

13 Díaz, *Historia*, Caps 6 and 8. For the Grijalva expedition see Henry Raup Wagner, *The Discovery of New Spain in 1518 by Juan de Grijalva*, Berkeley, California, Cortés Society, 1942, for the Spanish texts. Wagner argues that Díaz, despite his claims, was not a member of the Grijalva expedition. Although not fully persuaded, I have nonetheless placed more emphasis on the *Itinerario* of Juan Díaz, a secular cleric with the expedition (ibid., 69–83), and on the account of Fernández de Oviedo, printed in 1535, and appearing to incorporate a log of the expedition written, in Wagner's view, by the pilot Alaminos (ibid., 88–135).

14 Díaz, *Historia*, Cap. 11.

15 Díaz, *Historia*, Cap. 25; Landa, *Relación*, 13–14.

16 Landa, *Relación*, 15; Díaz, *Historia*, Caps. 26 and 29; Francisco Cervantes de Salazar, *Crónica de la Nueva España* (1560), Madrid, 1914, Caps. 25–9.

17 Gonzalo Fernández de Oviedo y Valdés, *Historia general y natural de las Indias (1535–1547)*, Madrid, 1959, 32: 3, 6; Díaz, *Historia*, Cap. 29; Landa, *Relación*, 8, n. 38.

18 A Mexican garrison survived at Xicalango, and presumably kept itself informed of events in the Aztec capital of Tenochtitlan. R.Y.1: 352, 364; 2:221–2.

19 Landa, *Relación*, 42.

2. Conquerors

1 For the *capitulación*, see Fr. Diego López de Cogolludo, *Los tres siglos de la dominación española en Yucatán o sea Historia de Esta Provincia (1654?)*, 2 vols., Mérida, Manuel Aldana Rivas, 1867–68 (hereafter Cogolludo, *Historia*), Lib.2, Caps. 2–4. Landa and Oviedo give the most complete early accounts of the conquest. The classic analysis remains that of Robert S. Chamberlain, *The Conquest and Colonization of Yucatan, 1517–1550*, Washington, Carnegie Institution, 1948, resting as it does on the exploitation of extant conquerors' accounts. Of these the most important is the *probanza* of Blas González, 1567, in Archivo General de Indias, Seville (hereafter A.G.I.), Patronato 68, no. 1, ramo 2.

2 Montejo v. Fiscal over removal from office, 1552, quoted Chamberlain, *Conquest*, 34.

3 Landa, *Relación*, 48; Oviedo, *Historia*, Lib. 32, Cap. 2; Probanza of Blas González.

4 Oviedo, *Historia*, Lib. 32, Cap. 3.

5 Oviedo, *Historia*, Lib. 32, Caps 2–8.

6 Ralph L. Roys, *The Political Geography of the Yucatan Maya*, Washington, Carnegie Institution, 1957, *passim*.

7 E.g. the remarkable vacillations of Macanahau, as described by Chamberlain, *Conquest*, 102–16

8 For the groupings Landa, *Relación*, esp. 17–40; *Relaciones de Yucatán*; Roys, *Political Geography*, *passim*.

9 *Crónica de Yaxkukul*, ed. Juan Martínez Hernández, Mérida, Talleres de la Compañía Tipográfica Yucateca, 1926, 6–7. Cf. 'Chronicle of Chac-Xuleb-Chen [Chicxulub]', Maya text and English translation in Daniel G. Brinton, *The Maya Chronicles (1882)*, Reprint, New York, A.M.S. Press, 1969.

10 On tainted water and the exuberant insect life, see G. C. Shattuck (ed.), *The Peninsula of Yucatan*, Washington, Carnegie Institution, 1933, esp. 207–14, 547–74.

11 E.g. the Parajas *probanza*, quoted Chamberlain, *Conquest*, 213.

12 R. Y. 1, 41–3.

13 Montejo to the Crown, Vera Cruz, 20 April 1529, *Col. de documentos inéditos relativos al descubrimiento, conquista y colonización de las antiguas posesiones españolas en América y Oceanía . . . muy especialmente del de Indias*, Madrid, 1864–84, 42 vols. (hereafter *D.I.I.*), 13, 89–91.

14 Montejo to the Crown, Salamanca de Campeche, 10 August 1534, quoted Chamberlain, *Conquest*, 164.

15 Landa, *Relación*, 54.

16 E.g. R.Y.1, 288–9.

17 Landa, *Relación*, 54–6.

18 Cogolludo, *Historia*, Lib. 3, Cap. 7.

19 Fr. Lorenzo de Bienvenida to the Crown, 10 February 1548, *Cartas de Indias*, Madrid, Ministerio de Fomento, 1877, 70–80; Chamberlain, *Conquest*, 233–6.

20 *Cabildo* of Mérida to the Crown, 14 June 1543, quoted Chamberlain, *Conquest*, 163.

21 Cogolludo, *Historia*, Lib. 2, Caps. 8–9; Chamberlain, *Conquest*, 146–9.

22 The first *tasación* or agreed tribute list for Yucatan was drawn up 1549. Not all areas were included in the list, which is published in Francisco del Paso y Troncoso (comp.), *Epistolario de Nueva España, 1505–1818*, México, 1939–42, 16 vols., 5, 103–81; 6, 73–112.

23 A large dispute is sidestepped here. Estimates of pre-contact population vary widely, from a high of eight millions offered by Helmuth O. Wagner, 'Subsistence Potential and Population Density of the Maya on the Yucatan Peninsula and Causes for the Decline in Population in the Fifteenth Century', *Verhandlungen des XXXVIII International Amerikannistenkongresses, Stuttgart-München, 1968*, Munich, Kommissionsverlag Klaus Renner, 1970, 1: 185–91, to a low of 300,000 suggested by Ralph Roys, 'Lowland Maya Native Society at Spanish Contact', in *Handbook of Middle American Indians*, Austin, University of Texas Press, 1965, 3: 661. For a discussion see Sherburne F. Cook and Woodrow Borah, *Essays in Population History: Mexico and the Caribbean*, Berkeley, University of California Press, 1972–79, 2: 22–40. Estimates for the post-1549 population differ because of variations in the conversion factor from tributaries to population. See Cook and Borah, *Essays*, 2: 1–79 for extended discussion of the whole colonial period, and Peter Gerhard, *The Southeast Frontier of New Spain*, Princeton, Princeton University Press, 1979. The cost in Spanish lives had been high. Cogolludo estimated that the conquest took more than 600 Spanish lives, with only 190 men living to claim their reward as conquerors. Cogolludo, *Historia*, Lib. 3, Cap. 15.

3. Settlers

1 Montejo to Montejo the Younger for the conquest of Yucatan, Ciudad Real de Chiapas 1540, quoted Chamberlain, 197–8; 218–19.

2 For a map of the early town, see J. Ignacio Rubio Mañé, *La Casa de Montejo en Mérida de Yucatán*, México, 1941, 16. For an account of its founding, see R.Y.1: 53–5.

3 Chamberlain, *Conquest*, 189.
4 Chamberlain, *Conquest*, 240, n. 8; R.Y. 1: 38ff., 2: 4, 64–5, 114–15, 131, 167–8, 178–81; Cogolludo, *Historia*, Lib. 5, Cap. 2.
5 Chamberlain, *Conquest*, 277–80.
6 F. V. Scholes, C. R. Menéndez, J. I. Rubio Mañé and E. B. Adams (eds.), *Documentos para la historia de Yucatán*, 3 vols., Mérida, Compañía Tipográfica Yucateca, 1936–38 (hereafter *DHY*), 2:45–53, 68–9; R.Y.1:55, 62; 2:35, 69–70.
7 See *tasación* of 1549, Paso y Troncoso, *Epistolario*, For an assessment of the oppressiveness of the 1549 requirements, see Scholes and Roys, *The Maya Chontal Indians of Acalan Tixchel*, 151–3. See also 470, n. 1. Scholes and Roys tells us that the aged, the ill, members of ruling families, and certain town officials were officially exempted. For the later García de Palacio's revisions, see ibid., 241. The Alcalde Mayor Quijada reported that by 1563 80,000 cotton mantles and a 'great quantity' of wax, together worth more than 250 thousand pesos, were being shipped from Yucatan's ports. Quijada to the Crown, 15 March 1563, Mérida, *Cartas de Indias*, 288. For cotton cultivation see Landa, *Relación*, 152, 200.
8 Chamberlain, *Conquest*, 343.
9 Gerhard, *The Southeast Frontier*, 25, Table B.
10 On the molestation of Indian women in Spanish service, see Don Diego Quijada to the Crown, 6 October 1561, R.Y.2: 260–1. On Spaniards marrying native women, see Juan Francisco Molina Solís, *Historia del descubrimiento y conquista de Yucatán*, México, Ediciones Mensaje, 1943, 2 vols., 2: 384–5. Scholes and Roys have retrieved much information on the *cacique* Don Pablo Paxbolon of Acalan-Tixchel, who married the daughter of a Spaniard named Diego de Orduña, after the death of his Maya wife. However Paxbolon was remarkable, both in his upbringing and in his expertise in mediating between the two cultures. Orduña was in all probability a trading partner. Scholes and Roys, *The Maya Chontal Indians of Acalan-Tixchel*, 248–9, 351. On 'lewd houses', see Fray Francisco de Toral to the Crown, 20 April 1567, *Cartas de Indias*, 242–5; Petition of Joaquín de Leguízamo, n.d., in France V. Scholes and Eleanor B. Adams, (ed. *Don Diego Quijada, alcalde mayor de Yucatán, 1561–1565*, 2 vols., Documentos sacados de los archivos de España, Biblioteca Histórica Mexicana de Obras Inéditas, nos. 14–15, México, Editorial Porrua, 1938, 2 vols., 207–8; Don Diego Quijada to the Crown, 6 October 1561, R.Y.2: 260–1.

4. Missionaries

1 For an attractive and long-needed brief account of the early days of the Franciscan order, and a useful collection of central documents, see Rosalind B. Brooke, *The Coming of the Friars*, New York and London, 1975. For the constitutions of the order, Rosalind B. Brooke, *Early Franciscan Government: Elias to Bonaventura*, Cambridge, 1959. There is a wealth of scholarly work on all aspects of the Franciscan enterprise in the New World, among which the works of the Spanish Franciscan Pedro Borges are outstanding; see his *Métodos misionales en la cristianización de América*, Consejo Superior de Investigaciones Científicas, Departmento de Misionología Española, Madrid, 1960, and his *El envío de misioneras a América durante la época española*, Salamanca, Universidad Pontifica, 1977. For a more recent overview, Lino Gómez Canedo, *Evangelización y Conquista: Experiencia Franciscana en Hispanoamérica*, México, Editorial Porrua, 1977. For Franciscans in Mexico the classic account is Robert Ricard, *La Conquête*

Spirituelle du Mexique (1933), translated into English by Lesley Byrd Simpson as *The Spiritual Conquest of Mexico*, Berkeley and Los Angeles, University of California Press, 1966. For the impulses behind missionary zeal John Leddy Phelan *The Millenial Kingdom of the Franciscans in the New World* (1956), 2nd edition, Berkeley and Los Angeles, University of California Press, 1970, is indispensable. See also 'Vida de Fr Martín de Valencia escrita por su compañero Fr Francisco Jiménez', ed. P. Anastasio López, *Archivo iberoamericano*, 26 (1926), and Inga Clendinnen, 'Disciplining the Indians: Franciscan Ideology and Missionary Violence in Sixteenth-Century Yucatan', *Past and Present*, 94 (1982), 27–48.

2 Ricard, *Spiritual Conquest*, 80.

3 E.g. Elizabeth Andros Foster (trans. and ed.), *Motolinía's History of the Indians of New Spain*, Westport, Conn., 1977; Fr Bernardino de Sahagún, Prologue to Book X, 'The People', *The Florentine Codex: General History of the Things of New Spain*, translated and annotated by Arthur J. O. Anderson and Charles E. Dibble, Santa Fe, School of American Research and the University of Utah, 1982, Introductory Volume, 79–80.

4 Fr Gerónimo de Mendieta, *Historia eclesiástica indiana: obra escrita a fines del siglo XVI*, ed. Joaquín García Icazbalceta, México, Porrua, 1971, Lib. 3, Cap. 28.

5 Mendieta, *Historia*, Lib. 3, Cap. 35.

6 *The Oroz Codex*, trans. and ed. Angélico Chávez, O. F. M. Washington, 1972, 183.

7 Mendieta, *Historia*, Lib. 3, Cap. 29.

8 For an example of the Crown's mean accounting, see Stella María González Cicero, *Perspectiva religiosa en Yucatán, 1517–1571*, México, El Colegio de México, 1978, 96.

9 Borges, *Métodos misionales*, 346, n. 35; *Oroz Codex*, 359. For a sensitive account of the distinctive Franciscan understanding of obedience, see David Knowles, *From Pachomius to Ignatius: A Study in the Constitutional History of the Religious Orders*, Oxford, 1966, esp. 80–8.

10 For examples, Motolinía, *History, passim; Oroz Codex, passim;* Mendieta, *Historia*, Lib. 5.

11 For the confused and contradictory evidence of earlier missionary activity see Chamberlain, *Conquest*, 311–13. For the missionary programme, Landa, *Relación, passim*, but esp. 68–75 and ns. 306, 308–14; Cogoluddo, *Historia, passim*, but esp. Libs. 5 and 6; Bernardo de Lizana, *Historia de Yucatán: Devocionario de Nuestra Señora de Izamal y conquista espiritual (1633)*, 2nd edition, México, Museo Nacional, 1893.

12 Landa, *Relación*, 73.

13 Fray Lorenzo de Bienvenida to the Crown, 10 February 1548, in *Cartas de Indias*, 70–82.

14 Ibid.

15 Landa, *Relación*, 68, n. 308; Molina Solís, *Historia del Descubrimiento*, 2: 350–7.

16 Landa, *Relación*, 51.

17 Fr Luis de Villalpando to the Crown, Mérida, 15 October 1550, in Gómez Canedo, *Evangelización*, 229–34

18 Ibid.

5. Conflict

1 'Ordenanzas del Lic. Tomás López', Cogolludo, *Historia*, Lib. 5, Caps 16–19.

2 E.g. R.Y.2: 209–10. See also 30–1, 67–79, 122–3, 187. For a chilling account of the

removal of the Chontal to Tixchel see Scholes and Roys, *Maya Chontal Indians*, 169–73. Orders for the gathering of Indians into convenient locations occur from the earliest days of Spanish settlement in the Indies, but the policy of *congregación* or *reducción* was not systematically implemented elsewhere, at least among settled Indian populations (e.g. in Peru and Central Mexico), for forty or more years after conquest, when it was executed by civil authorities in response to massive Indian population loss, and the consequent debilitation of communities. Edward Kurjack has argued that *congregación* in Yucatan was perhaps a response to early and massive population decline. Edward B. Kurjack, *Prehistoric lowland Maya Community and Social Organization: A Case Study at Dzibilchaltún, Yucatan, Mexico*, Pub. 38. New Orleans, Tulane University Press, 1974.

3 Landa, *Relación*, 72; Cogolludo, *Historia*, Lib. 6, Cap. 8.

4 'Proceso contra Francisco Hernández, 1556–1562, Archivo General de la Nación (A.G.N.)', Inquisición 6, no. 4, published in J. Ignacio Rubio Mañé (ed.), *Archivo de la Historia de Yucatán, Campeche y Tabasco*, 3 vols., México, 1943 (hereafter *A.H.Y.C.T.*), 2: 7–334. See also Rubio Mañé, Intro. XXI-XXXIII, and Scholes, in Scholes and Adams, *Don Diego Quijada*, 1: XX-XXVI.

5 Scholes and Adams, *Don Diego Quijada*, 1, 281–2.

6 For the confession, Rubio Mañé, *A.H.Y.C.T.* 2: 326–31.

7 Diego de Landa, Francisco de Navarro and Hernando de Guevara to the Council of the Indies, 3 April 1559, France V. Scholes, Carlos R. Menéndez, J. Ignacio Rubio Mañé and Eleanor B. Adams (eds.), *Documentos para la historia de Yucatán*, 3 vols., Mérida, 1936–1938 (hereafter *D.H.Y.*) 1: 83–4.

8 'Cargos de residencia contra el lic. Garci Jufre de Loaisa hechos por el alcalde mayor don Diego Quijada, Mérida, 2 de agosto 1561', and 'Sentencia del doctor Diego Quijada contra el lic. Garci Jufre de Loaisa, Mérida, 9 de agosto 1561', in Scholes and Adams, *Don Diego Quijada*, 1, 9–12.

9 Cabildo of Mérida to the Crown, Mérida, 6 October 1561, Scholes and Adams, *Don Diego Quijada*, 1: 13–16.

10 Don Diego Quijada to the Crown, 15 April 1561, *Cartas de Indias*, 369–79, esp. 373.

11 Miguel Serrano y Sanz, 'Vida y escritos de Fray Diego de Landa', Appendix B in Rubio Mañé, *A.H.Y.C.T.* 2: 435. Landa's translations have been lost. His *doctrina* was probably similar to the Nahuatl *doctrina* of Fray Alonso de Molina, used extensively in New Spain.

12 Cogolludo, *Historia*, Lib. 5, Cap. 14; Lizana, *Historia de Yucatán*, 56v.–60v.

13 Landa, *Relación, passim*, but esp. 89–91, 125–6, 194, 199, 204–5.

14 Landa, *Relación*, 127, 167, 207–8.

15 Landa, *Relación*, 43–4.

16 Landa, *Relación*, 169.

6. Crisis

1 Cogolludo, *Historia*, Lib. 6, Cap. 1; Landa, *Relación*, 68, n. 308. While arrivals in the peninsula are reasonably well recorded, departures have largely gone unrecorded. I have been unable to establish the precise number of Franciscans present in Yucatan in 1562. It was later claimed against Landa that he had driven several 'venerable and learned' friars out of the province when he became Provincial. Declaration made at the request of Bishop Francisco de Toral, January 1563, Scholes and Adams, *Don Diego Quijada*, 1: 257–8, 262, 270–1, 283.

2 Scholes and Adams, *Don Diego Quijada*, 1: 326; 2: 415–16.

3 'Declaraciones de algunos testigos sobre las investigaciones de las idolatrías de los Indios hecha por Fray Diego de Landa y sus compañeros en el año de 1562, Residencia de Quijada', *A.G.I.* Justicia, in Scholes and Adams, *Don Diego Quijada*, 1: 24–68. See esp. testimony of Bartolomé de Bohorques, 24–31. For a general account, see France V. Scholes and Ralph L. Roys, 'Fray Diego de Landa and the Problem of Idolatry in Yucatan', *Co-operation in Research*, Washington, Carnegie Institution, 1938, 585–620.

4 Sworn statement of Fray Pedro de Ciudad Rodrigo, 20 September 1562, Scholes and Adams, *Don Diego Quijada*, 1: 180.

5 Scholes and Adams, *Don Diego Quijada*, 1: 25.

6 Scholes and Adams, *Don Diego Quijada*, 1: 38.

7 H.C. Lea, *A History of the Inquisition of Spain* (1906–1907), 4 vols., New York, 1966, 3, esp. 19. Cf. Yolande Mariel de Ibáñez, *La Inquisición en México durante el siglo xvi*, México, 1946, 48.

8 Scholes and Adams, *Don Diego Quijada*, 1: 66.

9 Report of Sebastián Vázquez, 25 March 1565, Scholes and Adams, *Don Diego Quijada*, 2: 209–21, esp. 212–14.

10 For Bishop Zumárraga's inquisition, and a full discussion of the episcopal inquisition and the operations of the Tribunal of the Holy Office in the sixteenth century, see Richard E. Greenleaf, *Zumárraga and the Mexican Inquisition, 1535–1543*, Washington, D.C., 1962; Richard E. Greenleaf, *The Mexican Inquisition of the Sixteenth Century*, Albuquerque, 1969. For the detailed records of one torture session, see 'Proceso del Santo Oficio contra Miguel, indio, vecino de México, por idolatría', in *Procesos de indios idólatras y hechiceros*, Publicaciones del Archivo General de la Nación, iii, México, 1912, 134–9.

11 For the regulations, see Francisco Antonio Lorenzana, *Concilios provinciales primero y segundo, celebrados en la muy noble y muy leal ciudad de México presidiendo el Illmo y Rmo. Señor D. Fr Alonso de Montufar, en los años de 1555, y 1565*, México, 1769.

12 Petition of Fray Diego de Landa, 15 September 1562; Scholes and Adams, *Don Diego Quijada*, 1: 171.

13 Accounts of Bartolomé de Bohorques, 22 September 1562, Scholes and Adams, *Don Diego Quijada*, 1: 301–9. See also 1: 27, 39, 193–7, 296.

14 Petition of Fray Diego de Landa to Don Diego Quijada, 4 July 1562, Scholes and Adams, *Don Diego Quijada*, 1: 70.

15 Testimony of Bartolomé de Bohorques, 2 January 1565, Scholes and Adams, *Don Diego Quijada*, 1: 27. The testimony of the notary Juan de Villalobos suggests that the initiative was taken by Quijada, but as the scribe saw only the formal documents relating to the arrangement, and as Bohorques claimed he observed the whole sequence of events, I have preferred his account. But cf. testimony of Juan de Villalobos, 27 February 1565, Scholes and Adams, *Don Diego Quijada*, 2: 56–7, and that of Sebastián Vázquez, 25 March 1565, 2: 212.

16 Testimony of Juan Cuouh, 5 July 1562, Scholes and Adams, *Don Diego Quijada*, 1: 60–1.

17 Petition by Fray Diego de Landa to Don Diego Quijada, 4 July 1562, Scholes and Adams, *Don Diego Quijada*, 1: 69.

18 For the violence, and the *encomenderos'* attempts to intervene, see e.g. Scholes and Adams, *Don Diego Quijada*, 1: 222–5; 2: 212–14.

19 Testimony of Gómez de Castrillo, 22 January 1565, Scholes and Adams, *Don Diego Quijada*, 1: 43–4.

20 Testimonies of Francisco Jiménez and Juan de Palomar, 23 September 1562, Scholes and Adams, *Don Diego Quijada*, 1: 217–20. See also 1: 37, 68.

21 Testimony of Lorenzo de Monterroso, 26 January 1565, Scholes and Adams, *Don Diego Quijada*, 2: 46–55, esp. 48–9.

22 For details of Toral's life, see Eleanor B. Adams, *A Biobibliography of Franciscan Authors in Colonial Central America*, Washington, 1953, 78–9.

23 Sahagún, *Florentine Codex*, Prologue to Bk. I, Introductory vol., 46.

24 José Llaguno, *La Personalidad jurídica del indio y el III Concilio Provincial mexicano (1585)*, *México, Editorial* Porrua, 1963, 175–6; Fray Francisco de Toral to the Crown, 25 May 1558 and 20 February 1559, *Cartas de Indias*, 132–4, 138–40; Fray Francisco de Toral to the Crown, 28 May 1562, *D.H.Y.* 2: 23.

25 Testimony of Joaquín de Leguízamo, 19 January 1563, Scholes and Adams, *Don Diego Quijada*, 1: 264.

26 Fray Antonio de Tarancón to Fray Francisco de Bustamente, 26 February 1563, Scholes and Adams, *Don Diego Quijada*, 2: 23; Fray Lorenzo de Bienvenida to the Crown, 23 February 1563, 28.

27 Indictment against the Indians of Sotuta province, 11 August 1562, Scholes and Adams, *Don Diego Quijada*, 1: 71–2. See appendix for translation.

28 Testimony of Pedro Huhul of Kanchunup, 17 August 1562, Scholes and Adams, *Don Diego Quijada*, 1: 94. For the Sotuta testimonies, 1; 71–129.

29 Testimonies of Antonio Pech and Francisco Canche, 19 August 1562, Scholes and Adams, *Don Diego Quijada*, 1: 78–81. Francisco is incorrectly given the Christian name 'Melchor' at the beginning of his testimony (80) but signs as 'Francisco' (82). See appendix for translations.

7. Attrition

1 'Información hecha a pedimento del Provincial Fray Diego de Landa ante el doctor Quijada, 27 January 1563', Scholes and Adams, *Don Diego Quijada*, 1: 289–301, esp. 297.

2 Scholes and Adams, *Don Diego Quijada*, 1: 129–35.

3 Judicial proceedings of Fray Francisco de Toral, September 1562, Scholes and Adams, *Don Diego Quijada*, 1: 200.

4 For the Hocaba-Homun testimonies see Scholes and Adams, *Don Diego Quijada*, 1: 135–62.

5 Memorandum of what must be verified . . . in the Province of Sotuta, 9 September 1562, Scholes and Adams, *Don Diego Quijada*, 1: 204.

6 For Magaña's report, submitted 23 September 1562, Scholes and Adams, *Don Diego Quijada*, 1: 207–14.

7 Information taken at the request of Bishop Francisco de Toral, January 1563, Scholes and Adams, *Don Diego Quijada*, 1; 245–5; Fray Francisco de Toral to the Crown, 15 March 1563 and 3 March 1564, 2: 42–3, 68–73.

8 Statement of Fray Juan Pizarro and Fray Francisco de Miranda, 16 September 1562, Scholes and Adams, *Don Diego Quijada*, 1: 174.

9 *Auto* of Don Diego Quijada, n.d., Scholes and Adams, *Don Diego Quijada*, 1: 174; information gathered by Don Diego Quijada against the Bishop . . . 18 September 1562, Scholes and Adams, *Don Diego Quijada*, 1: 174–7.

10 Scholes and Adams, *Don Diego Quijada*, 1: 177–9.

11 E.g. Testimony of Bartolomé Rojo, 17 September 1562, Scholes and Adams, *Don Diego Quijada*, 1: 162–4.

12 The three were Francisco Pacheco, Bartolomé de Bohorques and Ginés Alvarez, Scholes and Adams, *Don Diego Quijada*, 1: 166–8, 218, 221–3.

13 Juan de Magaña to Alonso de Zorita, 24 September 1562, Scholes and Adams, *Don Diego Quijada*, 1: 182–4.

14 Fray Lorenzo de Bienvenida to the Crown, 23 February 1563, Scholes and Adams, *Don Diego Quijada*, 2: 7–9.

15 Scholes and Adams, *Don Diego Quijada*, 1: 249–89, for Toral's witnesses. For Landa, Scholes and Adams, *Don Diego Quijada*, 1: 289–343.

16 Scholes and Adams, *Don Diego Quijada*, 1: 294–5.

17 Fray Lorenzo de Bienvenida to the Crown, 23 February 1563, Scholes and Adams, *Don Diego Quijada*, 2: 9; Reply of Fray Diego de Landa to charges made against him, n.d., 2: 401.

18 Fray Juan Pizarro to Fray Diego de Landa, 21 March 1563, Scholes and Adams, *Don Diego Quijada*, 2: 58–62; Testimony relating to the sermon preached by Fray Juan Pizarro, 24 March 1562, 2: 62–5.

19 E.g. letter from ten *caciques* of New Spain to the Crown, 11 February 1567, *Cartas de Indias*, 367–8. For another, see William Gates, *Yucatan Before and After the Conquest* (2nd ed.), Baltimore, 1937, 117; Landa, *Relación*, 84, n. 350. (Tozzer gives the date of the *Cartas de Indias* letter incorrectly as 11 February 1565.)

20 Francisco de Montejo Xiu, Juan Pacab, Jorge Xiu and Francisco Pacab to the Crown, 12 April 1567, *Cartas de Indias*, 407–10.

21 Landa, *Relación*, 83–4. For the judgment and relevant testimonies, Scholes and Adams, *Don Diego Quijada*, 2: 396–435.

22 Royal officials of Yucatan to the Crown, 28 February 1563, Scholes and Adams, *Don Diego Quijada*, 2: 27–31; Fray Francisco de Toral to the Crown, 1 March 1563, 2: 38; *cabildo* of the city of Mérida to the Crown, 15 March 1563, 2: 46–52.

23 For the charges Vázquez was to investigate, Scholes and Adams, *Don Diego Quijada*, 2: 195–209; for his response, 209–21; for some of the testimonies he recorded, 1: 24–68.

24 Royal *cedula* naming Don Luis Céspedes governor of Yucatan and Tabasco, 3 June 1564, Scholes and Adams, *Don Diego Quijada*, 2: 225–9.

25 Don Diego Quijada to the Crown, 10 February 1565, Scholes and Adams, *Don Diego Quijada*, 2: 175. As late as May 1564 Quijada did not seem to realise his jeopardy: see Don Diego Quijada to the Crown, 20 May 1564, 2: 79–93.

26 Petition of Joaquín de Leguízamo, n.d., Scholes and Adams, *Don Diego Quijada*, 2: 207–8.

27 Report of Sebastián Vázquez, 25 March 1565, Scholes and Adams, *Don Diego Quijada*, 2: 221. See also 2: 258–98, and 305–7.

28 Sentence of the Council in the *residencia* of Don Diego Quijada, 30 October 1570, Scholes and Adams, *Don Diego Quijada*, 2: 379–92.

29 Don Diego Quijada to the Crown, 10 February 1565, Scholes and Adams, *Don Diego Quijada*, 2: 175.

30 *Cabildo* of the city of Mérida to the Crown; 1 May 1566, *Cartas de Indias*, 397–9.

31 Toral to the Crown, Mérida, 3 March 1564, Scholes and Adams, *Don Diego Quijada*, 2: 68–73; Toral to the Crown, Mérida, 5 April 1569, in Stella María González Cicero, *Perspectiva religiosa en Yucatán, 1517–1571*, México, El Colegio de México, 1978, 240–2.

32 Toral to the Crown, Mérida, 3 June 1564, Scholes and Adams, *Don Diego Quijada*, 2: 93–4.

33 Toral to the Crown, Mérida, 20 April 1567, *Cartas de Indias*, 242–5.

34 Toral to the Crown, 8 October 1566, in González Cicero, *Perspectiva Religiosa*, 229–31.

35 E.g. Toral to the Crown, 20 April 1567, *Cartas de Indias*, 242–5; Toral to the Crown, 22 April 1567, 5 April 1569 and 6 March 1569, in González Cicero, *Perspectiva Religiosa*, 235–6; 238–42.

36 Toral to the Crown, Mérida, 3 March 1564, Scholes and Adams, *Don Diego Quijada*, 2: 68–73.

37 Reply of the Crown to the Bishop of Yucatan, 4 July 1570, in González Cicero, *Perspectiva Religiosa*, 248–9.

38 Fray Alonso Thoral to the Crown, Campeche, 20 June 1566, in González Cicero, *Perspectiva Religiosa*, 218–21.

39 González Cicero, *Perspectiva Religiosa*, 103.

40 The Franciscans to the Crown, 24 February 1570, in González Cicero, *Perspectiva Religiosa*, 244–5.

41 Cogolludo, *Historia*, LIb. 6, Cap. 15. See also Memoria de los conventos, vicarías y pueblos, 1582, *D.H.Y.*, 2: 55–65 which indicates the extent of the Franciscan recovery: in that year there were twenty-four Franciscan parishes, and only four secular.

42 Cogolludo, *Historia*, Lib. 6, Cap. 16; Solorzano y Pereyra, *Política Indiana*, Lib. 6, Cap. 24.

43 'Pleito entre D. Francisco Veláquez de Gijón, Gobernador de Yucatán, y el Obispo Fray Diego de Landa, Año de 1574' (from *A.G.N.* Inquisición: Tomo 117) in Ernesto Ramos (ed.), *Colección Siglo XVI, número 7*, México, 1960.

44 Cogolludo, *Historia*, LIb. 6, Cap. 18.

8. Retrospections

1 Landa, *Relación*, 72. Much of this discussion is drawn from Clendinnen, 'Missionary Violence'.

2 Toral to the Crown, Mérida, 1 March 1563, Scholes and Adams, *Don Diego Quijada*, 2: 34–7; Toral to the Crown, Mérida, 3 March 1564, Scholes and Adams, *Don Diego Quijada*, 2: 68–73.

3 Ibid., 71. While it is likely that Juan de Mérida carried through the actual construction, the basic plan and the first labour were Landa's. Cogolludo, *Historia*, Lib. 5, Cap. 14.

4 Statement made by the Marqués del Valle, 27 November 1562, Scholes and Adams, *Don Diego Quijada*, 1: 186; Information given at the request of Provincial Diego de Landa before Dr Quijada, January 1563, Scholes and Adams, *Don Diego Quijada*, 1: 296; Responses of Fray Diego de Landa to the charges made by Fray Francisco de Guzmán, n.d., Scholes and Adams, *Don Diego Quijada*, 2: 416.

5 E.g. Hector Pérez Martínez (ed.), *Relación de las Cosas de Yucatán, por el Obispo de esa diocese*, México, 1938, intro., 34–6; Francis F. Blom, *The Conquest of Yucatan*, Boston, 1936, 110; William Gates, *Yucatan before and after the Conquest*, iii–iv. Serrano y Sanz is unusual in that he suggests the *Relación* was written before 1562, with the implication that references to the events of that year were inserted later by Landa's or another's hand. Serrano y Sanz, 'Vida y escritos', Rubio Mañé, *A.H.Y.C.T.* 2: 446–7. Tozzer, surprisingly, does not comment at all.

6 Landa, *Relación*, vii. For the possible omissions and transpositions, e.g. 184–6, ns.

962, 963, 965. A recent translator believes that 'the work in its original form was almost certainly dictated', on the grounds of the brusqueries of the style. A. R. Pagden (trans. and ed.), *The Maya: Diego de Landa's Account of the Affairs of Yucatan*, Chicago, 1975, intro. *passim*, but esp. 22.

7 Landa, *Relación*, 75–80.

8 Landa, *Relación*, 170–2. For the flowers, 194; for armadillos and opossums – and the wonder of diving pelicans – 202–4.

9 Sánchez de Aguilar, *Informe*, 295.

10 Sánchez de Aguilar, *Informe*, 283; Toral to the Crown, Mérida, 1 March 1563, Scholes and Adams, *Don Diego Quijada*, 2: 35–6.

11 Landa, *Relación*, 113, 155.

12 Landa, *Relación*, 114.

13 Landa, *Relación*, 117–20, 143.

14 Testimony of Juan Cuouh, Scholes and Adams, *Don Diego Quijada*, 1: 103–8, and appendix.

15 Memorial of Fray Diego de Landa, n.d., Scholes and Adams, *Don Diego Quijada*, 2: 416–23.

9. Finding out

The prefatory quotations for the whole 'Indian' section are drawn from *The Book of Chilam Balam of Chumayel*, in the Roys translation.

1 E.g. Gaspar Antonio Chi, *R.Y.*1: 42–5; *A.G.I.*, Mexico 104, Probanza of Gaspar Antonio Chi; Relación of Gaspar Antonio Chi (1582), Landa, *Relación*, Appendix C. See also 44–6, n. 219. Earlier texts are more rewarding: e.g. 'Crónica de Yaxkukul' and 'Chronicle of Chac-Xuleb-Chen', and the documents generated by the Mani Land Treaty of 1557, Roys, *Indian Background*, 175–94.

2 Nelson Reed, *The Caste War of Yucatan*, Stanford, Stanford University Press, 1964, 278–80.

3 See J. Eric S. Thompson, *A Commentary on the Dresden Codex; a Maya Hieroglyphic Book*, Philadelphia, American Philosophical Society, 1972; *Codex Peresiansis* (Codex Paris, Bibliothèque nacionale, Paris), Introduction and summary F. Anders, Graz, Akademische Druck-u, Verlagsanstalt, 1968; *Codex Tro-Cortesianus* (Codex Madrid, Museo de América, Madrid), Introduction and Summary F. Anders, Graz, Akademische Druck-u, Verlagsanstalt, 1967. For the description of the genre, Father Avendaño (1696), quoted in Philip Ainsworth Means, *History of the Spanish Conquest of Yucatan and of the Itzas*, Cambridge, Mass., Peabody Museum Papers, Harvard University, vol. 7, 1917, 141.

4 For the most accessible example, see Ralph L. Roys (trans. and ed.), *The Book of Chilam Balam of Chumayel* (1933), new edition Norman, University of Oklahoma Press, 1967. For a full listing of the books of Chilam Balam, and other Lowland Maya sources, see Charles Gibson and John B. Glass, 'A Census of Middle American Prose Manuscripts in the Native Historical Tradition', in *Handbook of Middle American Indians*, 15, ed. Howard F. Cline, Austin, University of Texas Press, 1975. See also Alfredo Barrera Vázquez and Silvia Rendón (eds.), *El libro de los libros de Chilam Balam*, México, Fondo de Cultura Económica, 1948. The most recent translation is that by Munro S. Edmonson, *The Ancient Future of the Itza: The Book of Chilam Balam of Tizimin*, Austin, University of Texas Press, 1982.

5 Michael D. Coe, *The Maya Scribe and his World*, New York, The Grolier Club, 1973.

6 Roys, *Chumayel*, 83; Gordon Brotherston, 'Continuity in Maya Writing: New Readings of Two Passages in the Book of Chilam Balam of Chumayel', in *Maya Archeology and Ethnohistory*, edited by Norman Hammond and Gordon R. Wiley, Austin, University of Texas Press, 1979, 241–58.

7 López Medel, *Ordenanzas*; Pedro Sánchez de Aguilar, 'Informe contra idolorum cultores del obispado de Yucatán', (*c.* 1613), in Francisco del Paso y Troncoso, *Tratado de las idolatrías, supersticiones, dioses, ritos, hechicerías y otras costumbres gentílicas de las razas aborígenes de México*, 2nd edition, México, Ediciones Fuente Cultural, 1953, 2: 250–2, 325.

10. Connections

1 López Medel, *Ordenanzas*; for Paxbolon France V. Scholes and Ralph L. Roys, *The Maya Chontal Indians of Acalan-Tixchel: A Contribution to the History and Ethnography of the Yucatan Peninsula* (1948), 2nd edition, Norman, University of Oklahoma Press, 1968, 175–8, 185–250, 254–64.

2 Landa, *Relación*, esp. 40, 99–101. Information in this section is drawn from the *Relación* unless otherwise noted. For kinship terms see Ralph L. Roys, 'Personal Names of the Maya of Yucatan', in *Contributions to American Anthropology and History*, 6, Washington, Carnegie Institution, 1940, 31–48; William A. Haviland, 'Rules of Descent in Sixteenth-Century Yucatan', *Estudios de Cultura Náhuatl*, 9 (1973), 135–50. For the household at contact, Fray Lorenzo de Bienvenida to the Crown, Mérida, 10 February 1948, in *Cartas de Indias*, 74; López Medel, *Ordenanzas*; 'Papeles relativos a la vista del oidor Dr Diego García de Palacio, 1583', *Boletín del Archivo General de la Nación*, 11, 1940, 385–483; Ralph L. Roys, France V. Scholes and Eleanor B. Adams, eds., 'Census and Inspection of the Town of Pencuyut, Yucatan, in 1583 by Diego García de Palacio, oidor of the Audiencia of Gautemala', *Ethnohistory*, 6 (1959), 195–225; Ralph L. Roys, France V. Scholes and Eleanor B. Adams, 'Report and Census of the Indians of Cozumel, 1570', in *Contributions to American Anthropology and History*, 6, Washington, Carnegie Institution, 1940, 1–30.

3 Inga Clendinnen, 'Yucatec Maya Women and the Spanish Conquest: Role and Ritual in Historical Reconstruction', *Journal of Social History*, 15 (1982), 427–41.

4 Cogolludo, *Historia*, Lib. 4, Cap. 5; Sánchez de Aguilar, *Informe*, 299; Roys, *Indian Background*, 29–30.

5 E.g. Landa, *Relación*, 87; Juan Bote, R.Y.1: 287–8; Pedro de Santillana, R.Y.1: 254–5; Juan de Magaña, R.Y.1: 187. Much of the *relación* material relating to tribute levels has been handily assembled in Robert S. Chamberlain, *The Pre-Conquest Tribute and Service System of the Maya as a Preparation for the Spanish Repartimiento-Encomienda in Yucatan*, Coral Gables, 1951.

6 For pre-Conquest trade, see chapter 1, note 2. For 'secular' feasts, Landa, *Relación*, esp. 90–8. For an impressive attempt to identify the cultural dynamics of population movements, see Nancy M. Farriss, 'Nucleation versus Dispersal: The Dynamics of Population Movement in Colonial Yucatan', *Hispanic American Historical Review*, 58 (1978), 187–216.

7 The best discussion of the Maya calendars remains that of J. Eric S. Thompson, *Maya Hieroglyphic Writing: An Introduction*, 2nd edition, Norman, University of

Oklahoma Press, 1960. For a series of *katun* prophecies see Roys, *The Book of Chilam Balam of Chumayel*, 144–63.

8 Roys, *Indian Background*, 10.

9 Michael Coe has presented an elegant and ingenious model of a complex rotational political system which he claims perhaps operated within Maya communities and which replicates the transference of responsibility between deities. His argument is seductive, but I am troubled that Landa, so acute an observer, leaves no account of such a system. M. D. Coe, 'A Model of Ancient Community Structure in the Maya Lowlands', *Southwestern Journal of Anthropology*, 21 (1965), 97–114. Coe's case is strengthened by Father Avendaño's 1696 account of the sacred books of prophecy of the Peten Maya. These, he tells us, showed 'not only the count of the said days and months and years, but also the ages (*katunes*) and prophecies which their idols and images announced to them, or, to speak more accurately, the devil by means of the worship which they pay to him in the form of some stones. These ages are thirteen in number; each age has its separate idol and its priest, with a separate prophecy of its events. These thirteen ages are divided into thirteen parts, which divide this kingdom of Yucatan and each age, with its idol, priest and prophecy, rules in one of these thirteen parts of this land, according as they have divided it.' Means, *History of the Spanish Conquest*, 141.

10 Karl K. Ruppert, J. Eric S. Thompson and Tatiana Proskouriakoff, *Bonampak, Chiapas, Mexico*, Washington, Carnegie Institution, 1955.

11 E.g. Landa, *Relación*, 94, 144; R.Y.1, 185.

12 Quoted Chamberlain, *Conquest*, 136.

13 For some of the confusions, Landa, *Relación*, 16–40, and accompanying notes. For a gallant attempt to sort them out, Arthur G. Miller, 'Captains of the Itza: Unpublished Mural Evidence from Chichén Itzá', in *Social Process in Maya Prehistory*, edited by Norman Hammond, London, Academic Press, 1977, 197–225, and 'The Little Descent: Manifest Destiny from the East', in *Actes du XLII Congrès des Américanistes, Paris, 1976–8*, Paris, Société des Américanistes, 1979, 221–36. For the native/stranger tension in rulership, Marshall D. Sahlins, *Historical Metaphors and Mythical Realities: Structure in the Early History of the Sandwich Islands Kingdom*, Ann Arbor, University of Michigan Press, 1981.

14 Sánchez de Aguilar, *Informe*, 293; Cogolludo, *Historia*, Lib. 4, Cap. 5; Roys, *Chumayel*, 76.

15 Barrera Vázquez and Rendón, *El Libro de los libros de Chilam Balam*. One scholar claims that 'soon [after the conquest] almost every village or town in the northern half of the peninsula had a copy either of these early chronicles ... or of later ones written by their own native priests ...'. Alfredo Barrera Vázquez in Alfredo Barrera Vázquez and Sylvanus Griswold Morley, 'The Maya Chronicles', *Contributions to American Anthropology and History*, 48, Washington, Carnegie Institution, 1949, 10.

16 Landa, *Relación*, esp. 98, 110; Roys, 'Personal Names', *Titles of Ebtun*, 13.

17 R.Y.2: 28, 187–8, 207; Thompson, *Maya History and Religion*, 277–8. For the close identification between bees, plants and humans see Roys, *Chumayel*, 95.

18 Landa, *Relación*, esp. 97.

19 Landa, *Relación*, 88, 125; Roys, *Chumayel*, 95, 114, 130.

11. Continuities

1 The 1549 tribute required each married man, or more properly each married couple, to present one cotton *manta* of about ten square yards or twelve square *varas*, and a number of European hens, together with maize, beans, beeswax and honey. For an estimation of the value of the *manta* in *reales*, and an astute assessment of the oppressiveness of requirements, see Scholes and Roys, *The Maya Chontal Indians of Acalan Tixchel*, 151–3, and 470, n. 1. See also Villalpando to the Crown, 15 October 1550, in Gómez Canedo, *Evangelización*.

2 Roys reports that the *almehenob* – the local nobility – even though otherwise indistinguishable from commoners were accorded their titles by those commoners well into the nineteenth century. Roys, *Titles of Ebtun*, 47.

3 Sánchez de Aguilar, *Informe*, 290; Cogolludo, *Historia*, Lib. 9, Cap. 1.

4 Roys, *Chumayel*, 83, 79.

5 Roys, *Titles of Ebtun*, Intro, Appendix E and 93, n. 2.

6 Roys, *Chumayel*, 89–90.

7 Roys, *Titles of Ebtun*, 21–38.

8 Antonio de Ciudad Real, 'Relación de las cosas que sucedieron al R. P. Comisario General Fray Alonso Ponce . . . (1588)', in *Colección de documentos inéditos para la historia de España*, vols. 57 and 58, Madrid, 1872. Partial translation by Ernest Noyes, *Fray Alonso Ponce in Yucatan 1588*, New Orleans, Tulane University Press, 1932, 327.

9 Landa, *Relación*, 164–5; Cogolludo, *Historia*, Lib. 4, Cap. 5.

12. Assent

1 Sánchez de Aguilar, *Informe, passim* but esp. 210–11, 201. See also R.Y.2: 28, 147, 190, 212; Cogolludo, *Historia*; F. V. Scholes, R. L. Roys, E. B. Adams, 'History of the Maya Area', *C.I.W. Yearbook*, 43, July 1943/June 1944; Eva Alexander Uchmany de la Peña, 'Cuatro casos de idolatría en el area maya ante el Tribunal de la Inquisición', *Estudios de Cultura Maya*, 6 (1967), 267–300.

2 Allen F. Burns, 'The Caste War in the 1970s: Present Day Accounts from Village Quintana Roo', in *Anthropology and History in Yucatan*, edited Grant D. Jones, Austin and London, Texas University Press, 1977, 261. Some of the following discussion has been rehearsed in Inga Clendinnen, 'Landscape and World View: The Survival of Yucatec Maya Culture under Spanish Conquest', *Comparative Studies in Society and History*, 22 (1980), 374–93.

3 Roys, *Titles of Ebtun*, 8, 424–7.

4 Roys, *Indian Background*, 175–94.

5 A. R. Pagden, *The Maya: Diego de Landa's Account of the Affairs of Yucatan*, Chicago, 1975, plate 7.

6 E.g. France V. Scholes and Ralph L. Roys, 'Fray Diego de Landa and the Problem of Idolatry in Yucatan', *Cooperation in Research*, Washington, Carnegie Institution, 1938, 586–620; Tozzer in Landa, *Relación*, 81, n. 344; William Madsen, 'Religious Syncretism', in *Handbook of Middle American Indians*, Austin, University of Texas Press, 1976, vol. 6, 369–91; D. E. Thompson, 'Maya Paganism and Christianity: a History of the Fusion of Two Religions', in *Middle American Research Institute Publication*, 19, New Orleans, Middle American

Research Institute, Tulane University, 1954; Richard E. Greenleaf, 'The Mexican Inquisition and the Indians: Sources for the Ethnohistorian', *The Americas: A Quarterly Review of Inter-American Cultural History*, 34 (1978), 315-44.

7 The Sotuta province testimonies we have were taken from Indians from seven villages over a six-day period. Indians from another village, Tixcacal, had their confessions recorded during the enquiry, but they have been lost. Scholes and Adams, *Don Diego Quijada*, 1: 199. It is clear that Landa selected only some confessions to be recorded, as there is no record of confessions from some Indians known to have made elaborate verbal statements, e.g. from the village of Usil alone, Magaña makes clear that Melchor Yam, Juan Cauich and Francisco Chuc made verbal confessions. Scholes and Adams, *Don Diego Quijada*, 1: 209-10.

8 Alfred Tozzer is the only historian I know to have offered a figure on the number of victims. Without discussion as to method, he arrives at 168, killed in eighty-nine separate events in Hocaba-Homun and Sotuta provinces. Alfred M. Tozzer, 'Chichen Itza and its Cenote of Sacrifice', *Memoirs of the Peabody Museum of Archaeology and Ethnology*, vols. 11 and 12, Cambridge, Mass., 1957. One must infer from his analysis of offerings at the Sacred Cenote that he counted every reference made in the confessions as relating to a unique event. For a full discussion of his (and my) criteria, see Inga Clendinnen, 'Reading the Inquisitorial Record in Yucatan: Fact or Fantasy?', *The Americas*, 38 (1982), 327-45.

9 Scholes and Adams, *Don Diego Quijada*, 1: 98-9.

10 Roys, *Indian Background*, 181, 186.

11 All the confessions were dated, and although the notary grouped them according to their village of origin, it seems he preserved the order in which the testimonies were taken each day. Francisco Camal of Tibolon, whose confession was taken on 17 August, identifies the preceding witness as Francisco Tuz, whose confession precedes Camal's in the testimonies as we have them. Scholes and Adams, *Don Diego Quijada*, 1: 122-5.

12 Scholes and Adams, *Don Diego Quijada*, 1: 72-8, 114-19, 125-8.

13 Scholes and Adams, *Don Diego Quijada*, 1: 78-82.

14 Scholes and Adams, *Don Diego Quijada*, 1: 115-19, 120-1, 125-8.

15 E.g. Tozzer, 'Chichen Itza and its Cenote of Sacrifice.'

16 Which is not to deny that there were traditional rituals associated with *cenotes* and wells, e.g. Scholes and Adams, *Don Diego Quijada*, 1: 100. In 1978 archeological investigation in the Caves Branch area of Central Belize indicated ritual activity deep within the caves. Skeletons, most being of children about five years of age, were found along with ritual objects. Tentative dating is for the late Pre-classic to Post-classic. Barbara McLeod and Dennis E. Puleston, 'Pathways into Darkness: The Search for the Road to Xibalba', in Merle Greene Robertson and Donnan Call Jeffers (eds.), *Tercera Mesa Redonda de Palenque*, 4, Monterey, Calif., 1978, 72.

17 Cook and Borah put the peninsula population in 1580-85 at 140,000. Cook and Borah, *Essays in Population History*, 2: 48.

18 For an example see the testimony of the *ah-kin* Francisco Chuc of Sahcaba translated in the appendix. For the usual construction of the village churches see Francisco de Cárdenas Valencia, *Relación historial eclesiástica de la provincia de Yucatán de Nueva España, escrita en el año de 1639*, México, Editorial Porrua, 1937, 110-11; Scholes, Menéndez, Rubio Mañé, Adams, *D.H.Y.*, 2: 114.

19 Scholes and Adams, *Don Diego Quijada*, 1: 103-8. See appendix for translation of Couoh's testimony.

20 Landa, *Relación*, 73. The Mani youths were old enough to have wives, who also received new clothes to wear at the grand Mani *auto de fe*. Scholes and Adams, *Don Diego Quijada*, 1: 301–10. Cogolludo, who reduces the two lads to one, identifies the discoverer as porter of the monastery, which would suggest his complete divorce from native life. Unhappily, Cogolludo is chronically unreliable. Cogolludo, *Historia*, Lib., 6, Cap. 1.
21 Scholes and Adams, *Don Diego Quijada*, 1: 114.
22 Evon Z. Vogt, *Tortillas for the Gods: a Symbolic Analysis of Zinacantecan rituals*, Cambridge, Harvard University Press, 1976.
23 Scholes and Adams, *Don Diego Quijada*, 1: 100–3, and appendix.
24 Reed, *Caste War*; Charlotte Zimmerman, 'The Cult of the Holy Cross: An Analysis of Cosmology and Catholicism in Quintana Roo', *History of Religions*, 3 (1963), 50–71. For the significance of the cross to the Maya before the arrival of the Spaniards, see Merle Green, Robert L. Rands, and John A. Graham, *Maya Sculpture*, Berkeley, 1972. See also Landa, *Relación*, 42, n. 211.
25 John McAndrew, *The Open-Air Churches of Sixteenth-Century Mexico*, Cambridge, Harvard University Press, 1965, 247–54, esp. 251 and Plate 115. Father Avendaño reported a representation of the First Tree of the World he saw among the pagan Itza at Tayasal in 1696. It took the form of a flaring stone and mortar column supported on a pedestal, with a mask of Ah Cocahmut, 'Son of the Very Wise God', set at the base. Means, *History*, 135–6.
26 Landa, *Relación*, 161–4.
27 Scholes and Adams, *Don Diego Quijada*, 1: 107.
28 Alfredo Barrera Vázquez, *El libro de los cantares de Dzitbalché*, México, Instituto Nacional de Antropología e Historia, 1965. For Landa's account, Landa, *Relación*, 117–18.
29 Scholes and Adams, *Don Diego Quijada*, 1: 122.
30 Thompson, *Maya History and Religion*, 170–2.
31 For the Mexican festival, Inga Clendinnen, 'The Cost of Courage in Aztec Society', *Past and Present*, 107 (1985), 44–89. For the Maya festival, Landa, *Relación*, 118–20.
32 Barrera Vázquez, *El libro de los cantares*, 77–8; Landa, *Relación*, 117–18.
33 Peter T. Furst, 'Fertility, Vision Quest and Auto-Sacrifice: Some Thoughts on Ritual Blood-Letting Among the Maya', in Merle Greene Robertson (ed.), *The Art, Iconography and Dynastic History of Palenque*, Part 3, Pebble Beach, Calif., 1976, 183; David Joralemon, 'Ritual Blood-Sacrifice among the Ancient Maya', in Merle Greene Robertson (ed.), *Primera Mesa Redonda de Palenque: Part II*, Pebble Beach, Calif., 1974, 59–75.
34 Scholes and Adams, *Don Diego Quijada*, 1: 152.
35 For the conversion campaigns see Ricard, *Spiritual Conquest*, esp. chap. 5; Pedro Borges, *Métodos misionales*.
36 Scholes and Adams, *Don Diego Quijada*, 1: 59–63; 'Avisos de muy illustre y reverendísimo señor don Fray Francisco de Toral, primer obispo de Yucatán, Cozumel y Tabasco ... para los padres curas y vicarios de este obispado y para los que en su ausencia quedan en las iglesias', n.d.; Scholes, Menéndez, Rubio Mañé, Adams, *D.H.Y.* II, 27.
37 McAndrew, *Open-Air Churches*, chap. 6 and 352–9, 515–24.
38 Sánchez de Aguilar, *Informe*, 290, 303; Cogolludo, *Historia*, Lib. 9, Cap. 1; Lib. 7, Cap. 15; Lib. 11, Cap. 14.

39 Roys, *Chumayel*, 126–7. For another example of voluntary incorporation, resting in this case on archaeological evidence, see Arthur G. Miller and Nancy M. Farriss, 'Religious Syncretism in Colonial Yucatan: The Archeological and Ethnohistorical Evidence from Tancah, Quintana Room', in N. Hammond and G. Willey (eds.), *Maya Archaeology and Ethnohistory*, 223–40. Such incorporations imply nothing about acceptance of Spanish clerical authority. The resident curate to Cozumel, appointed in 1582, was mournfully persuaded he would suffer a fatal canoe accident in the treacherous waters between island and mainland should he interfere with local religious practices, that having been the fate of his predecessor. Sánchez de Aguilar, *Informe*, 275.
40 Scholes and Adams, *Don Diego Quijada*, 1: 76.

Epilogue: Confusion of tongues

1 Roys, *Chumayel*, 132–63 but esp. 138. See also Anne C. Collins, 'The Maestros Cantores in Yucatan', *Anthropology and History in Yucatan*, ed. Grant D. Jones Austin, University of Texas Press, 1977. Just what effect that northern decision for acceptance of Christianity had on the independent Itza of the south can only be guessed at. The Peten Itza have their own sorry 'confusion of tongues' story. In 1614 an Itza embassy indicated to Spanish authorities at Mérida their readiness to submit when the time was ripe. To the Spaniards submission was a political act, and not to be waited on. Nearly a century of miscommunication and sporadic violence ended with the Itzas' military subjugation. The story is told in brief by Victoria Reifler Bricker, *The Indian Christ, the Indian King*, Austin, University of Texas Press, 1981, 21–4, and at length by Juan de Villagutierre Sotomayor, *Historia de la conquista de la provincia de el Itzá 1701*, Guatemala, Sociedad de Geografía e Historia, 1933. 'Confusion of Tongues' for these kinds of simultaneous monologues is the formulation of Clifford Geertz, 'Thick Description: Toward an Interpretive Theory of Culture' in his *The Interpretation of Cultures*, New York, Basic Books, 1973, 2–30.
2 Sánchez de Aguilar, *Informe*, esp. 281, 294, 301, 318; Cogolludo, *Historia*, 252.
3 Roys, *Chumayel*, 106–7.
4 Roys, *Chumayel*, 92. Eric Wolf, in his influential and justly popular book *Sons of the Shaking Earth*, Chicago, University of Chicago Press, 1959 acknowledged that 'there is much that is Indian in the Catholicism of Middle America', but claims the conversion was successful because 'when an Indian speaks of a human being today he does not say "a man"; he says "a Christian", a believer'. (167). The criterion for 'successful conversion' sustaining my analysis is very different, and derives from Clifford Geertz's definition of ordered social change. He argues that such change must involve 'the attainment of members of the group of novel conceptions of the sorts of individuals and the sorts of groups (and the nature of the relationships between such individuals and groups) that comprise their immediate social world . . . such an attainment of novel conceptual forms depends in turn on the emergence of institutions through whose very operations the necessary categorizations and judgments can be developed and stabilized'. Clifford Geertz, *Social History of an Indonesian Town*, 1965, M.I.T. Press, 5. To extend the criteria to the sphere of religion, and to 'directed acculturation' or conversion, we would expect substantial reorganization of the concept of the self, of the individual to other groups, and of the individual to the cosmos. (The pragmatic accommodations,

politic submissions, or relabellings of deities sometimes called 'conversions' would therefore be put out of court.) There is no indication of such a reorganisation in Maya thinking.

Select Bibliography

Note: Nancy M. Farriss' fine study of the Maya throughout the colonial period, *Maya Society under Colonial Rule: The Collective Enterprise of Survival*, Princeton, Princeton University Press, 1984, unfortunately appeared too late for me to profit from it. I can only most warmly recommend it.

Adams, Eleanor B. *A. Biobibliography of Franciscan Authors in Colonial Central America*, Washington, 1953.

Ancona, Eligio. *Historia de Yucatán desde la época más remota hasta nuestros días*, 3 vols., Mérida, 1878–79.

Andrews, Anthony P. 'The Salt Trade of the Maya', *Archaeology*, 33 (1980), 24–33.

Barrera Vázquez, Alfredo, ed. *Códice de Calkini*, Campeche, Talleres Gráficos del Estado, 1957.

Barrera Vázquez, Alfredo, ed. *El libro de los cantares de Dzitbalché*, México, Instituto Nacional de Antropología e Historia, 1965.

Barrera Vázquez, Alfredo, and Morley, Sylvanus Griswold, 'The Maya Chronicles', *Contributions to American Anthropology and History*, 10, no. 48, Washington, Carnegie Institution, 1949.

Barrera Vázquez, Alfredo and Rendón, Silvia, eds. *El libro de los libros de Chilam Balam*, México. Fondo de Cultura Económica, 1948.

Bataillon, Marcel. *Erasmo y España*, 2nd ed., México, Fondo de Cultura Económica, 1966.

Berger, John. *Pig Earth*, New York, 1979.

Borah, Woodrow. 'The Historical Demography of Aboriginal and Colonial America: An Attempt at Perspective', in *The Native Population of the Americas in 1492*, edited by William M. Denevan, Madison, University of Wisconsin Press, 1976, 13–34.

Borges, Pedro. *Métodos misionales en la cristianización de América*, Consejo Superior de Investigaciones Científicas, Departamento de Misionología Española, Madrid, 1960.

Borges, Pedro. *El envío de misioneras a América durante la época española*, Salamanca, Universidad Pontifica, 1977.

Bricker, Victoria R. 'The Caste War of Yucatan: The History of a Myth and the Myth of History', in *Anthropology and History in Yucatan*, edited by Grant D. Jones, Austin, University of Texas Press, 1977, 251–8.

Bricker, Victoria R. *The Indian Christ, the Indian King*, Austin, University of Texas Press, 1981.

228

Brinton, Daniel G. *The Maya Chronicles (1882)*, Reprint, New York, A.M.S. Press, 1969.

Brotherston, Gordon. 'Continuity in Maya Writing: New Readings of Two Passages in the Book of Chilam Balam of Chumayel', in *Maya Archeology and Ethnohistory*, edited by Norman Hammond and Gordon R. Willey, Austin, University of Texas Press, 1979, 241–58.

Burns, Allen F. 'The Caste War in the 1970s: Present Day Accounts from Village Quintana Roo', in *Anthropology and History in Yucatan*, edited Grant D. Jones, Austin and London, Texas University Press, 1977.

Cárdenas Valencia, Francisco de. *Relación historial eclesiástica de la provincia de Yucatán de la Nueva España escrita en el año de 1639*, México, Editorial Porrua, 1937.

Caro Baroja, Julio. *The World of the Witches*, Chicago, University of Chicago Press, 1964.

Carrasco, Pedro. 'The Civil-Religious Hierarchy in Mesoamerican Communities: Pre-Spanish Background and Colonial Development', *American Anthropologist*, 63 (1961), 483–97.

Carrasco, Pedro. 'The Joint Family in Ancient Mexico: The Case of Molotla', in *Essays on Mexican Kinship*, edited by Hugo G. Nutini, Pedro Carrasco and James M. Taggart, Pittsburgh, University of Pittsburgh Press, 1976, 45–64.

Cartas de Indias. Madrid, Ministerio de Fomento, 1877.

Cervantes de Salazar, Francisco. *Crónica de la Nueva España (1560)*, Madrid, 1914.

Chamberlain, Robert S. *The Conquest and Colonization of Yucatan, 1517–1550*, Washington, Carnegie Institution, 1948.

Chamberlain, Robert S. *The Pre-Conquest Tribute and Service System of the Maya as Preparation for the Spanish Repartimiento-Encomienda in Yucatan*, University of Miami Hispanic-American Studies, no. 10, Coral Gables, Florida, University of Miami Press, 1951.

Chapman, Anne C. 'Port of Trade Enclaves in Aztec and Maya Civilization', in *Trade and Market in Early Empires*, edited by Karl Polanyi, C. M. Arensberg, and H. W. Pearson, New York, The Free Press, 1957, 114–53.

Chi, Gaspar Antonio. 'Relación,' (1582), M.S. trans. by R. L. Roys, in A. M. Tozzer (ed.), *Landa's Relación de las cosas de Yucatán, a translation*, Cambridge, Peabody Museum, 1941, 230–2.

Christian, William A., Jr. *Local Religion in Sixteenth-Century Spain*, Princeton, Princeton University Press, 1980.

Ciudad Real, Antonio de. *Relación de las cosas que sucedieron al R. P. Comisario General Fray Alonso Ponce . . . (1588)*, in *Colección de documentos inéditos para la historia de España*, vols. 57 and 58, Madrid, 1872. Partial translation in Ernest Noyes, *Fray Alonso in Yucatan 1588*, New Orleans, Tulane University Press, 1932.

Clendinnen, Inga. 'Landscape and World View: The Survival of Yucatec Maya Culture under Spanish Conquest', *Comparative Studies in Society and History*, 22 (1980), 374–93.

Clendinnen, Inga. 'Disciplining the Indians: Franciscan Ideology and Missionary Violence in Sixteenth-Century Yucatan', *Past and Present*, 94 (1982), 27–48.

Clendinnen, Inga. 'Reading the Inquisitorial Record in Yucatan: Fact or Fantasy?', *The Americas*, 38 (1982), 327–45.

Clendinnen, Inga. 'Yucatec Maya Women and the Spanish Conquest: Role and Ritual in Historical Reconstruction', *Journal of Social History*, 15 (1982), 427–41.

Clendinnen, Inga. 'The Cost of Courage in Aztec Society', *Past and Present*, 107 (1985), 44–89.

Codex Dresden. Thompson, J. Eric S. *A Commentary on the Dresden Codex: a Maya hieroglyphic book,* Philadelphia, American Philosophical Society, 1972.

Codex Madrid. Codex Tro-Cortesiansis (Codex Madrid, Museo de América, Madrid) Introduction and summary F. Anders, Graz, Akademische Druck-u, Verlagsanstalt, 1967.

Codex Paris. Codex Peresiansis (Codex Paris, Bibliothèque nacionale, Paris) Introduction and summary F. Anders, Graz, Akademische Druck-u, Verlagsanstalt, 1968.

Codex Perez. See Craine, Eugene R. and Reindorp, Reginald C.

Coe, Michael. 'A Model of Ancient Community Structure in the Maya Lowlands', *Southwestern Journal of Anthropology,* 21 (1956), 97–114.

Coe, Michael. *The Maya Scribe and his World,* New York, The Grolier Club, 1973.

Coe, Michael D. 'Death and the Ancient Maya', in *Death and the Afterlife in Pre-Columbian America,* edited by Elizabeth P. Benson, Washington, Dumbarton Oaks, 1975, 87–104.

Cogolludo, Diego López de. *Los tres siglos de la dominación española en Yucatán o sea Historia de Esta Provincia (1654?),* 2 vols. Mérida, Manuel Aldana Rivas, 1867–68.

Colección de documentos inéditos relativos al descubrimiento, conquista y organización de las antiguas posesiones españolas de América y Oceanía, sacados de los archivos del reino, y muy especialmente del de Indias, 42 vols, Madrid, 1864–84.

Colección de documentos inéditos relativos al descrubrimento, conquista y organización de las antiguas posesiones españolas de ultramar, 25 vols, Madrid, 1885–1932. ('Relaciones de Yucatán', vols. 11 and 13.)

Collins, Anne C. 'The *Maestros Cantores* in Yucatan', in *Anthropology and History in Yucatan,* edited by Grant D. Jones, Austin, University of Texas Press, 1977, 233–47.

Cook, Sherburne F. and Borah, Woodrow. *The Indian Population of Central Mexico, 1531–1610,* Berkeley, University of California Press, 1960.

Cook, Sherburne F. and Borah, Woodrow. *Essays in Population History: Mexico and the Caribbean,* 3 vols. Berkeley, University of California Press, 1972–79.

Cortés, Hernán. *Cartas de relación (1522–1525),* edited by Manuel Alcalá, México, Editorial Porrua, 1963.

Craine, Eugene R. and Reindorp, Reginald C. eds. *The Codex Pérez and the Book of Chilam Balam of Mani,* Norman, University of Oklahoma Press, 1979.

Cuevas, Mariano, ed. *Documentos inéditos del siglo XVI para la historia de México,* Mexico, 1914.

Culbert, T. Patrick, ed. *The Maya Collapse,* Albuquerque, University of New Mexico Press, 1973.

Denevan, William M., ed. *The Native Population of the Americas in 1492,* Madison, University of Wisconsin Press, 1976.

Dening, Greg. *Islands and Beaches,* Melbourne, 1980.

Diáz del Castillo, Bernal. *Historia verdadera de la conquista de la Nueva España,* Introducción y notas de Joaquín Ramiro Cabañas, 2 vols., México, Editorial Porrua, 1966.

Diccionario de Motul maya-español, atribuído a Fray Antonio de Ciudad Real . . ., edited by Juan Martinez Hernández, Mérida, Talleres de la Compañía Tipográfica Yucateca, 1929.

Edmonson, Munro S. *Nativism, Syncretism and Anthropological Science,* New Orleans, 1960.

Edmonson, Munro S. *The Ancient Future of the Itza: the Book of Chilam Balam of Tizimin,* Austin, University of Texas Press, 1982.

Farriss, Nancy M. 'Nucleation versus Dispersal: the Dynamics of Population Movement in Colonial Yucatan', *Hispanic American Historical Review*, 58 (1978), 187–216.

Furst, Peter T. 'Fertility, Vision Quest and Auto-Sacrifice: Some Thoughts on Ritual Blood-Letting among the Maya', in Merle Greene Robertson (ed.), *The Art, Iconography and Dynastic History of Palenque*, Part III, Pebble Beach, California, 1976.

Geertz, Clifford. *The Interpretation of Cultures*, New York, Basic Books, 1973.

Gerhard, Peter. *The Southeast Frontier of New Spain*, Princeton, Princeton University Press, 1979.

Gibson, Charles and Glass, John B. 'A Census of Middle American Prose Manuscripts in the Native Historical Tradition', in *Handbook of Middle American Indians*, 15, ed. Howard F. Cline, Austin, University of Texas Press, 1975.

Gómez Canedo, Lino. 'Fray Lorenzo de Bienvenida y los orígenes de las misiones de Yucatán (1537–1564)', *Revista de la Universidád de Yucatán*, 18 (1976), 46–68.

Gómez Canedo, Lino. *Evangelización y Conquista: Experiencia Franciscana en Hispanoamérica*, México, Editorial Porrua, 1977.

González, Blas. 'Probánza de méritos y servicios de Blas González, conquistador', ed. R. S. Chamberlain, *Hispanic American Historical Review*, 25 (1945), 526–36.

González Cicero, Stella María. *Perspectiva religiosa en Yucatán, 1515–1571*, México, El Colegio de México, 1978.

Greene, Merle, Rands, Robert and Graham, John A. *Maya Sculpture*, Berkeley, 1972.

Greenleaf, Richard E. *Zumárraga and the Mexican Inquisition, 1536–1543*, Washington, 1962.

Greenleaf, Richard E. 'The Inquisition and the Indians of New Spain: A Study in Jurisdictional Confusion', *The Americas*, 22 (1965), 138–66.

Greenleaf, Richard E. *The Mexican Inquisition of the Sixteenth Century*, Albuquerque, 1969.

Greenleaf, Richard E. 'The Mexican Inquisition and the Indians: Sources for the Ethnohistorian', *The Americas: A Quarterly Review of Inter-American Cultural History*, 34 (1978), 315–44.

Hammond, Norman, ed. *Social Process in Maya Prehistory*, London, Academic Press, 1977.

Hammond, Norman and Willey, Gordon R. eds. *Maya Archeology and Ethnohistory*, Austin, University of Texas Press, 1979.

Haviland, William A. 'Rules of Descent in Sixteenth-Century Yucatan', *Estudios de Cultura Náhuatl*, 9 (1973), 135–50.

Hellmuth, Nicholas M. 'Choltí-Lacandon (Chiapas) and Petén-Ytzá Agriculture, Settlement Pattern and Population', in *Social Process in Maya Prehistory*, edited by Norman Hammond, London, Academic Press, 1977, 421–48.

Hernaez, Francisco Javier, ed. *Colección de bulas, breves y otros documentos relativos a la iglesia de América y Filipinas dispuesta, anotada y illustrada*, Brussels, 1879.

Hunt, Marta E. 'Colonial Yucatan: Town and Region in the Seventeenth Century', Ph.D. dissertation, University of California, Los Angeles, 1974.

Hunt, Marta E. 'Processes of the Development of Yucatan, 1600–1700', in *Provinces of Early Mexico*, edited by Ida Altman and James Lockhart, Los Angeles, U.C.L.A. Latin American Center, 1976, 33–62.

Jones, Grant D. 'Southern Lowland Maya Political Organization: A Model of Change from Protohistoric through Colonial Times', in *Actes de XLIIe Congrès*

232   *Select bibliography*

International des Américanistes, Paris, 1976–8, Paris, Société des Américanistes, 1979, 83–94.

Joralemon, David. 'Ritual Blood-Sacrifice among the Ancient Maya', in Merle Greene Robertson, ed., *Primera Mesa Redonda de Palenque*, Part II, Pebble Beach, California, 1974, 59–75.

Keegan, John. *The Face of Battle*, New York, Penguin, 1978.

Kubler, George A. *Mexican Architecture of the Sixteenth Century*, 2 vols., New Haven, Yale University Press, 1948.

Kubler, George A. 'On the Colonial Extinction of the Motifs of Pre-Columbian Art', in *Essays in Pre-Columbian Art and Archaeology*, by Samuel K. Lothrop *et al.*, Cambridge, Mass., Peabody Museum of American Archaeology and Ethnology, Harvard University, 1961, 14–34.

Kubler, George A. *Studies in Classic Maya Iconography*, New Haven, Connecticut Academy of Arts and Sciences, 1969.

Kurjack, Edward B. *Prehistoric Lowland Maya Community and Social Organization: A Case Study at Dzibilchaltún, Yucatan, Mexico*, New Orleans, Middle American Research Institute, Tulane University, 1974.

LaFarge, Oliver and Byers, Douglas S. *The Year-Bearer's People*, New Orleans, Middle American Research Institute, Tulane University, 1931.

Landa, Diego de. *Landa's Relación de las cosas de Yucatán*, translated and edited by Alfred M. Tozzer, Cambridge, Mass., Peabody Museum, Harvard University, 1941.

Lawrence, Peter. *Road Belong Cargo*, Manchester, 1964.

Lea, H. C. *A History of the Inquisition in Spain* (1906–1907), 4 vols., New York, 1966.

León-Portilla, Miguel, ed. *Visión de los vencidos: Relaciones indígenas de la conquista*, México, Universidad Nacional Autónom de México, 1959.

León-Portilla, Miguel. *Tiempo y realidad en el pensamiento maya*, México, Universidad Nacional Autónoma de México, 1968.

Lizana, Bernardo de. *Historia de Yucatán: Devocionario de Nuestra Señora de Izamal y conquista espiritual (1633)*, 2nd ed., México, Museo Nacional, 1893.

Llaguno, José. *La personalidad jurídica del indio y el III Concilio Provincial mexicano (1585)*, México, Editorial Porrua, 1963.

López de Cogolludo, Diego: *see* Cogolludo, Diego López de.

López, P. Anastasio. 'Vida de Fr Martín de Valencia escrita por su compañero Fr Francisco Jiménez', *Archivo iberoamericano*, 26 (1926).

López de Gómara, Francisco. *Cortés: The Life of the Conqueror by his Secretary* (1552), translated and edited Lesley Byrd Simpson, Berkeley and Los Angeles, University of California Press, 1966.

Lorenzana, Francisco Antonio. *Concilios provinciales primero y segundo, celebrados en la muy noble y muy leal cuidad de México presidiendo el Illmo. y Rmo. Señor D. Fr Alonso de Montufar, en los años de 1555, y 1565*, Mexico, 1769.

McAndrew, John. *The Open-Air Churches of Sixteenth-Century Mexico*, Cambridge, Mass., Harvard University Press, 1965.

McLeod, Barbara and Puleston, Dennis E. 'Pathways into Darkness: The Search for the Road to Xibalba', in Merle Greene Robertson and Donnan Call Jeffers (eds.), *Tercera Mesa Redonda de Palenque*, 4, Monterey, Calif., 1978.

Madsen, William, 'Religious Syncretism', in *Handbook of Middle American Indians*, 6, Austin, University of Texas Press, 1967, 369–492.

Mariel de Ibáñez, Yolande. *La Inquisición en México durante el siglo XVI*, México, 1946.

Martínez Hernández, Juan, ed. *Crónica de Yaxkukul*, Mérida, Talleres de la Compañía Tipográfica Yucateca, 1926.

Maudslay, A. P. *Archeology-Biologia Centrali-Americana*, 5 vols., London, 1889–1902.

Means, Philip A. *History of the Spanish Conquest of Yucatan and of the Itzas*, Cambridge, Mass., Peabody Museum Papers, Harvard University, 1917.

Medina, José Toribio, ed., *La Primitiva Inquisición (1493–1569)*, 2 vols., Santiago de Chile, 1914.

Mendieta, Fray Gerónimo de. *Historia eclesiástica Indiana*, ed. Joaquín García Icazbalceta, México, Porrua, 1971.

Miles, S. W. 'The Sixteenth-Century Pokom-Maya: A Documentary Analysis of Social Structure and Archaeological Setting', *Transactions of the American Philosophical Society*, n.s. 47, pt 4, Philadelphia, American Philosophical Society, 1957, 731–81.

Miller, Arthur G. 'Captains of the Itza: Unpublished Mural Evidence from Chichén Itzá', in *Social Process in Maya Prehistory*, edited by Norman Hammond, London, Academic Press, 1977, 197–225.

Miller, Arthur G. 'The Maya and the Sea: Trade and Cult at Tancah and Tulum, Quintana Roo, Mexico', in *The Sea in the Pre-Columbian World*, edited by Elizabeth P. Benson, Washington, Dumbarton Oaks, 1977, 97–138.

Miller, Arthur G. 'The Little Descent: Manifest Destiny from the East', in *Actes du XLII Congrès des Américanistes, Paris, 1976–8*, Paris, Société des Américanistes, 1979, 221–36.

Miller, Arthur G. and Farriss, Nancy M. 'Religious Syncretism in Colonial Yucatan: The Archaeological and Ethnohistorical Evidence from Tancah, Quintana Roo', in *Maya Archaeology and Ethnohistory*, edited by Norman Hammond and Gordon R. Willey, Austin, University of Texas Press, 1979, 223–40.

Molina Solís, Juan Francisco. *Historia de Yucatán durante la dominación española*, 3 vols., Mérida, 1904–13.

Molina Solís, Juan Francisco. *Historia del descubrimiento y conquista de Yucatán*, 2 vols., México, Ediciones Mensaje, 1943.

Morley, Sylvanus G. *The Ancient Maya*, 3rd ed., revised by G. W. Brainerd, Stanford, Stanford University Press, 1956.

Motolinía, Fray Toribio de. *Motolinía's History of the Indians of New Spain*, trans. and ed. Elizabeth Andros Foster, Westport, Conn., 1977.

Noyes, Ernest. *Fray Alonso Ponce in Yucatan 1588*, New Orleans, Tulane University Press, 1932.

Nutini, Hugo G. 'The Nature and Treatment of Kinship in Mesoamerica', in *Essays on Mexican Kinship*, edited by Hugo G. Nutini, Pedro Carrasco and James M. Taggart, Pittsburgh, University of Pittsburgh Press, 1976, 3–27.

Oakes, Maud. *The Two Crosses of Todos Santos: Survivals of Mayan Religious Ritual*, New York, Pantheon, 1951.

Oroz Codex, The. Trans. and ed. Angélico Chávez, O.F.M., Washington, 1972.

Oviedo y Valdés, Gonzalo Fernández de. *Historia general y natural de las Indias (1535–1547)*, Madrid, 1959.

Pagden, A. R. trans. and ed. *The Maya: Diego de Landa's Account of the Affairs of Yucatan*, Chicago, 1975.

'Papeles relativos a la visita del oidor Dr. Diego García de Palacio, año de 1583.' *Boletín del Archivo General de la Nación*, 11 (1940), 384–483.

Paso y Troncoso, Francisco del (comp.). *Epistolario de Nueva España 1505–1518*, 16 vols., México, 1939–42.

Paso y Troncoso, Francisco del. *Tratado de las idolatrías, supersticiones, dioses, ritos, hechicerías, y otras costumbres gentílicas de las razas aborígenes de México*, 2 vols., México, 1954.

Patch, Robert W. 'A Colonial Regime: Maya and Spaniard in Yucatan,' Ph.D. dissertation, Princeton University, 1979.

Pérez, Juan Pío. *Diccionario de la lengua Maya*, Mérida, Imprenta Librería de Juan Molina Solís, 1866–77.

Pérez Martínez, Hector, ed. *Relación de las Cosas de Yucatán, por el Obispo de esa diocese*, México, 1938.

Phelan, John L. *The Millenial Kingdom of the Franciscans of the New World*, 2nd ed., Berkeley and Los Angeles, 1970.

'Pleito entre D. Francisco Velázquez de Gijón, Gobernador de Yucatán, y el Obispo Fray Diego de Landa, Año de 1574', in Ernesto Ramos (ed.), *Colección Siglo XVI Núm. 7*, México, 1960.

Pohl, Mary. 'Ritual Continuity and Transformation in Mesoamerica: Reconstructing the Ancient Maya "Cuch" Ritual', *American Antiquity*, 46 (1981), 513–29.

Pollock, Harry E. D., Roys, Ralph L., Proskouriakoff, Tatiana and Smith, A. Ledyard *Mayapan, Yucatan, Mexico*, Washington, Carnegie Institution, 1962.

Procesos de indios idólatras y hechiceros, Publicaciones del Archivo General de la Nación, 3, México, 1912.

Redfield, Robert. *The Little Community*, Chicago, 1940.

Redfield, Robert. *The Primitive World and Its Transformations*, Cornell, 1953.

Reed, Nelson. *The Caste War of Yucatan*, Stanford, Stanford University Press, 1964.

Reina, Ruben E. *The Law of the Saints: A Pokoman Pueblo and Its Community Culture*, Indianapolis, Bobbs-Merrill, 1966.

'Relaciones de Yucatán', in *Colección de documentos inéditos relativos al descubrimiento, conquista y organización de las antiguas posesiones españolas de Ultramar*, 2nd series, vols. 11 and 13, Madrid, Real Academia de la Historia, 1898–1900.

Remesal, Antonio de. *Historia general de las Indias Occidentales, y particular de la governación de Chiapa y Guatemala (1619)*, 2 vols., Guatemala, Tipografía Nacional, 1932.

Ricard, Robert. *La Conquête Spirituelle du Mexique (1933)*, translated by L. B. Simpson as *The Spiritual Conquest of Mexico*, Berkeley and Los Angeles, University of California Press, 1966.

Robertson, Merle Greene, ed. *Primera Mesa Redonda de Palenque*, Parts 1 and 2, Pebble Beach, California, Robert Louis Stevenson School, 1974.

Robertson, Merle Greene, ed. *The Art, Iconography and Dynastic History of Palenque*, Part 3, Proceedings of the Segunda Mesa Redonda de Palenque, Pebble Beach, California, Robert Louis Stevenson School, 1976.

Roys, Ralph L. *The Ethno-Botany of the Maya*, New Orleans, Middle American Research Institute, Tulane University, 1931.

Roys, Ralph L. 'Antonio de Ciudad Real, Ethnographer', *American Anthropologist*, n.s. 34 (1932), 118–26.

Roys, Ralph L. ed. *The Titles of Ebtun*, Washington, Carnegie Institution, 1939.

Roys, Ralph L. 'Personal Names of the Maya of Yucatan', in *Contributions to American Anthropology and History*, 6, Washington, Carnegie Institution, 1940, 31–48.

Roys, Ralph L. ed. 'The Prophecies for the Maya Tuns or Years in the Books of Chilam Balam of Tizimin and Mani', in *Contributions to American Anthropology and History*, 10, Washington, Carnegie Institution, 1949, 157–86.

Roys, Ralph L. 'Conquest Sites and the Subsequent Destruction of Maya Architecture in the Interior of Northern Yucatan', *Contributions to American Anthropology and History*, 11, Washington, Carnegie Institution, 1952, 129–82.

Roys, Ralph L. *The Political Geography of the Yucatan Maya*, Washington, Carnegie Institution, 1957.

Roys, Ralph L., ed. 'The Maya Katun Prophecies of the Books of Chilam Balam. Series 1' in *Contributions to American Anthropology and History*, 12, Washington Carnegie Institution, 1960, 1–60.

Roys, Ralph L. 'Literary Sources for the History of Mayapan', In *Mayapan, Yucatan, Mexico*, by Harry E. D. Pollock *et al.*, Washington, Carnegie Institution, 1962, 24–86.

Roys, Ralph L. ed. *Ritual of the Bacabs*, Norman, University of Oklahoma Press, 1965.

Roys, Ralph L. 'Lowland Maya Native Society at Spanish Contact', in *Handbook of Middle American Indians*, 3, Austin, University of Texas Press, 1965, 659–78.

Roys, Ralph L. ed. *The Book of Chilam Balam of Chumayel*, 2nd ed., Norman, University of Oklahoma Press, 1967.

Roys, Ralph L. *The Indian Background of Colonial Yucatan (1943)*, Reprinted, Norman, University of Oklahoma Press, 1972.

Roys, Ralph L., Scholes, France V. and Adams, Eleanor B., eds. 'Report and Census of the Indians of Cozumel, 1570', in *Contributions to American Anthropology and History*, 6, Washington, Carnegie Institution, 1940, 1–36.

Roys, Ralph L., Scholes, France V. and Adams, Eleanor B., eds. 'Census and Inspection of the Town of Pencuyut, Yucatan, in 1583 by Diego García de Palacio, oidor of the Audiencia of Guatemala', *Ethnohistory*, 6 (1959), 195–225.

Rubio Mañé, J. Ignacio. *Alcaldes de Mérida de Yucatán, 1542–1941*, México, 1941.

Rubio Mañé, J. Ignacio. *La Casa de Montejo en Mérida de Yucatán*, México, 1941.

Rubio Mañé, J. Ignacio, ed. *Archivo de la Historia de Yucatán, Campeche y Tabasco*, 3 vols., México, 1943.

Ruppert, Karl, Thompson, J. Eric S. and Proskouriakoff, Tatiana, *Bonampak, Chiapas, Mexico*, Washington, Carnegie Institution, 1955.

Ruz Lhuillier, Alberto. *Costumbres funerarias de los antiguos mayas*, México, Universidad Nacional Autónoma de México, Seminario de Cultura Maya, 1968.

Sabloff, Jeremy A. and Freidel, David A. 'A Model of a Pre-Columbian Trading Center', in *Ancient Civilization and Trade*, edited by Jeremy A. Sabloff and C. C. Lamberg-Karlovsky, Albuquerque, University of New Mexico Press, 1975, 369–408.

Sabloff, Jeremy A., and Rathje, William L. 'The Rise of a Maya Merchant Class', *Scientific American*, 233 (1975), 72–82.

Sabloff, J. A. and Rathje, William L., eds. *Changing Pre-Columbian commercial systems: the 1972–73 seasons at Cozumel, Mexico*, Monographs of the Peabody Museum, Harvard University, No. 3, Cambridge, Mass., 1975.

Sahagún, Fray Bernardino de. *The Florentine Codex: General History of the Things of New Spain*, translated and annotated by Arthur J. O. Anderson and Charles E. Dibble, 13 parts, Santa Fe, The School of American Research and the University of Utah, 1950–82.

Sahlins, Marshall D. *Historical Metaphors and Mythic Realities: Structure in the Early History of the Sandwich Islands Kingdom*, Ann Arbor, University of Michigan Press, 1981.

Sánchez de Aguilar, Pedro. *Informe contra idolorum cultores del obispado de Yucatán dirigido al Rey N. Señor en su Real Consejo de las Indias (c. 1613)*, in Francisco del Paso y Troncoso, *Tratado de las idolatrías, supersticiones, dioses, ritos, hechicerías y otras costumbres gentílicas de las razas aborígenes de México*, 2 vols., 2nd ed., México, Ediciones Fuente Cultural, 1953.

Scholes, France V., and Adams, Eleanor B., eds. *Don Diego Quijada, Alcalde Mayor de Yucatán, 1561-1565*, 2 vols., Mexico, Editorial Porrua, 1938.

Scholes, France V., Menéndez, Carlos R., Rubio Mañé, J. Ignacio and Adams, Eleanor B. eds. *Documentos para la historia de Yucatán*, 3 vols., Mérida, Compañía Tipográfica Yucateca, 1936-38.

Scholes, France V., and Roys, Ralph L. 'Fray Diego de Landa and the Problem of Idolatry in Yucatan', in *Cooperation in Research*, Washington, Carnegie Institution, 1938, 585-620.

Scholes, France V., and Roys, Ralph L. *The Maya Chontal Indians of Acalan-Tixchel: A Contribution to the History and Ethnography of the Yucatan Peninsula* (1948), 2nd ed., Norman, University of Oklahoma Press, 1968.

Scholes, France V., and Thompson, J. Eric S. 'The Francisco Pérez "Probanza" of 1654-1656 and the "Matrícula" of Tipu (Belize)', in *Anthropology and History in Yucatan*, edited by Grant D. Jones, Austin, University of Texas Press, 1977, 43-68.

Shattuck, G. C. ed. *The Peninsula of Yucatan*, Washington, Carnegie Institution, 1933.

Siemens, Alfred H., and Puleston, Dennis E. 'Ridged Fields and Associated Features in Southern Campeche: New Perspectives on the Lowland Maya', *American Antiquity*, 37 (1972), 228-39.

Sierra O'Reilly, Justo. *Los indios de Yucatán (1848-1851)*, edited by Carlos R. Menéndez, 2 vols., Mérida, Compañía Tipográfica Yucateca, 1954-57.

Stephens, John L. *Incidents of Travel in Central America, Chiapas and Yucatan*, 2 vols., New York, 1841.

Stephens, John L. *Incidents of Travel in Yucatan (1843)*, 2 vols., New York, Dover Press, 1963.

Strickson, Arnold, 'Hacienda and Plantation in Yucatan: An Historical-Ecological Consideration of the Folk-Urban Continuum in Yucatan', *América Indígena*, 25 (1965), 35-65.

Thompson, Donald E. 'Maya Paganism and Christianity: A History of the Fusion of Two Religions', in *Middle American Research Institute Publication*, 19, New Orleans, Middle American Research Institute, Tulane University, 1954, 1-36.

Thompson, J. Eric S. *Maya Hieroglyphic Writing: An Introduction*, 2nd ed., Norman, University of Oklahoma Press, 1960.

Thompson, J. Eric S. *The Rise and Fall of Maya Civilization*, 2nd ed., Norman, University of Oklahoma Press, 1966.

Thompson, J. Eric S. *Maya History and Religion*, Norman, University of Oklahoma Press, 1970.

Thompson, J. Eric S. 'A Proposal for Constituting a Maya Subgroup, Cultural and Linguistic, in the Petén and Adjacent Regions', in *Anthropology and History in Yucatan*, edited by Grant D. Jones, Austin, University of Texas Press, 1977, 3-42.

Todorov, Tzvetan. *The Conquest of America: the Question of the Other*, trans. from the French by Richard Howard, New York, 1982.

Tozzer, Alfred M. *A Comparative Study of the Mayas and the Lacandones*, New York, Macmillan, 1907.

Tozzer, Alfred M. *A Maya Grammar*, Cambridge, Peabody Museum, Harvard University, 1921.

Tozzer, Alfred M. *Landa's Relación de las cosas de Yucatán: a translation*, Cambridge, Mass., Peabody Museum, Harvard University, 1941.

Tozzer, Alfred M. 'Chichen Itza and Its Cenote of Sacrifice', *Memoirs of the Peabody Museum of Archeology and Ethnology*, 2 vols., Cambridge, Mass., 1957.

Uchmany de la Peña, Eva A., 'Cuatro casos de idolatría en el area maya ante el Tribunal de la Inquisición', *Estudios de Cultura Maya*, 6 (1967), 267–300.

Villa Rojas, Alfonso. *The Maya of East Central Quintana Roo*, Washington, Carnegie Institution, 1945.

Villa Rojas, Alfonso. 'Notas sobre le tenencia de la tierra entre los mayas de la antiguedad', *Estudios de Cultura Maya*, 1 (1961), 21–46.

Villagutierre Sotomayor, Juan de. *Historia de la conquista de la provincia de el Itza (1701)*, Guatemala, Sociedad de Geografía e Historia, Tipografía Nacional, 1933.

Vogt, Evon Z. *Zincantán: A Maya Community in the Highlands of Chiapas*, Cambridge, Mass. Belknap Press of Harvard University Press, 1969.

Vogt, Evon Z. 'The Genetic Model and Maya Cultural Development', in *Desarrollo Cultural de los mayas*, 2nd ed., edited by Evon Z. Vogt and Alberto Ruz Lhuillier, Mexico, Universidad Nacional Autónoma de México, 1971, 9–48.

Vogt, Evon Z. *Tortillas for the Gods: a Symbolic Analysis of Zinacantecan Rituals*, Cambridge, Mass., Harvard University Press, 1976.

Wachtel, Nathan, *The Vision of the Vanquished: The Spanish Conquest of Peru through Indian Eyes*, New York, Barnes and Noble, 1977.

Wagner, Helmuth O. 'Subsistence Potential and Population Density of the Maya on the Yucatan Peninsula and Causes for the Decline in Population in the Fifteenth Century', in *Verhandlungen des XXXVIII Internationalen Amerikanistenkongresses, Stuttgart-München, 1968*, Munich, Kommissionsverlag Klaus Renner, 1970, 1: 185–91.

Wagner, Henry R. ed. *The Discovery of New Spain in 1518 by Juan de Grijalva*, Berkeley, California, Cortés Society, 1942.

Wagner, Henry R. ed. *The Discovery of Yucátan by Francisco Hernandez de Córdoba*, Berkeley, California, Cortés Society, 1942.

Wallace, Anthony F. C. 'Revitalization Movements', *American Anthropologist*, 58 (1956), 264–81.

Wauchope, Robert. *Modern Maya Houses: A Study of Their Archaeological Significance*, Washington, Carnegie Institution, 1938.

Willey, Gordon R., 'External Influences on the Lowland Maya: 1940 and 1975 Perspectives', in *Social Process in Maya Prehistory*, edited by Norman Hammond, London, Academic Press, 1977, 57–75.

Willey, Gordon R. and Bullard, William R. Jr. 'Prehistoric Settlement Patterns in the Maya Lowlands', in *Handbook of Middle American Indians*, 2, Austin, University of Texas Press, 1965, 360–77.

Wolf, Eric R. 'Closed Corporate Peasant Communities in Mesoamerica and Central Java', *Southwestern Journal of Anthropology*, 13 (1957), 1–18.

Wolf, Eric R. *Sons of the Shaking Earth*, Chicago, University of Chicago Press, Phoenix Books, 1959.

Worsley, Peter. *The Trumpet Shall Sound*, London, 1957.

Zimmerman, Charlotte. 'The Cult of the Holy Cross: An Analysis of Cosmology and Catholicism in Quintana Roo', *History of Religions*, 3 (1963), 50–71.

Index

DATE DUE

Index 243